The Invention
of the Jew

The Invention of the Jew

Jewish-American Education Novels
(1916-1964)

Bernard Sherman

Thomas Yoseloff

New York • South Brunswick • London

Library of Congress Catalogue Card Number: 68-27194

Thomas Yoseloff, *Publisher*
Cranbury, New Jersey 08512

Thomas Yoseloff Ltd
108 New Bond Street
London W. 1, England

SBN
498-06595-2

Printed in the United States of America

Dedicated to my teacher, Ernest Samuels;
to my friend, Benjamin Weintroub;
and to my wife, Marilyn.

Acknowledgments

I wish to thank the following people for their cooperation, without which this study would have been impossible: Professors Ernest Samuels, Harrison Hayford, and Richard Ellmann of Northwestern University for their encouragement, insightful guidance, and the inspiring example of their own work; Benjamin Weintroub for his suggestions and the use of his private library; the librarians of the Deering Library of Northwestern University for their cooperation; David Mark, Arthur Granit, Harold U. Ribalow, Yuri Suhl, and Albert Halper for their kindness and patience in granting me interviews and answering written inquiries.

Grateful acknowledgment is also made to the following for permission to quote from copyright material: Albert Halper, *The Golden Watch*, New York, Henry Holt and Company, 1953, by permission of Albert Halper; Alfred Kazin, *A Walker in the City*, New York, Harcourt, Brace and World, Inc., 1951, by permission of Harcourt, Brace and World, Inc.; Isaac Rosenfeld, *Passage From Home*, New York, The World Publishing Company, 1961, by The World Publishing Company; Henry Roth, *Call It Sleep*, New York, Pageant Books, 1960, by Cooper Square Publishers, Inc., New York.

Contents

The Invention
of the Jew

"*The circumstance of being born a Jew in America was a very special one in that it announced not only the specialness of being born, but a kind of extra specialness, the specialness of having been a Jew or being a Jew. This, however, remained a mysterious thing: one did not know exactly what it was and so one had to invent being a Jew. This seems to me to involve many glorious possibilities.*"

PHILIP ROTH

"*Second Dialogue in Israel*" *Congress Bi-Weekly, Vol. 30, No. 12, P. 30.*

1

Education Novels and Fiction by Jewish-Americans

DEFINING JEWISH-AMERICAN NOVELS

The objective assessment of Jewish-American literature as a distinct genre is a purpose of this study. The realization of this purpose is hindered by differing opinions appearing throughout the century regarding the nature of democracy and the Jewish-American ethos. To many, the term "Jewish-American" connotes the stubborn maintenance of outworn customs, a failure of the melting pot. Others, advancing the idea of cultural pluralism, argue for the vigor of an America which has not submerged ethnic differences. To them, the existence of a body of fiction exploring the peculiar nature of the American Jew indicates not the failure of assimilation, but vitality of democracy.

13

Before this last decade, the writer was hindered rather than helped by having the label "Jewish" attached to his work. Such an identity might discourage the non-Jewish public and, perhaps, even the Jewish one. Fiction so labeled was likely to be received indifferently by general reviewers and to create insupportable expectations among reviewers for the Jewish-interest periodicals. The critic who would seek to consider this body of writing as a genre also has been hampered. He must discover the similarities in materials and methods among Jewish-American writers at the peril of offending those sensitive to special notice; at the same time, he must point out any excellence achieved by the Jewish writers, risking the charge of ethnocentricity.

The difficulties of the historian of Jewish-American literature are further increased by the absence of an accepted definition of that literature. Such a definition would indicate the qualities that justify a separate classification of the books but would not obscure their universal properties and their availability to the general reader.

Previous attempts to define the Jewish-American novel have been numerous, but inconclusive. The definitions are found in the prefaces, reviews, and articles in which critics attempted to account for Jewish-American writing as an entity. They range from the exact to the vague. Four appreciably different definitions will be considered in the order of their abstractness, from the most specific to the most nebulous.

The narrowest of these definitions—that of J. Waller in "The Jewish Book Myth"[1]—distinguishes between Jews as members of an ethnic group by virtue of their birth and Hebrews as professing adherents of the religion of Judaism. According to this definition, a Jewish book should reflect the ideals of Judaism. Books that simply describe the Jewish writer's people as Farrell and Saroyan describe their ethnic groups would not be called Jewish books.

Henry Roth, the author of *Call It Sleep* (1934), has described the spirit motivating his novel as the "Hebrew uprightness of . . . orthodoxy," which created a "sort of general mystical state" in him, although he had abandoned religion.[2] The novel itself reflects a perfervid and mystical intensity and the search for consummation through religion. Indeed, it grants the reader insight into the relation of the religious temperament to fiction. But to regard the sole, or even primary, source of *Call It Sleep* as Judaism would be an oversimplification. The library as well as the synagogue, the heterodoxies of Freud and Marx as well as the orthodoxies of the *Torah*, influence the book. In contrast to Roth in *Call It Sleep*, Jewish-American novelists characteristically have not been religious, nor have they been theologians. Rabbis, who by definition fulfill the requirement that the author of Jewish books know about Judaism, have written theological works and published their collected sermons rather than composed novels.[3]

To accept the religious definition would simplify the task of the historian by reducing the number of novels in the Jewish-American category to a minute fraction of the hundreds which have appeared in the listings of the *Jewish Book Annual* or in Joseph Mersand's survey of Jewish-American literature, *Traditions in American Literature* (1939). But what is to be made of all the rest of these novels; what of all the characters with their intriguing, iterative syndromes; what of the recurrent settings, the Lower East Side, Williamsburg, Chicago's West Side? It is too simple to say that a wise author writes about what he knows. What is needed is an exploration of the materials and the concomitant themes: assimilation, the conflict of generations, economic strife,

the anomie of city life—the clash of values acutely sensed
by marginal man.

The second definition of a Jewish book seeks to move
beyond the limitation of religion. It turns to the exploration of Jewish traits, attitudes, sensibilities—terms which
cast a disturbing shadow of racism. For example, in the
novels of Samuel Ornitz and Ludwig Lewisohn are found
psychiatrists distressed at the number of "neurasthenics"
among the Jews. Running down the list of Jewish authors
and considering the traits traditionally applied to Jews,
Louis Kronenberger finds that such a list as "skepticism,
humor, melancholy, prophecy, brilliance, bitterness, pity,
and irony" is simply not sufficiently inclusive.[4] The most
troublesome charge laid against the critic is that, in
defining Jewish writing, he fails to produce delimiting
qualities unique to the Jews. To ascribe a set of character
traits indeed may be an exercise more obfuscating than
enlightening. However, the exploration in fiction of the
effect of social forces upon personality is another matter,
one within the province of the critic.

Neither definition is the way to initiate a literary study
dealing with the interrelationships of materials, styles,
and ideologies. Dramatic situations rising from character
and setting—the components of the novel, that is—provide a more fruitful starting point. But further refinement of definition is necessary.

The third definition is simply a general rubric applied
to Jewish literature: "the cry for social justice." (Unfortunately, the phrase is so comprehensive that it could
include much of twentieth-century literature.) Jewish
poetry has been analyzed by Philip M. Raskin with the
hope of abstracting some *leitmotif;* plays by Jewish play-
wrights such as Clifford Odets, Elmer Rice, and Arthur
Miller have been similarly scrutinized by Charles Glicksberg; Ben Field's novels were examined by their author
for the same purpose.[5] Each found that the distinctively

Jewish element was the demand—very often in fervid, prophetic, even mystical terms—that man fulfill his highest possibilities, that he achieve a Messianic release in a world in which mind and justice were triumphant. The locus of this spirit of social compassion is the prophetic vision of Isaiah, a central concept of Judaism and, therefore, a spirit especially appropriate in Jewish writing (although it is, as well, one general in literature). Nonetheless, the term offers no solution to the problem of definition because it is so inclusive.

The fourth definition of Jewish literature calls for the inner self of the author to be recognizably Jewish. It requires the author to accept this fact of his consciousness as an integral part of his work. One advocate of this definition was Ludwig Lewisohn,[6] who underwent the process of accepting the Jewish strains of his consciousness with a soul-shaking labor described in the two volumes of his autobiography, *Up Stream* (1922) and *Mid-Channel* (1929). Unfortunately, to call for the Jewish author to abstract the identifiably Jewish features of his subconscious and to purge his work of the "inauthentic" in the process is to demand the impossible. Since the Jewish author often has rejected the official institutions of Jewish-American life and has attempted to create an art drawn from the uncontrolled elements of his unconscious, any definition of his art must include the ambiguous and unclassifiable.

For the purpose of this study, a Jewish-American novel will be considered such if it describes Jews experiencing the problems that were substantially, but not exclusively, theirs. The problems (religious doubt, the clash of generations, assimilation, the marginal relation to American culture) produce an interrelated, repeated set of dramatic situations. The significance of the study of Jewish-American novels as such lies in the particular and peculiar literary uses to which the writers put their themes and their materials. That is to say, it lies in the relationship between the circumstances of Jewish life in America and the fiction which grows out of those circumstances. The existence of a unique outlook or method of expression identifiable as "Jewish" must be determined by first examining the fiction. The above definition points directly at the material of the novels. It avoids fruitless controversies more self-defensive than enlightening and promotes an inductive method.

One further consideration is authorship. While Jewish characters appear in novels by non-Jews (Fitzgerald's Wolfsheim, Hemingway's Robert Cohn, and Wolfe's Esther Jack are the most familiar examples), they do so generally in a peripheral rather than a central way, developing a situation or illustrating some thesis not specifically related to Jewishness. Books by non-Jews in which the Jew appears centrally, such as Myra Kelly's East Side stories and Henry Harland's novels written under the *nom de plume* of Sidney Luska,[7] attempt to exploit the exotic aspects of Jewish life for local-color effect. Jewish writers were capable of seeking the appeal of the exotic, but their more characteristic purpose was to make their subject familiar rather than strange to the reader.

This study proposes to limit the authors included to Jews on the assumption that the Jewish writer, particularly when he writes autobiographically, brings insights to his fictional treatment of Jews not available to the non-Jewish writer. At any rate, non-Jewish authors have seldom written domestic novels about Jews, perhaps because of the quantity of novels being produced by writers with more authentic credentials. (Fiction by Jewish authors treating a milieu not specifically Jewish may be regarded simply in the tradition of American literature.)

There remains the problem of finding some focus which

will bring the lineaments of the Jewish-American novel
into greatest clarity, revealing its true spirit.

THE CATEGORY OF EDUCATION NOVEL

Certain subjects recurring in the Jewish-American novel
can be grouped into major categories. Most often the
subject is a social problem; the novel is a problem novel.
The reports of new novels in the *Jewish Book Annual*
reveal that in certain years a number of books concerning
say, intermarriage or anti-Semitism appear. As the particular social problem reaches some resolution or loses its
force of interest, it is less frequently treated. The Jew
as soldier in World War II is such a topic, one which
preoccupied non-Jewish writers as well as Jews. As the
rather narrow scope of the topic was exhausted and the
service in general became a matter of indifference to the
public, the number of such novels decreased. Other important subjects earlier in the century were ghetto conditions, Russian Jew versus German Jew, and the garment industry.

One category of the Jewish-American novel transcends
the topicality and the forced, tendentious tone of the
problem novel. Harold Ribalow drew up a list of fifty
basic works of Jewish fiction from 1917 to 1951 for the
Chicago Jewish Forum.[8] An examination of the list reveals that twenty of the fifty novels depict the initiation
into experience of a boy or youth, tracing his passage
from innocence to awareness, his realization of the particular meaning of the life of a Jew in the American city—
in short, the *Bildungsroman* theme turned to a particular
time and place. The Yiddish terms for such a novel are
identical to the German: *Bildungsroman* and *Erziehungs-
roman*.[9] Equivalent terms in English are the adolescent
novel (which delimits the age group of the protagonist

too sharply since boyhood novels cover the same ground and should be included), the initiation novel, and the education novel. The last term will be the most commonly used in this study because it is accurate and concise.

The education novel exactly reproduces the central experience of American Jewry: the movement from the enclosed *shtetl* (Eastern European village) environment, with its highly ordered and pervasive moral system (diffused by peasant lore and a necessarily realistic view of humanity), to the exacting demands of an industrial society. Unlike other immigrant groups, the Jews had regarded themselves as being in diaspora even in Europe. (A central tenet of Judaism is that every Jew is an exile who must some day return to Jerusalem.) America, coming with such suddenness to so many, intensified the cleavage between the domestic religious culture of the Jews and their external lives in a country which regarded them as an anomaly. The novel repeats the pattern of this process by describing a youth outgrowing the protection of the home and encountering the beckoning life without.

The fictional form which revealed this experience has been called "the Jewish novel of education" by Jacob Sloan, who finds it inevitable that Jews should write such novels.[10] Living themselves the dual lives of American Jews, writers such as Ludwig Lewisohn, Delmore Schwartz, and Isaac Rosenfeld have found this form to provide an appropriate structure for the inward-turning process which they underwent. Sloan defines the novel of education as "a journey of exploration in which traditional values are being considered, accepted, rejected, or transfigured."

Philip Roth has recalled an experience which indicates the potency for Jewish writers of the education novel. He related the incident during a symposium, "Jewishness and the Creative Process," without mentioning that his own *Goodbye, Columbus* is itself such a novel, dealing as it does with the introduction of a poor youth into the parvenu suburban culture. While teaching a writer's workshop at the University of Iowa, Roth was surprised to get from each of the five Jewish men in the class a story with the same theme, although it was handled differently by each. The story describes a Jewish boy or adolescent and his relations with his family. A sister always appears, though the writer actually may not have had one. The father invariably is silent, while the mother and sister seem to hover over the youth. The resolution of the story is the protagonist's introduction to sex by a *shiksa* (a non-Jewish girl) who in no way resembles the mother or sister. The repetition of this story over the last fifty years may be taken to imply that it is a "central Jewish fantasy," as Roth calls it.[11] It is not so much the *shiksa* who is the essential component of the fantasy (Roth's Neil Klugman is initiated into sex by a certain Brenda Patimkin), but the protagonist, a youth leaving his family for the world beyond the Jewish orbit which the family represents. In a later story, "Civilization and Its Discontents," Roth moved even closer toward this fantasy with the character of Monkey, a Southern-born non-Jew.

The Adolescent Novel in General Fiction

The comparison of Jewish-American education novels with the American adolescent novels, a parallel term, reveals some sharp similarities and some significant differences. The similarities may be assigned to the conditions which dictate the terms of all such novels, the differences to the singularities of the Jewish ethos. J. Tasker Witham's study, *The Adolescent in the American Novel: 1920-1960*, makes the following generalizations about novels with adolescent protagonists: (1) the majority are first novels; (2) they are autobiographical; (3) most deal with males and in a frank manner; (4) the protagonist is a sensitive would-be artist of some kind.[12] These characteristics are true of the Jewish novel of adolescence. Witham attributes them to the tendency of the beginning novelist to follow the dictum, "Write about what you know."

Witham proposes another set of generalizations. Novels of the Twenties and Thirties are likely to extend the action beyond the adolescence of the protagonist. (The onset of puberty may be taken as the chief mark of adolescence.) Adolescent novels of that period are sociological in approach, whereas novels of the Forties and Fifties are psychological in orientation and cover a shorter period in the protagonist's life. The difference here is a major one. Most of the Jewish-American novels of the Forties and Fifties continue a concern with societal circumstances equal in importance to the psychological. Furthermore, the Jewish novelist is more likely than the non-Jewish novelist to structure his treatment of the personality of the protagonist around family interrelationships.

The Family Novel

A second category, the family novel, the saga of generations, forms another sub-group within Jewish-American literature which challenges the education novel for supremacy as the major type. Elias Tobenkin's *House of Conrad* (1918), Myron Brynig's Singerman series, and more recently Miriam Osterman's *Damned If You Do, Damned If You Don't* (1962) follow this tradition. More significant than these family chronicles to Jewish-American letters is the novel that explores the immediate relationships within the family as an organism undergoing stress. The Jews are noted for the importance they give to the family, and it is the family in conflict that is the universal determinant of the Jewish novel more surely even than Judaism. The education novel, with its inside view, affords an unequaled vantage point from which to observe the conflict of values that rent Jewish family life.

To some degree, the Jewish author found it difficult to achieve sufficient objectivity to approach the family conflict with undistorted perspective. In such cases, the portrayal of the mother tends to get out of hand; she is more strident and hysterical than seemed intended by the author, as in Henry Denker's *My Son, the Lawyer* (1950) and Herman Wouk's *Marjorie Morningstar* (1955). In the better controlled of the education novels, family conflict is the nightmare wherein are re-enacted the frustrations and shocks of the urban day.

The hopes which brought the family to America were invested in the lives of the children, whose fulfillment, achieved through freedom from poverty and pogroms, was to repay the parents for the disruption of their own lives. Family tradition primarily charged the son with the obligation of achieving success; urban processes dictated that the price of that success was to be the abandonment of Jewish traditions. The sons who chose a literary career were in a unique position to explore every nuance of the clash of values between worlds, using the conflict as they did as the very means of gaining the fulfillment expected of them.

Beside providing a subject, the education novel also offers the author a framework that lends itself to a range of themes, some of which can be subsumed under other titles such as "conversion to Socialism" or "ghetto novel." In Jewish fiction, the education novel is used in a twofold way, then: first, to explore a youth's initiation into the adult world and, second, as a rhetorical device to carry out an examination of social conditions. In the latter function, the youthful protagonist reacts like litmus paper, recording the effect on human personality of destructive social conditions all the more clearly because of his original purity.

The total of novels about Jewish-American life in the last fifty years (their number was much lower in the preceding years) is in the hundreds, with a correspondingly greater number of short stories. The Jewish-American education novel, defined as an extended work of fiction by a Jew about a Jewish youth who is undergoing his initiation into the American urban experience, totals about eighty, including novels of every quality down to the paperback gang novel. The education novels to be examined in this study will be somewhat fewer—about forty, those that most aptly illustrate one trend or another of the education novel.

LITERARY CRITICISM OF JEWISH-AMERICAN FICTION

Jewish-American fiction comprises an extensive body of literature, but surprisingly little serious critical attention was devoted to it until recent years. The greatest part of the criticism has appeared as book reviews in periodicals. Harold Ribalow has pointed this out, perhaps too bleakly, in "Zion in Contemporary Fiction": "In the literary histories, in the critical journals, in the volumes of criticism, these Jewish writers are eliminated as though they never existed."[13] Needless to say, the recent vogue of this fiction has increased the number of articles.

Specialists in this field still are few. Ribalow, anthologist and editor, is himself the critic most devoted to this literature. Others who at present are expert in the field are: Milton Hindus, literary historian; Charles Angoff, novelist; Leslie Fiedler, critic; Irving Malin, critic; and Sol Liptzin, literary scholar.

Maurice Samuel, who has enjoyed a long career as a translator and a popularizer of Yiddish literature, discloses in his autobiography, *Little Did I Know* (1964), a long delayed desire to write a full-scale treatment of Jewish-American literature. Ribalow indicates that publishers have approached him to undertake the same task, but he finds it too time-consuming an enterprise.[14] One suspects that a certain intractability in the material itself beyond its bulk may be one of the reasons for the limited critical and historical treatment.

It is true that a few pages are devoted to Jewish writing in Hebrew or Yiddish as an ethnic field in the United States in the Bibliography and Supplement to the *Literary History of the United States,* but no treatment is to be found in the *History* itself.[15] The major part of Jewish writing has been in English and seldom has been treated as such. Recent book-length studies are Irving Malin's *Jews and Americans* (1965), David S. Lifson's *The Yiddish Theatre in America* (1965), and Sol Liptzin's *The Jew in American Literature* (1966).

The success of Bernard Malamud, Saul Bellow, and Philip Roth has resulted in a great many articles. Indeed, collections of essays have been compiled treating the small *oeuvre* of J. D. Salinger. It is possible even to say that a breakthrough finally has been made, as do the editors of the anthology bearing that title: *Breakthrough: A Treasury of Contemporary American-Jewish Literature* (1964).

EARLIER CLASSIFICATIONS OF THE JEWISH-AMERICAN NOVEL

A listing of some articles with the varying schema they assign to the corpus of Jewish-American fiction is instructive. In the introduction to *Breakthrough,* Irving Malin and Irwin Stark propose as the chief themes of the literature: (a) "The Old Country," the persistent influence of the old ways in the new land; (b) "Fathers and Sons," the dramatization of the old and new; (c) "The Sense of the Past," the recollection of the historic past of Judaism; (d) "Dualities," contradictions and ambiguities; (e) "The Heart," the sense of suffering and compassion; (f) "Transcendence," the achievement of unity.[16]

A statement of the themes of this literature resembling that in *Breakthrough* was made by Irving Howe in "The Stranger and the Victim: the Two Jewish Stereotypes of American Fiction."[17] The title indicates his thesis, that the treatment by Jew or non-Jew draws on two myths with antecedents far back in European tradition. Howe's categories state the themes in a form which combines periods and styles: (a) "Poverty as Local Color," he cites *Haunch, Paunch and Jowl* and *Jews without Money;* (b) "The Great Romance" (mamma and son), *Call It Sleep;* (c) "The Father as Patriarch," *The Island Within* and *Sons of the Fathers;* (d) "The Bohemian Rejection," a variant of assimilation, *A Jew in Love;* (e) "Nothing to Lose but Your Chains," the problem novel beginning in the Depression, Ben Compton in *U. S. A.;* (f) "The Artist as Businessman," *What Makes Sammy Run?;* (g) and "The Jew as Placard," the thesis novel, *Wasteland.*

Such were the conditions of Jewish-American life that the Jewish novel is parallel to the urban novel. *The American City Novel* by Blanche Gelfant, a literary genre study, includes several Jewish-American education novels. Most of these fall under Mrs. Gelfant's first category, "the portrait study." The plot of such novels consists of a series of "educating incidents" impressing the hero with the meaning, values, and manners of the city. [18] The other two principal modes of the city novel are the "synoptic study," with its group hero, and the "ecological study," with its exploration of the manner of life in a small area of the city. A study both synoptic and ecological is Meyer Levin's *The Old Bunch* (1937), which follows a number of youths through the education experience. Also classified as a synoptic study could be David Mark's *The Neighborhood* (1960), which appeared after Gelfant's study was completed. Mark himself has accepted both the education novel and the ecological study as appelations for his novel.[19] Another of Gelfant's sub-types is the novel of sentiment, after the manner of Betty Smith's *A Tree Grows in Brooklyn*. In this group belongs Sam Ross's *The Sidewalks Are Free* (1950). Using more or less factitious means, such novels attempt to evoke a sentimental response in the reader. Gelfant's categories are valid and illumine the question of Jewish writing as city writing. Gelfant's statement of purpose for her study is a model for the literary genre study: to define the class by "intention, materials, and motifs; to suggest the social backgrounds out of which it has emerged and upon which it has developed" (p. viii).

Leslie Fiedler in *The Jew in the American Novel*, applying the technique of the myth critic, lists the categories as: (a) "Zion as Eros," the ghetto novel as the "erotic-assimilationist novel," employing the love story to dramatize the act of assimilation; (b) "Zion as Armageddon," the proletarian novel; and (c) "Zion as Main Street," the middle-brow novel.[20] The above groupings, overlapping as they do, indicate the feasibility of categorizing the Jewish-American novels in order to better understand the genre.

THE CATEGORIES IN THE PRESENT STUDY

The categories in the present study group education novels chronologically. Each of the groups represents a school sharing common themes and style: Chapter Two,

"First Generation: The Socialist Imagination," the early model ghetto novel; Chapter Three, "Second Generation: The Child of the Depression," the next generation's more doctrinaire approach; Chapter Four, "Getting Older: The Time of Alienation," the post-Marxist malaise; Chapter Five, "Bemused Again: The Dream of Success," another essay of an old theme; Chapter Six, "Second Childhood: The Nostalgic Backward Glance," the revival of the ghetto for sentimental purposes; and Chapter Seven, "Third Generation: The Black Comedians," the satirical criticism of today's affluent Jew.

The first group of education novels intimately delineates the experience of the first-generation American, the immigrant ghetto experience. The accent is upon the externalized representation of social and economic forces. These novels offer the least sensitive and persuasive treatment of unfolding youth to be found in the education novel. The protagonist is often seen as an artist searching for fulfillment in the *golus* (diaspora). The portrayal is self-pitying, but also, self-revealing. An alternative type within this group offers a reverse portrait, the rogue-hero. The authors of this group of books were European-born and informed by the Jewish Bundist socialist tradition.

In its second phase, the education novel was written by a generation born in America. They were at one remove from their predecessors—from the Lower East Side across the river to Brownsville—and they showed less compassion for the suffering immigrants and more impatience with their limitations. The authors of the first group of novels had abandoned Orthodox Judaism as a personal belief but were conversant with its rituals and sympathetic with their fellow Jews, whom they saw as members of the working class ripe for conversion to socialism. The second generation, liberated from traditional Jewish life by virtue of their birth in the United States, lacked intimacy with Jewish customs. Their immediate concern, like that of the first-generation writers, was the condition of poverty and the criticism of capitalism; but the concern had hardened into a purely Marxist one as they turned East, mistaking the proletarian tunic, which now concealed the Czarist uniform so plain to their fathers, for the symbol of classlessness.

Their subject, like that of their predecessors, was the discord between generations. But it was seen entirely from the viewpoint of the son, whose very choice of vocation, novelist, was the sign of disaffection with his parents, who were by now *petits bourgeois* and, in a sense, more Americanized than he. The writers of the first generation were likely to be journalists, possibly in the Jewish press. The second generation were more likely to think of themselves primarily as novelists, although the material difficulties of that calling often forced them to be journalists as well.

An appropriate title for the second group of novels is "The Child of the Depression"; the novels in this group were produced in the Great Depression and reflect it inescapably.

Anti-Semitism was the overriding subject for the war years, one which lent itself to the exploration of the self-contained world of the searching youth only in a peripheral way. The education novel did not appear unless the novel of army life is counted.

As a result of the post-war mood of disillusion and the retreat of the liberals (who formed, after all, the only camp for Jewish intellectuals), there appeared the novel of alienation—the existentialist, victim novel. As Jew, as intellectual, as disaffected son, the protagonist of the education novel reappeared with new relevance. As the novelist turned farther inward, he found that most introspective of characters to offer an appropriate symbol for the soul-searching process. For a time it seemed that

it was the Jew who, in his being and his historical mis-
fortunes, prefigured the fate of Western man himself.
The Jewish-American novel thus entered the mainstream
of Western world literature.

The great preoccupation of Jewish-American novelists
with the money society did not vanish as prosperity became an entrenched way of life, however. A group of education novels appearing after World War II again took
up the examination of the American dream of success.
These omitted the last-minute conversion to Marxism
which often served as a convenient resolution of the
earlier protest novels.

By mid-century it was possible for writers to turn back
to the ghetto or slum life of their parents and grandparents for purposes other than the revelation of conditions
under capitalism. The passage of time and the failure of
contemporary culture to provide stability brought the
earlier period into a different perspective. The virtues of
that time, the warmth of the holidays, the innocence and
optimism, became more apparent in the nostalgic backward glance. These books range from comedy relying on
memories of the candy store to serio-comic re-creations
of the dynamics of neighborhood life.

The current manifestation of the education novel re-
vives the long-time preoccupation with the values of
American money society, but with less reverence for Jewish life than was ever before evidenced by Jewish-American writers. Kingsly Amis' *One Fat Englishman* (1963)
describes such novels wittily as the "Neo-Gothic, meta-
fantasy" school.

THE STRATEGY OF THE EDUCATION NOVEL

As their titles suggest, these groupings, with one exception, are temporal categories. Within given, brief
periods, with some overlapping, writers of education

novels shared the same ideology and employed the same literary devices. The differences among novels within a group are due primarily to qualitative disparities among the writers.

The use of Jewish themes and the return of the writer to his boyhood may be seen as the artful employment of the materials for the sake of their interest to the reader as well as for their meaning to the writer.

The use of the Jewish character for its resonance as a stereotype (or archetype, if one prefers) is most apparent in two of its guises. The young New York Jew with his Depression cry of "Why?" is a readily available figure. In *Waiting for the End* (1964), Leslie Fiedler raises the figure to major significance: "The autobiography of the urban Jew whose adolescence coincided with the Depression, and who walked the banks of some contaminated city river with tags of Lenin ringing in his head . . . has come to seem part of the mystical life history of a nation."[21] The second of these central images is the alienated Jew, the anti-hero existentialist sufferer, whose estrangement parallels the condition of twentieth-century man.

The accuracy of these images of the Jew is not at issue here. The make-up of radical groups, voting patterns and occupational indices, religious affiliations, and psychological reports on the degree of anomie may or may not indicate that American Jews lived a more complex life than the above stereotypes indicate. According to Dennis Wrong in "Jews, Gentiles, and the New Establishment," intellectually elite circles hold an image of the Jews which attributes to them "intellectuality, political liberalism, intense parental solicitude with close bonds between mothers and sons . . . volubility and emotional expressiveness, fear of violence, and ironic humor."[22] These traits appear repeatedly in the Jew's image of himself in the education novel, which customarily employs

2

First Generation: The Socialist Imagination

THE EARLY MODEL APPEARS

The Jewish-American education novel begins with a group of books written between 1916 and 1930. Seven of these will be considered in this chapter. The novels and authors share many similarities, and thus some generalizations will be attempted. Two of the novels (*The Abyss* and *The Sidewalks of New York*) are sentimental melodramas written for a popular audience; they will be mentioned only briefly.

The first of these, Nathan Kussey's *The Abyss,* appeared in 1916 as part of a trilogy issued under the Macmillan imprint. It proposed to transcribe (providing sufficient public interest were maintained over fifteen hundred pages) an "epic of the streets" to be called

"Children of the Abyss."[1] In the same year, Elias Tobenkin's first novel, *Witte Arrives*, presented an extended
and unsensational treatment of the immigrant experience.[2]

In the next year the novel appeared which is taken to
mark the beginning of the tradition of serious Jewish-
American fiction, Abraham Cahan's *The Rise of David
Levinsky*.[3] This frank and unflattering study of the Jewish immigrant losing his religion as he gained his America
could not have been published unless certain events had
prepared the way.

Cahan had been championed as a realist by William
Dean Howells. Howells had urged him to write a novel,
found him a publisher, Appleton, and wrote a favorable
review of the book, *Yekl: A Tale of the New York
Ghetto* (1896).[4] The small sale of the book caused Cahan to defer his novelistic career for journalism until
twenty years had passed.[5]

By then the muckraking magazines had helped to build
a willing readership for scenes of poverty. Ghetto life
had appeared in Jacob Riis's *How the Other Half Lives*
(1890) and Hutchins Hapgood's *The Spirit of the
Ghetto* (1902). *McClure's Magazine* had published the
sketches on which *The Rise of David Levinsky* was based.
Heretofore, the poor had appeared in fiction not so much
to promote social amelioration, as to produce the effect
of quaintness; the local-color school offered some excuse
for scenes of ghetto life.[6]

Another factor more directly favored the appearance
of the ghetto novel at this time. A group of adventure-
some publishers, appearing after World War I to chal-
lenge the established firms, made a place for Jewish novels on their lists. Boni and Liveright, founded in 1917
and noted later for its publication of Dreiser and O'Neil,
published the most sensational of the books in this chapter, *Haunch, Paunch and Jowl* (1923). After the retire-

ment of Boni in 1918, associates of the firm started their own houses. Among those listed in *Literary History of the United States* as related to the parent house in some way were Pascal Covici of Chicago (*Sidewalks of New York*, 1927), Charles Boni (*By the Waters of Manhattan*, 1930), Horace Liveright (*Aaron Traum*, 1930), and Liveright Publishing Corporation (*Jews without Money*, 1930). Others firms derived from the parent house which were to figure as publishers of Jewish subject novels in later years were Simon and Schuster, Random House, Julian Messner, Covici-Friede, and Viking. The notable 1936 *Fortune* article, "Jews in America," states that prior to 1915 practically no Jews were influential in the publishing industry. Their list of Jewish-owned publishing houses is composed of former Liveright associates. The majority of books about Jews in America has been published by these houses.[7]

Other novels to be included in this chapter follow. The rogue-hero tradition in the novel of Jewish-American life (a persistent one despite the complaints of the Jewish community), begun with *The Rise of David Levinsky*, was continued with *Haunch, Paunch and Jowl* by Samuel Ornitz in 1923. A third youthful rogue appeared in Nat J. Ferber's *The Sidewalks of New York* in 1927, the second of our inconsequential melodramas. *The Island Within* by Ludwig Lewisohn and *The Boy in the Sun* by Paul Rosenfeld (two rare education novels by German Jews) appeared in 1928. *Aaron Traum* (1930) by Hyman and Lester Cohen marks the end of this early model of the Jewish-American education novel. In 1951, Samuel Ornitz published *Bride of the Sabbath,* perhaps in expiation for his *Haunch, Paunch and Jowl*. Because it so resembles in subject matter, style, and ideology the early models, *Bride of the Sabbath* will be taken up in this chapter.[8]

The care which Cahan and the other
period devoted to detailing the social and
toms and the eccentricities of immigrant b
the local-color tradition. The authors also s.
genuine desire of the best local colorists to
true picture of the group they describe. They w
to bring an intimate knowledge to their books,
their perspective and their conclusions were some
distorted by too close an involvement. Most of these
authors learned English as a second language, and they
were not able entirely to overcome this handicap. Their
novels are marked by solecisms and crudity.

The best of these books—those by Cahan and Ornitz
—retain their vitality and can be read today for much the
same reasons that Zola and Norris are read. With passion and sympathy, they create a vanished world. With
a concern for the destiny of a people, they depict the arduous urban existence at the turn of the century when the
problems caused by the industrial revolution were clearly
discernible: the displacement of the worker, rootlessness,
the dissolution of what John Dewey called "The Household and Neighborhood System" in *The School and Society* (1896).

The Early Model in the Context
of Socialist Thought

The figure of Abraham Cahan illustrates the social
and political matrix of the early model author. Daniel
Bell draws a distinction between Cahan and the generation of American-bred writers. In his view, Jewish writing in America up to the 1940's dealt with two motifs:
the "experiences of the fathers and the experiences of the
sons." That is, Cahan, along with Asch, Pinski, and I.
J. Singer (writers in Yiddish) dealt with life in the

shtetl (Eastern European village in the pale of Jewish settlement) or with immigrant struggles. Gold, Schneider, Gollomb, and Ornitz wrote about the struggle of the sons to escape from the old world into the new either by embracing materialism or joining the radical movement.[9] Cahan's insight into the problems of both the sons and the fathers was remarkable; his own education and career account for it.

Cahan followed the path from closed village to open metropolis. After an Orthodox Jewish elementary education in Russia, he sought to become Westernized; his secondary education was in a Russian government school designed to give Jews a non-Judaic curriculum. Cahan associated with the Jewish radical groups in nearby Vilna, a center of the Jewish Bundist movement at the time of his youth.[10] At that time, many Jews spoke Yiddish in their daily affairs and Hebrew as a religious language; their knowledge of Russian was scanty. A few escaped from the *shtetl* by learning literary Russian, the key to the Western world. Cahan went to the United States, where he mastered English to become a journalist. He turned to Yiddish in order to reach the Jewish immigants with the message of socialism. His two novels were written in English, however; and his character David Levinsky exemplifies the transition from the *shtetl* to the city.

The other authors of the first group—Hyman Cohen (who collaborated with his son, Lester), John Cournos, Elias Tobenkin, and Samuel Ornitz—also learned English as a new language and also were shaped by the Bundist culture of Eastern Europe.[11] As immigrant Jews from the pale of settlement (the region in Czarist Russia where Jews were required to live), they disavowed *shtetl* life; as intellectuals, they were international socialists; as New York East Siders, they were familiar with the garment industry. Their books reflect all three influences.

Socialism in the Early Model

Socialism and the novel of social protest were not the exclusive fictional material of the immigrant writers. Indeed, Walter Rideout, in *The Radical Novel in the United States*, sees the immigrant as a seldom treated, minor subject in the socialist novel, citing *Witte Arrives* as one example. He defines "Socialist" novels as those which advocate socialism, explicitly or implicitly. For novels of general social protest he reserves the vaguer term "socialistic." The question of whether or not a novel protesting conditions under capitalism is implicitly advocating socialism is a fine one. At any rate, the books taken up in this chapter examine the immigrant fate from the viewpoint of social protest.[12]

All but one of Rideout's five major categories for the socialist novel ("Conversion, the coming of Socialism, labor struggles, the decadence of the rich, and prostitution") appear in the early model of the education novel. They can be reviewed.

The process of achieving a better life occupies the protagonist, but he does not usually turn to the career of agitator. His conversion is more ambiguous. Lesser characters, however, embrace socialism with the apparent approval of the author. Labor struggles are prominent. Garment making is the only real industry in the novels, and the garment workers engage in a model and victorious labor struggle.

The upper levels of society do not appear as they do in novels by non-Jews in which the Jew is a character. The portrait of Simon Rosedale in *The House of Mirth* (1905) fixes the position of the German Jew. Edith Wharton, whose knowledge of the nuances of social position was sure, presents him as the most blatant of climbers. Seen from below by the Russian Jews who pop-

ulate the early model novels, the German Jew appeared
to be at the top; seen from within by Ludwig Lewisohn
in *The Island Within,* he was, indeed, in Rosedale's
position. Scathing indictments of Tammany leaders and
the parvenu garment manufacturer are frequent, but
these can hardly be called "the decadent rich."

The socialist novel included prostitutes. In the early
model of the education novel, Jewish postitutes figure in
a doctrinaire way—as fallen flowers crushed by urbanization and poverty. The more daring girl, attracted by
the freedom of the new environment, finds herself evicted
by an Orthodox father. The theme of fallen woman did
not evoke the most sophisticated response from the
authors. In *The Sidewalks of New York,* racist theory
supersedes socialistic dogma as the fiery Italian blood of
Goldie, the illegitimate issue of Annie Freedman and
Tony Petruccio, spurs her into the rage needed to battle
her way out of a white slaver's den with a chair leg.

Socialism, introduced as a part of the major theme—
the initiation of the youthful Jew into the secular world
—is treated in the context of the Jewish ethos. The
conflict implicit in the lives of Jewish Bundist Socialists,
who attempted to maintain ethnic and even religious
connections while trying to live out their socialist beliefs, appears in the novels, for example, in the unsuccessful struggle of Orthodox parents against secular learning
for the souls of their offspring. Sometimes the conflict
is embodied in a character such as Uncle Mendel in
Bride of the Sabbath who takes his children out of *heder*
(afternoon religious school), only to set them to studying Graetz's secular *History of the Jews.*

The authors seem to have resolved the polarity of
Judaism and socialism in their own minds. Although their
criticism of Jewish businessmen, judges, and philan-
thropists sometimes earned them the reproach of the
Jewish community, they produced this criticism in a spirit

of social protest which "was Judaism secularized," as Moses Rischin characterizes Jewish socialism. He cites Abraham Cahan as one who found socialism to be a religion.[13] The call for justice which infuses Judaism was easily translated into the Bundists' call for, at the very least, a little more honesty. If the trappings and rituals of Judaism were abandoned, sympathy for suffering Jews and understanding of their character and lives were not.

A recurrent image in the Jewish socialist imagination linked Karl Marx with Moses. Both were deliverers, Moses of the Jewish people, Marx of all mankind. *Zade* (grandfather) in *Bride of the Sabbath* compares the two, calling Marx the "Moses for all the enslaved." Recalling the reluctance of the Jews to follow Moses out of Egypt, he arraigns the Jewish "bosses" who betray the workers: "der Marx wrote Torah when he said we are true to our class first."[14] More than a rationalization, the linking of Marx and Moses is a symbolic expression of the prophetic but divided strain in Jewish socialist thought.

Cahan, Ornitz, and Tobenkin portray the discord between religious observance and fealty to the collective movement; but they remain within the orbit of their people, lovingly describing the customs and the character types whom they condemn, at the same time, for their folly in refusing socialism.

PLOT AND CHARACTER IN THE EARLY MODEL

In its first stage the education novel employed the simple biographical narrative. The protagonist is an innocent, readily mirroring the effects of ordinary immigrant experiences. Most frequently, the novels begin with brief scenes of boyhood in Russia; the voyage to America follows; the greatest part of the novel describes youthful tribulations with family, school, and job. The last section of the novel brings the protagonist into his twenties as he settles upon a career and realizes that the struggle for social justice must be continued within narrow limits. In short, the story is that of innocence transformed into awareness—the education novel theme.

Two of the novels, *The Rise of David Levinsky* and *Haunch, Paunch and Jowl,* turn the theme. In these, the protagonist is a scoundrel. Although not totally bereft of the edifying ambitions of the good hero, he nonetheless devotes his energies to the unethical or dishonest pursuit of material gain. As the novel closes, he is at the end of his career, ruefully reflecting on a choice which has brought him treasure but not emotional fulfillment.

Characters other than the protagonist assume a subsidiary position in the plot. They are a stock group, but a lively one: *melamdim* (*heder* teachers); garment center drudges, either careworn or blazing with socialistic fervor; Tammany satraps; "allrightnik" bosses, widening their distance from the workers through conspicuous consumption. Of greatest importance is the family.

In these early specimens, the siblings do not interact with the protagonist to any degree. They function, rather, as exemplars of the various paths taken by the second generation in the ghetto, following their inclinations into such occupations as garment-factory proprietorship, the stage, and sports.

Parents offend actuarial tables in these first books by dying often and early. In this respect, reality is exaggerated for melodramatic effect. The early death of a parent occurs in all but one of the books; fully five of the seven protagonists eventually are deprived of both parents. Witham in *The Adolescent in the American Novel* estimates the number of novels which portray an incomplete family, including siblings, at one-eighth of the total of all adolescent novels, a number far lower than in the early model.[15]

The father, although not the dim apparition of later Jewish novels, is more likely a blusterer in the house than a patriarch. The curse of the fathers is their inability to grasp American economic conditions. This is complicated by a character flaw; they can best be described as *luft-menschen* (literally "airmen") who flit about unsteadily from one unsound scheme to another, chasing success. In the figure of Semyon Gombarov in John Cournos' *The Mask* (1919), the father is an enlightened atheist, a "kindly anarchist." But he, like the more standard father who tries to maintain some sort of religious life, is inept at making a living. Gombarov brings his ill-fated invention of a gold-like alloy to America only to have his laboratory burn down a second time. The father in *Aaron Traum* likewise has invented something promising, gliders for sewing-machine pedals to simplify the laborious foot movement; but, ignorant of the law, he signs his rights away.

The mothers are not as fully characterized as the fathers. The mother in *The Abyss* is brave and tender, combining a skill in making *gefüllte fisch* with an unaccented English, although her son speaks an unnerving combination of baby talk and Newark slum speech. A conventional figure, she soon dies, permitting the plot to move on to the scenes of vagabond life which are its real interest.

Although it is far from being the first Jewish-American novel, *The Rise of David Levinsky* is the earliest of lasting literary interest and, therefore, is an appropriate choice to begin the detailed examination of education novels.

THE RISE OF DAVID LEVINSKY

The best remembered ghetto novel is *The Rise of David Levinsky* by Abraham Cahan, the long-time editor of the *Jewish Daily Forward* and a major figure in Jewish-American culture.

The elements common to ghetto fiction appear in the book: "the first person as narrator, the flashbacks, the anecdotal style, the homely detail."[16] Cahan employs these with seriousness, eschewing sentimental effect, but not such sentimental materials as the orphaned *Yeshiva* (divinity school) boy and the unrequited love affairs. His unblinking view of human nature, his frank treatment of the sensual Levinsky, and his ordered depiction of the destruction of religious sensibilities under the press of urban necessity place the novel in the category of Naturalism rather than local color.

The book is classified as a Naturalistic novel by Henry Popkin. He places it specifically in the tradition of Dreiser's Frank Cowperwood novels as a sympathetic analysis of an American rise to wealth.[17] Reflecting social history, Levinsky the Russian Jew achieves neither Cowperwood's financial power nor his intimacy with men of importance. Dreiser's *Sister Carrie* is a more likely progenitor than the Cowperwood books for the plot of a *naïf* thrust into an indifferent city, the rising action expressed through sexual entanglements, and the ending in which the unfulfilled protagonist bemusedly ponders his fate. Another similarity to Dreiser is Cahan's ability to dignify the illicit infatuations of pulp love tales. In each man, a serious philosophy of life, determinism, manages to redeem a humorless, graceless prose style.[18]

David in Europe

The European experience of David prefigures his later transformation from raw immigrant to young businessman. Because David is twenty at the time of his emigration, his training as Talmudist has been completed. However, Levinsky is not really a holy man; his character is more complex and more receptive to Americanization as Cahan defines it. At the same time, he is, superficially, the most devout and Judaicized of the protagonists in this study.[19]

Only the first two hundred pages of the novel, Books I to V, treat the boyhood and youth of David Levinsky. The form of the book is that of the biographical education novel, but instead of stopping at the point where Levinsky's future becomes apparent, the novel covers his entire life span. The novel ends with Levinsky in his autumnal years, bemoaning the disappearance of his true self, the innocent *Yeshiva* boy.

As a boy, Levinsky is apt at learning and is destined for the rabbinical school—two characteristics of the education-novel protagonist. The young Talmudic student flirts with the emancipated daughter of a benefactor as she seeks amusement in the provincial village. Possessing the ardent nature and sexual susceptibility of the protagonist as youth, David exchanges the *kaftan* (long gaberdine coat) for the uniform of the *Gymnasist* (high school student) in play with Mathilda. Thus, as John Higham points out in his introduction to the book, David's fall from the absolute purity of the *Yeshiva* scholar really marks the start of his Americanization. Previously, he had been exposed to Westernizing influences—as a boy his daydreams mingled Russian cossacks with David and Goliath—but he had resisted the tempting secular works in Yiddish. Satan, as Levinsky calls his temptation, enters his world in feminine guise.

The pogrom of Elisabethgrad in 1881 starts a general Jewish migration to America. (In an aside, Cahan brings the book forward to 1917 to predict that "the great Russian Revolution" will make the Jews feel that Russia can be their true home.) David's imagination is caught up: "The United States lured me not merely as a land of milk and honey, but also, and perhaps chiefly, as one

of mystery, of fantastic experiences, of marvelous trans-
formations."[20] The theme of a life-long quest is struck
with some irony; the transformation will occur, but it
will be a disappointing one. David is enabled to emi-
grate, not by the sum he has saved by skimping on meals,
but by the money Matilda gives him as she grows fearful that his infatuation may lead to public embarrass-
ment.

At debarcation, David learns the value of his seminary
education. A shipboard friend who is an experienced
tailor is immediately snatched up by an "allrightnik," a
successful former immigrant. David, having no such marketable skill, is dismissed with a quarter and the directions
to the Lower East Side. One of David's several for-
tuitous benefactors presents him with an American suit,
a haircut which shears off his *payos* (side curls), and five
dollars with which he buys a basket of pins and cuff but-
tons. But the irrevocable step into the New World is
taken one day when he has his beard shaved. His stated
reason is an overheard remark that it makes him look
like a greenhorn; but the real motive, as the action quickly
reveals, is his desire to seduce his landlady.

Jewish Socialism and Naturalism in
The Rise of David Levinsky

Like other Jewish Socialists, Cahan infused his Marxist
theory with Jewish thought. Oscar Handlin characterizes
Cahan's brand of socialism in *Adventure in Freedom,*
calling Cahan a socialist—but not a revolutionist—whose
pen was bitter describing the sweat shop or tenement but
saccharine describing the universal values of family life.
Cahan's solution for ghetto ills was reform through labor organization and the Socialist Party.[21] David's
religious period is not merely a false prelude to his real
psychic life as a petty capitalist. Rather, his two lives

are contrasted; the loss of faith is given as the sign of readiness to adopt capitalistic enterprise. This dichotomy reinforces the rebirth theme of the novel (the immigrant is reborn at Ellis Island),[22] but no attempt is made to relate the novel's religious elements to a systematic Socialist critque of society. In an abstract passage in which Cahan's voice speaks as one with Levinsky's, the failure of Orthodox Judaism to hold its followers beyond the walls of the *shtetl* is laid to its inflexibility rather than to industrial society. So closely is inner faith interwoven with external sign that the donning of a starched collar and tie open vistas of disbelief.[23]

David fills the void of vanished faith with theories evolved from his observations as an unscrupulous businessman and codified by his studies in odd moments on the road. Like a Dreiser or a Jack London character, he is profoundly influenced by Herbert Spencer's *Sociology* and *Social Statics*. His hatred of the Cloakmakers' Union leaders—"so many good-for-nothings" jealous of successful businessmen—and pride in his own success lead him to regard the "Struggle for Existence" and "the Survival of the Fittest" as almost plagiarisms of his own thought.

Mulling over his elated discovery of these formal expressions of his theories, he recalls a Jewish parable of chickens fighting for food. It expresses in the more modest terms appropriate to his station the illustration of the squid and the lobster which embodies the theory of evolutionary struggle for Dreiser's Cowperwood.

An important principle of the Naturalist novel, particularly in its European antecedents, lies in the depiction of a particular trade and the character changes it works upon its practitioners, e.g., Zola's Gervaise, who is brutalized by the laundry. The transformation of character in the coarsening Naturalistic fashion can be seen in *The Rise of David Levinsky*. Failing in his ambition to ob-

tain a college education, Levinsky assiduously studies the
manners of Americans. His life becomes a kind of manual
of comportment for assimilationists. Some of the rules:
a long cigar lends its bearer dignity, but a stub is de-
meaningly un-American; conservative brown suits create
an air of dignity; finally, to gesticulate when talking discloses the alien religion. (As editor of the *Forward,*
Cahan carried out a similar program of Americanization,
informing his readers of the arcane rules of proper conduct.) This kind of polish serves only to veneer the use
of devious methods that has debased Levinsky. His real
school has been the garment industry. In it he has learned
to suppress irredeemably his finer instincts.

Another principle of Naturalism is followed by Cahan. In the novel of brutalization, a turning point marks
the beginning of the inexorable downward process, a
chance occurrence of minor import, such as the kiss of
Gervaise and Coupeau in the laundry in *L'Assommoir.*
Levinsky blames a spilt bottle of milk for thwarting his
scholarly ambitions and turning him toward business:
his employer's reprimand for his clumsiness makes him
resolve to go into business for himself, using the sum he
has been saving for tuition. As in the naturalistic predecessors, the triviality of the event suggests social forces
in operation more impelling than chance.

The novel's thorough treatment of the garment industry, labor problems, and immigrant life earns it a
place in the group of novels critical of the business ethic
appearing during this period, which stretches, say, from
Mark Twain's *The Gilded Age* to Sinclair Lewis' *Babbitt.*
Levinsky is a Jewish Babbitt, his acceptance of American
free-enterprise philosophy undermined by doubt and the
desire for a more poetic life.

Aaron Traum

Lester Cohen, like Cahan, Tobenkin and Cournos, was a journalist, a contest editor for the *New York Graphic*. His first novel, *Sweepings* (1926), a family saga of a Boston merchant, was something of a popular success in the 1920's. In the composition of his Jewish novel, *Aaron Traum*, Lester was joined by his father, Hyman, a Chicago physician and Yiddish poet, to whom *Sweepings* had been dedicated. The spirit which infuses *Aaron Traum* is the one common to these early models of the education novel—Bundist socialism. If one were to guess at the guiding hand of the book, one would choose the father; the tradition which informs it is more clearly the European Jewish-Socialist one than the American one of the second generation.

Aaron Traum follows the biographical pattern much in the fashion of the other early models. Traum's boyhood is covered, his youth as a garment worker and strike leader, and his period of wandering. At the close of the novel, Traum in his late twenties ends his searching and dreaming as he finds his true vocation, with improbable precipitousness, as a wood sculptor.

Also employed in the novel are the typical elements of the novel of youth in this stage of its development. In the first scene, Aaron, at his mother's graveside, is about to leave for America. He has been raised by his stepmother—a tug at the heartstrings especially popular among family-minded Jewish readers. His father is the familiar *luftmensch* inventor. His dreams of some mechanical contrivance to make his fortune are expressed in Jewish terms: he communes prophetically with Jehovah, letting the practical world go by. The brothers are obvious symbols of the alternate paths taken by the young Jew in America: soft-faced Sammy, squeaking away at *Kol Nidre* to become Sascha of the violin, and stony-faced Maxie, shadow-boxing about the basement to become a ring champion.

The hero, too, is standard. An Oliver Twist, he is sent to work at eleven. His original career plan in Europe—to be a rabbi—is frustrated by poverty. The surname, Traum, the German word for "dream," indicates Aaron's character and the theme of the book: the search of a sensitive youth for his lost Jewish boyhood and for an edifying life in America. The linking of Traum with the biblical name Aaron suggests that this is the struggle of all Jews in America.

Aaron Traum as a Naturalist Work

A novelistic tradition as well as a socialistic one informs *Aaron Traum*. The appearance of vulgar characters and the minute examination of their occupations was prepared by the European and American Naturalists. A touchstone to identify American Naturalist writing is the Spencer[24] reading hero. Dreiser, London, and practically all the novelists of the early model mention *Social Statics* or another of the books of the canon. Aaron Traum, in the tumult of the crowded ghetto basement, studies the *First Principles*. Traum's combination of great physical strength, brawling ability, and intellect makes him resemble Martin Eden more than, say, a Zangwill peddler. In such a way did the Jewish-American novelist elude the stereotype of the Jew in English fiction, finding a nobler form to embody the Jewish spirit.

Aaron Traum is most clearly in the tradition of American Naturalism when, in the manner of Frank Norris' *McTeague,* it combines deterministic thought with melodramatic action. The authors of *Aaron Traum* resemble Norris in their espousal of determinist doctrine and their melodramatic illustration of it. Such a combination occurs as Aaron observes his Uncle Skolnick, the King of the Pushcarts, enter a Houston Street house of prostitution one lively Tammany election night. Aaron falls back thinking, reviewing the "miasmic ensemble," realizing that "the disorders of humanity were not entirely due to the capitalistic system." In the terminology of the determinist novelist, he envisions the Darwinian struggle within an indifferent Nature:

He caught an inkling of something beyond the confines of systems and philosophies—so many men, so many diverse appetites. . . . Earth—the caldron of creation . . . the primordial unrest of earth flowing in the veins of men . . . men seek—blindly, nobly, confusedly . . . the veins of men leaden with lust, salty with tears. . . . Man—ferment of earth . . . a thousand blood mixtures are his—goals to reach before the end . . . for a moment the spirit climbs toward the light—groping, forgetting, remembering. . . . Remembering what?—an illusion traced in the sands of time. And the primordial darkness waits, and wearies not, waiting for the return of the bit of ooze that has spluttered out of the caldron of the earth. Time is long, life is short—man is what he needs to be—snatch, then, in your moment, at star or flesh-pot . . . ahoy! . . . ahoy! . . . before the great darkness engulfs. . . .[25]

His extended reflection is interrupted by the sight of Uncle Skolnik emerging from the low den and tumbling down the stairs stricken with *angina pectoris*. Uncle has chanced upon his own fallen daughter.

While the depiction of the garment industry in *Aaron Traum* does not attempt the documentary completeness of the later proletarian industrial novel, it does survey the various kinds of garment industry jobs and Lower East Side shops as Aaron progresses up the ladder of labor skills. His first job at the age of thirteen is shirt tacker in a strangely empty shop. Aaron quits when he learns that he is a scab. His next job is more congenial. His employers, the Rifkin brothers, had taken scholastic honors in Odessa and the appealing "air of the Russian intelligentsia hung about them."[26] Here he learns Hood's

"The Song of the Shirt," an appropriate lyric. Such a shop was not at all unlikely. Morris Hillquit describes an early job in a congenial shirtmaking shop where the operators spent as much time discussing social and literary topics and heartily singing revolutionary songs as they did working. Hillquit's listing of the aims of the United Hebrew Trades, which he helped found in 1888, confirms the close link between labor-union activity and socialism in the early Jewish labor movement. The aims were "(1) mutual aid and cooperation among the Jewish trade unions of New York; (2) organization of new unions; (3) the propaganda [sic] of Socialism among the Jewish workers." In order to carry out his organizing, Hillquit learned Yiddish.[27]

Prosperity takes the shop downtown and changes the rest day from the true Sabbath, Saturday, to the Christian Sunday. The entirely Jewish staff is divided on this; but Aaron is not ready for this change, although he is now fifteen and has mastered the advanced skill of "sleeve throwing." Soon Aaron is an apprentice cloakmaker in his brother's shop, but the job is no sinecure. Bernard Traum is a selfish "allrightnik," determined to make his way in America unimpeded by sympathy for family or fellow man.

Aaron's education is furthered by Socialist-minded fellow workers. He discovers the Grace Aguilar library and a bookstore where doctrinaire journals and pulp serials open his mind to the wider world.[28] He studies Spencer, Henry George, and Edward Bellamy; but imaginative literature rouses him most: Balzac, Ibsen, and Zola. Late one night after reading Flaubert's *Salammbô*, he walks the streets, revisiting his former lodgings and exulting in his true rebirth—not in the immigrant hold of a ship, nor in the shops, but in the library.

By now Aaron is a model proletarian hero—six feet

of bone and muscle, with broad shoulders and a strong face. His sharpened sensibilities and his solidarity with the workers bring him leadership of the garment-workers' union and membership in the brigade of "The Strong"—street fighters against the police and strike-breaking sluggers. Emulating Ibsen's Dr. Stockmann, he becomes a teacher in the shops, finally organizing an adult education circle taught by East Side writers and scholars. (Similarly using physicians and philosophers, Jacob Gordon, playwright and editor of journals of the Yiddish theater, founded the Educational League in 1900. The hero of Joseph Gollomb's *Unquiet,* an education novel of 1935, served in such a school, called "Breadwinner's College."[29]) Presumably on free nights, Aaron mounts a soap box in Rutgers Square to preach the gospel of socialism which he has absorbed in the streets from East Side speakers and, more intensively, from police clubs, as the authors put it.

Despite its episodic plotting and labored prose, *Aaron Traum* rises above the melodrama of strike scenes and Tammany villains. The minor figures are a gallery of ghetto types, displaying the variety and vigor with which Jews responded to the city. Aaron Traum retains a certain interest as a late portrait of that Jack London anomaly, the social-Darwinian superman. A Jewish basis is laid for Traum's dreaming and searching. It is "the age-long preoccupation of his forebears with learning, commentation [sic], dreams obscure and revelations everlasting."[30] His education in shop, free library, and radical bookstore also forms his character. The pages describing Traum's socialistic education and his superhuman labors in the "cause" are the most vivid in the book. The intense emotionality which gives *Martin Eden* the power that novel yet retains is akin to the spirit of *Aaron Traum,* a similar biography of education.

The Uncle as Conscience
Witte Arrives

Elias Tobenkin's *Witte Arrives* and Samuel Ornitz's *Haunch, Paunch and Jowl* exemplify the use of a minor character to embody the conscience of the protagonist. In each an uncle, as the unmarried brother, demonstrates in his life history the ideals of revolution. Other examples of the type are the journalist Mendel Walkowitz in *Bride of the Sabbath,* the revolutionist Grisha in *Unquiet,* and Nathan Polansky in *My Son, the Lawyer* by Henry Denker. By the Sixties, with Uncle Asher in Philip Roth's *Letting Go,* the type has degenerated from the dedicated foe of the Czar to a seedy Bohemian, living with a *shiksa,* and incapable of demonstrating an edifying lifestyle to the searching nephew.

Uncle Simeon Witkowski in *Witte Arrives* seems to have materialized from the bucolic daydreams of the protagonist. Bearded and consumptive-looking, fitting the cartoon image of the revolutionist, Simeon arrives, as an electrifying apparition, in the midwestern town where young Emil Witte lives with his father, whose devotion to the Sabbath has kept him strapped to the peddler's pack. Years before, Simeon had abandoned his Talmudic studies in Vilna, taking up Russian in order to acquire a secular education and, presumably, falling in with the Bundists. One thing led to another and he was sent to Siberia, charged with attempting to assassinate Czar Alexander III.

Uncle Simeon's function in the novel is to pronounce some simple Marxist theories and to dramatize the conversion of young Witte. Simeon's socialistic view of history through the ages is recounted in detail. He explains to his young nephew that the nihilist struggle against the Czar is only a prelude to the war against the entire economic and social system. The serenity in America will be followed by upheaval in the twentieth century. Giving young Witte a copy of the *Communist Manifesto,* Simeon returns to the struggle abroad. He leaves no forwarding address but grimly suggests a subscription to *Free Leaves,* the party organ which carries death notices. As a result of his teachings and heroic example, Emil is converted to socialism.

HAUNCH, PAUNCH AND JOWL

A contrast to the use in *Witte Arrives* of the uncle as pure spirit, with little plot integration, is found in *Haunch, Paunch and Jowl.*[31] Since Meyer Hirsch is a rogue-hero, his uncle as conscience has an evil voice. Philip Gold, rather than his scheming nephew, has the education-novel hero's talent for intellection. A meeting of a mixed group of leftists (non-resistant, socialist, revolutionist, and anarchist) inspires Philip to devise his theory of success: climbing upon the backs of the workers and then circumventing the hated German-Jewish bosses by dealing directly with immigrant labor. He urges Meyer to use the freedom of America to exploit whomever one pleases, reminding him that in Europe their family was not respectable and that it is up to them to become distinguished ancestors. The reversal of fortunes in America—which found the *shayne leite* (educated folk) in the sweat shops of the *grobe* (the gross) who had the shrewdness and flexibility to rise to the top —was a favorite theme of the immigrant novel. The mister becomes a *shister* (shoemaker) and the *shister* a mister, as the folk expression had it.

Both men rise. Uncle Philip bests the hated German Jews and enters their society by marrying one of their homelier daughters. In a parallel development, Meyer Hirsch achieves a Tammany judgeship, having started his legal practice with his former boyhood gang who now require considerable legal aid. Meyer's nature is ardent, however; his viscera dominates. Unlike Uncle Philip, who is satisfied with a loveless marriage and dies wasted by cancer of the stomach, Meyer enjoys a lively love-life and grows stout on rich Jewish cooking. His long-time pursuit of an ethereal social worker, the expression of his higher urges, is frustrated. She marries a wealthy sociologist, an occurrence not without precedent in the ghetto in that period—at least two marriages of poor Jewish girls to liberal millionaires made headlines.

The parallel is further maintained in politics. Meyer has taken the demotic road of Tammany. Blackmail brings him a judgeship, but a scandal frustrates his ultimate ambition, the governor's chair. Philip dreams on the national level; as a high-tariff Republican he might become the Plenipotentiary to Islam, Turkey having the only ambassadorship open to a Jew.[32]

The Judaism of Philip and Meyer

The Philip Gold sub-plot adds a needed dimension to the novel. More complex than Meyer, Philip is, nonetheless, more single-minded. His apostasy from the human race is a deliberate one, a decision based on the irrational emotion of hate, but carried out with the logic of *pilpul* and the tenacity of the erstwhile Talmudist. (*Pilpul* was a rigorous, mind-sharpening, argumentative method of examining the religious texts.) In the service of the American god of Mammon, Philip enlists the undeviating severity which is the only legacy of his years of Judaic studies. In contrast, the source of Meyer's decision for Mammon is his training in the streets; the exciting Ludlow Street Gang easily outweighs the influence of the despairing *melamed* of the little ghetto *heder*. As a result of their Americanization, both men are untouched by the moral strictures of Judaism; but it is Meyer who, uninformed by a transcendent culture, vaguely daydreams of a finer existence.

Both men are irreligious; but Meyer, as a politician, must keep up appearances and, in fact, plays the "professional Jew" with relish. In the course of depicting Meyer as a surface Jew, Ornitz zestfully portrays an assemblage of hypocrites—from the Congressman, an officer in a Jewish fraternal order who has one speech (concerning Russian pogroms), to the ambitious young Reform rabbi whose only talent is to flatter his wealthy parishioners.

Meyer is the worst hypocrite. His *bar mitzvah* (confirmation) means only release from the confinement of *heder* with its "insatiable monster, [the] God of Vengeance."[33] The *heders* in the Pale were not superior to the ones in America, nor were the *melamdim* of a different sort. It was the solidarity and conformity of the *shtetl* that minimized the number of Meyer Hirsches. Meyer's evil character is not simply the stereotype of the Jew of English literature brought to these shores. To be sure, such a reading is possible from without, whence he may appear to be the shrewd self-serving Jew. From the inside, however, this is a tale of the deviating Jew. As an adolescent, Meyer helps his gang stone the freethinkers at The Talkers' Cafe, where non-believers dine on a fast day and advertise an audacious Yom Kippur Picnic. The incident is probably based on The Grand Yom Kippur Ball held in 1890. (Yom Kippur is the Day of Atonement, a solemn fast day.) Meyer promptly goes uptown to take his dinner, famished by the exercise. In the kind of incident which brought the book the resentment of the Jewish community, he finds the restaurant crowded with his "hungry co-religionists." It is the busiest day of the year.

The opinions voiced by a minor character reflect the

views of the author more precisely than do those of
Meyer, the narrator, since the latter are overlaid with
a self-defensive cynicism. Dr. Lionel Crane, Harvard-
accented, tall, tastefully turned out in "simple cane"
and pince-nez, theorizes about the "Jewish Question." It
will continue in America until the Jews drop their
"bizarre Jewishness" and outlandish attire. Crane ex-
coriates the professional Jews who raise alarums over
every grievance and calls instead for self-criticism of the
kind, presumably, that Ornitz supplies in this novel.
Crane condemns the few Jews who are guilty of "usury,
faginism, receiving solen goods, corrupting officials, pro-
curing, brothel-keeping, sharp-dealing, legitimatizing the
cheating and over-charging of Gentiles, labor-sweating."
Medical imagery infuses the talk of Crane, a specialist in
"Race Psychopathology." He proposes a therapy of
self-probing which may induce a burn but which will
cleanse the Jews of the neurasthenic, insane, feeble-
minded, and diabetic.[34]

Neither the diagnosis nor the astringent prescription
seems to have been very acceptable to the Jewish readership. The fears that Ornitz may have felt in writing this
boldly polemic book break through to the surface in
Crane's monologue: "I know I will be called the enemy
of my people, hounded, cursed, spat upon, . . . called
a renegade, turncoat, the paid tool of the Anti-Semites
. . . *I will take the sick ego of my people to the clinic.*"[35]

BRIDE OF THE SABBATH

Ornitz again essayed the novel of Jewish content almost thirty years later in *Bride of the Sabbath,* a book
that was to have neither the infamous reputation of
Haunch, Paunch and Jowl nor its readership. While a
new era in Jewish life as well as in American literature
had appeared since the writing of the earlier book, the

plot, style, and ideas of *Bride of the Sabbath* place it alongside its early model predecessors rather than among the books which return to the turn of the century with the objective viewpoint of a later generation. There is even a regression of sorts. Abandoning the rogue protagonist, Ornitz employs the biographical plot, portraying the wholly admirable dreamer-idealist of the early model, a less sophisticated device than that of the rogue. Although *Bride of the Sabbath* manages to overcome its anachronism, even to display a certain vitality, its chief interest lies in the Bundist socialist ideas of the author. If Ornitz had not refined his novelistic technique, neither had he qualified very much the ideas of his youth.

It is these ideas which give the book its dated tone. The American-born novelist, turning back to the period when his parents or grandparents faced ghetto issues, brings a nostalgic viewpoint to bear; Ornitz takes up each vanished issue as if it still called for a commitment. He levels scorn at the Tammany complex of judge, lawyer, ward heeler, and policeman. Finding such a document, a veritable encyclopedia of the attitudes and issues of an earlier day, is like finding a living fossil; and the novel can be dissected for the same purpose as fossils are: to determine the nature of an organism by studying its parts, with the archaeologist's interest in a past era rather than the biologist's concern with present ecology.

One can surmise that the omniscient narrator's ideas are those of the author simply because they are expressed by the voice of Ornitz, candid and in his own person, casually jumping ahead to cite future events such as the coming of the Third Reich. The use of different characters to express alternative positions on the political spectrum is not ignored, however. Uncle Mendel Walkowitz, a columnist for the *Daily Yiddish Advance* (the *Forward*), professes views more radical than those

of the narrator. Saul Kramer, the protagonist, is the
more conservative voice of Ornitz. Scorned for his mod-
eration by Uncle Mendel, Kramer espouses the new
theory of social psychology. Three major voices speak,
then, and a multitude of topics of Jewish life are treated.

The Narrator's Voice

The voice of Ornitz is most concerned with detailing
life on the Lower East Side from the Spanish-American
War to World War I—from Saul Kramer as a toddler
to Saal Cramer (he is thus renamed by a Tammany min-
ion) as a young social worker. Jewish holidays are
described feelingly. Even more esoteric Judaica appear:
the *mikva* (ritual bath), the *payos* (side curls), *tsitsis*
(fringed undergarment), and the *bris* (ritual circumcision). Some of the local phenomena are colorful traces of
a vanished past, e.g., the underground birth-control
clinic which recommends that the harried wife escape
her husband by taking a promenade; the Free Burial Society, a *shtetl* institution which imported well; the fad
for Malted Milk, regarded as protection against tuber-
culosis; and soda water which caused the spread of the
candy store. Much of this is presented as straight social
history, bolding overlaid on the story, but intriguing.

The treatment of other matters is even less studied.
The reader is told that Henry Ford was yet to affect ad-
versely every Jew in the world and "contribute materially
to the rise of Hitler"[36] and that Henry James, a "Hell-
enizer," abandoned his heritage to become an Englishe-
man. This last appears in a breezy seven-page essay on
assimilation: "Lest we forget: Jewish asthma, how de-
ceitful; a Jewish million dollars, how boastful; and Jew-
rotic, how clannish."[37] This is Ornitz at his worst.

When Ornitz is able to couple social history to the
plot, there is considerable impact, e.g., the picket-line

struggles of the grandfather, who has organized the
Orthodox garment workers employed for lower wages
in shops that permit them to observe Saturday as the
Sabbath. In another such effective scene, Hymie Resnik,
a strikebreaker with Tammany influence, is clubbed and
arrested. Saul, a liberal concerned with Hymie's civil
rights, delays an assignation with his labor-organizer
girlfriend. At the station house, Saul is distressed to see
the fawning care accorded to Hymie; he returns to the
girl, but the moment is lost. In such a way does Ornitz
utilize situation to exemplify theme.

The novel includes much spoken Yiddish given in its
English translation, a means of determining the verbal
facility of the Jewish-American writer as much as the
authenticity of his credentials as a Jew. Ornitz's method
is to express the idioms peculiar to Yiddish by literal
translation, e.g., "Hear in" for *Her sich ein;* "What
make you, chossen!" for *Was machst du, chossen* (bride-
groom) ; and "Mr. Jacob-the-Tall-One" for *Herr Yakov-
der-Haycher.* While such phrases are sometimes incongruous, they do have a certain dignity because they are
never used solely for comic effect.

Historical verisimilitude is sought by the inclusion of
such actual events as the Triangle Waist Factory fire
of 1911 and the funeral parade of a chief rabbi, and of
such minor characters as Maude Stokely, a Christian
Socialist do-gooder, and her husband, a Bukharin anarchist sculptor, who entertain Bohemians in their Washington Square South apartment, recalling Mabel Dodge's
"Evenings."

The custom of drawing upon historical events and
personages in this period was not limited to Jewish
writers, of course. Realistic novelists have long grappled
with the question of how much actuality to inject into
their imaginative structure. The Triangle fire figured in
some of the radical and non-radical fiction of the period

as a sort of *cause célèbre*. Elias Tobenkin used it in *The Road* (1922). To change the name needs little imagination. In Zoe Beckley's *A Chance to Live* (1918), it is the "Circle Waist Company"; in *Unquiet* the circle is squared; and, geometry being exhausted, it becomes the "Tip Top Shirtwaist Company" in *Bride of the Sabbath*.

A Radical's Voice

Ornitz' more radical voice, Uncle Mendel, "a Yiddish journalist, a freethinker, a socialist, and a first-class Epikaros" (Ornitz' term for apostate), expresses scorn for all the rites of Judaism. Uncle Mendel writes antisynagogue pieces and defies a Jewish audience with antireligious "truths." But his socialism is that of the older generation. He has abandoned the religion but not the people, who can, after all, serve as a model for proletarian struggle. His greatest moment comes when he is arrested with Bella Taub (Emma Goldman) for assassinating President McKinley. Soon he is back, jaunty as ever in his Bohemian getup, commenting with Marxist wisdom about the ineffectiveness of individual protest. Although his costume is complete, from slouch hat to pointed goatee, flowing tie, and light walking stick, Uncle Mendel is more substantial than a caricature—and not only because the outlines of historical referents are apparent. (A possible prototype is Michael Zametkin, a socialist lecturer, publicist, and editor.) Uncle Mendel is a type, but his important function in the novel makes him more than a doctrinal puppet.

The Protagonist's Voice

Saul Kramer, the third voice, represents the secular drive of the second generation toward Americanism. With the usual symbolism of the immigrant novel, he was conceived in the Old Country but born in the New World. His unconventionality is foreshadowed at his birth when he wets the *Mohel's* (ritual circumcisor) beard; his grandmother dubs him an *Azis Panim* (flier in the face). The same description was given of another protagonist of the education novel, Vanya Gombarof of Cournos' autobiographical *The Mask*. By definition, the secular author/protagonist was an enlightened Jew, an apostate. Exceeding probability, a grape falls into Saul's mouth at the circumcision, leading to another grandmotherly prediction, that he will be a glutton and rich. But this time she is wrong. Saul's hunger will be for experience.

Saul finds the ghetto to be a complex place. His grandmother was responsible for his early upbringing and has so insulated him that a beardless male face frightens him. Ultra-orthodoxy is one pole, then, of Jewish life in the ghetto. The other pole is socialism and trade-union activity. This polarity is symbolized by the portraits which face each other in Saul's household: Karl Marx, the master of international socialism, and Theodor Herzl, the founder of political Zionism. As an Epikaros, Saul reaches beyond both aspects to become a "liberal," a social psychologist, employing the Freudian science which Uncle Mendel (and frequently Ornitz) discounts.

As in most ghetto biographical novels, the search for fulfillment and a life that is ethically viable forms the basis of the plot. Saul's liberalism leads him to Christian socialism and beyond it to Tolstoy's "Resist not evil." Failing to anticipate the revival of non-resistance, Ornitz as narrator tells us that this is too weak a strategy to succeed in the world.

Although the web of theories articulated by the three voices of the novel are generally extraneous to the action, the novel is not devoid of craft. The plot also delineates Ornitz' theory of the meaning of Jewish life in America.

The unconsummated love for Saul of Pauline Kaplan forms part of a triad of love affairs, each representing for Saul a possible destiny in Jewish-American life. Forced out of school to help support her consumptive father, the American-born Pauline becomes a lowly "baster," like a greenhorn. She rejects everything Jewish in her drive to material success. She lives the life of conspicuous consumption—a non-Jewish life, lived by Jews, as Ornitz sees it. The second possible fate for Saul is the enlightened, labor-socialist one, embodied in "Wild Becky" Rosenberg, a firebrand of the needle trades. (A similar character appears as Becky Nadelman, "Needleman," in *Unquiet*.) A veteran of picket battles, she wears the daring "Annette Kellerman" one-piece swimsuit in idyllic days off the line. Becky marries an ex-Catholic radical. But the great love of Saul's life is a dancer. A Catholic unable to accept her divorce as a fact, Nancy tries to convert Saul, who finds the consummation of their love frustrated by her vision of the Virgin. Nancy becomes a lay worker in a hospital for the incurably ill. Saul has accepted none of these destinies.

In the last scene of the book, Saul accidentally knocks off his glasses and says *"Mazel Tov"* (good luck) as they shatter; unconsciously, he recalls the destruction of the Temple in Jerusalem. He turns back to the ghetto, finally and exaltedly accepting his destiny as a Jew, but also celebrating the "bride he had led to espouse Christ—Mazel Tov!"[38] At last, we learn the identity of Saul Kramer's true bride, the Bride of the Sabbath. His fate is to live a true Jewish life.

Bride of the Sabbath is an appropriate title. The *Shabbes Kaleh* (the Sabbath Queen) is the symbolic figure for the Sabbath. The coming of the seventh day is marked by her visit to every Jewish home. The Sabbath is the central Jewish holiday; but one must look to the European *shtetl* to discover the web of associations and customs woven around it. The unity of life within enclaves in small towns or larger cities such as Odessa permitted such customs as the complete cessation of work during the hours of the Sabbath, the observation of the religious ceremonies within the home and *shul* (synagogue), the preparation of food cooked in advance, and the avoidance of riding or the carrying of money or other objects. With its carefully ordered preparations, its alternation of worship, fellowship, and rest, and its escape from the mundane, the day achieved a spirit never possible in the New World. The exploitation of workers by paying them less in shops that closed on Saturday has been treated in novels, but there is nothing in Jewish-American fiction comparable to, say, the scenes in Sholom Aleichem which revolve around the efforts of the traveler to reach home in time for the Sabbath or for Tevye the dairyman to provide for the important *shabbes* dinner.

THE BOY IN THE SUN and THE ISLAND WITHIN

Two slim novels which appeared in 1928 are strikingly similar in many respects. Both are rare in expressing the education-novel theme from the viewpoint of the German Jews who, despite their advanced Westernization and secularization, have never been prominent in the efflorescence of Jewish novels in the United States.[39] Paul Rosenfeld's *The Boy in the Sun* sold modestly and was soon forgotten; Ludwig Lewisohn's *The Island Within* ran to thirty printings and is one of the landmarks of Jewish-American fiction.

The careers of the two men can be contrasted. Rosenfeld lived and worked modestly, devoting his life to modern music. He wrote only the one novel. Despite his small frame, his death was the occasion for a memorial volume remarkable for the devotion of such men as Ed-

mund Wilson and Sherwood Anderson. Lewisohn enjoyed a more flamboyant career, fraught with contro-
versy, and produced a great number of novels and books
of criticism. Both men are largely forgotten.[40]

Each novel describes the life of a youth in a comfortable, Upper West Side Manhattan home. The theme of
youth encountering experience is linked to the theme of
anti-Semitism. The preoccupation with poverty, the garment industry, and socialism found in the novels by
Russian Jews is absent. These were not, after all, the
experience in this milieu. What is found instead in each
novel is a sensitive look at the subtleties of discrimina-
tion as they are encountered by the assimilated, non-
Orthodox Jew as he attempts to move freely into the
parlors of established New York society—not at its
highest levels, but at the level just below.

The Island Within is the more objective of the two
novels. It provides historical speculation delivered by a
self-conscious narrator. The plot is more spacious, prefaced by the history of the Levy family through several
European generations, told in terms of the discrimina-
tion they encounter in the university and the professions
in Germany. The legal and social obstacles thrown up
in their path are all the harder for them to understand
because they have adopted the external appearance, customs, and patriotism of their fellow Germans. In the
United States, assimilation is equally difficult. The focus
of this problem in *The Island Within* is the protagonist's
sister. Rather hysterically, she finds herself blocked from
admission to a private academy for girls. Her somewhat
richer friends have exhausted the ten per cent Jewish
quota, the upper limit for maintaining a Christian clien-
tele, according to the headmistress. This incident and a
subsequent attempt by the girl to convert to a prospective
fiancé's Christianity is observed, bemusedly, by the
younger brother, who himself later marries a non-Jew

and much later finds his way back to unassimilated Judaism, the same journey that Lewisohn took.

Rosenfeld's book, *The Boy in the Sun,* deals with the same material, the subtle encounters with anti-Semitism of the upper middle class, in a more compressed manner than *The Island Within,* omitting the historical flashbacks and covering a shorter span of the protagonist's life. The portrait of the father, ending his days in exhausting poverty, recalls incidents of Rosenfeld's life.

The anti-Semitism encountered by an assimilating German Jew is not the principal identifying characteristic of the early education novel. The recurrent subjects of that novel in its early stage are rebirth upon entering Ellis Island, privation in the ghetto of New York City, socialism, labor strife and working conditions in the garment industry, and the loss of religion and ritual customs by the Eastern European Jew. These were to be repeated in a new form in the decade which followed the years of the early model.

Notes to Chapter 2

1. Nathan Kussey, *The Abyss* (New York: The Macmillan Co., 1916). Another education novel appearing as the first of a trilogy is John Cournos' *The Mask* (New York: George H. Doran Co., 1919).

2. Elias Tobenkin, *Witte Arrives* (New York: Frederick A. Stokes Co., 1916).

3. Abraham Cahan, *The Rise of David Levinsky* (New York: Harper and Brothers, 1917; Harper Torchbook, 1960, ed. John Higham.)

4. Higham, *ibid.,* p. ix.

5. Moses Rischin, *The Promised City* (Cambridge: Harvard University Press, 1962), pp. 124-125.

6. According to Montagu F. Modder's *The Jew in the Literature of England* (New York: Jewish Publication Society, 1939), the first appearance of the ghetto as an exotic subject was in Leopold Kompert's *Scenes from the Ghetto,* which was translated from the German and published in London in 1882, not long before Henry Harland was describing the New York ghetto in his novels. Modder credits Israel Zangwill's *Children of the Ghetto* (1892) with being the first English-language treatment of the basic theme of Jewish fiction: the conflict

68   THE INVENTION OF THE JEW

between Jewish faith and secular, democratic forces. That novel was commissioned by the Jewish Publication Society of America as a "Jewish *Robert Elsmere*": John Gross, "Zangwill in Retrospect," *Commentary,* XXXVIII, No. 6 (Dec. 1964), 54. Abraham Cahan's *Yekl, A Tale of the Ghetto* was published in 1896. The appearance of the ghetto as a subject in English and American fiction was almost simultaneous.

7. *Literary History of the United States,* p. 1132; Louis Kronenberger, "Gambler in Publishing: Horace Liveright," *The Atlantic,* CCXV, No. 1 (Jan. 1965), 97; *Fortune,* XIII, No. 2 (Feb. 1936), 79–144.

8. Ludwig Lewisohn, *The Island Within* (New York: Harper and Bros., 1928); Paul Rosenfeld, *The Boy in the Sun* (New York: The Macauley Co., 1928); Samuel Ornitz, *Haunch, Paunch and Jowl* (New York: Boni & Liveright, Inc., 1923); Nat J. Ferber, *The Sidewalks of New York* (Chicago: Pascal Covici, 1927); Hyman and Lester Cohen, *Aaron Traum* (New York: Horace Liveright, 1930); Samuel Ornitz, *Bride of the Sabbath* (New York: Rinehart & Co., Inc., 1951).

9. Daniel Bell, "A Parable of Alienation," in *Mid-Century,* ed. Harold U. Ribalow, (New York: The Beechhurst Press, 1955), p. 141.

10. Nathan Glazer, *American Judaism* (Chicago: The University of Chicago Press, 1957), p. 68.

11. The writers who will appear in the third chapter, Mike Gold, Isidore Schneider, Meyer Levin, Daniel Fuchs, and Henry Roth, were either born in America or were brought here as children. Their consciousness was formed in the United States. Primarily, their language was English, although Yiddish may have been spoken in their home and they may have learned to read Hebrew without understanding its meaning.

12. Walter Rideout, *The Radical Novel in the United States* (Cambridge: Harvard University Press, 1956), pp. 73 ff.

13. Rischin, *Promised City,* p. 166.

14. Ornitz, *Bride of the Sabbath,* p. 73.

15. J. Tasker Witham, *The Adolescent in the American Novel* (New York: Frederick Ungar Publishing Co., 1964), p. 82.

16. Jane Hayman, "Futile and Uncertain," *Commentary,* XXXI, No. 6 (June 1961), 550.

17. Henry Popkin, "Jewish Writers in England," *Commentary,* XXXI, No. 2 (Feb. 1961), 136. Isaac Rosenfeld shares this reading of the book as Naturalist in "David Levinsky: The Jew as American Millionaire," in *An Age of Enormity,* ed. Theodore Solotaroff (Cleveland: The World Publishing Co., 1962), pp. 273–281.

18. At one time Cahan planned to write a treatise on Darwinism. John Higham, in the introduction to the Harper Torchbook edition, cites the American dream of success in W. D. Howells' *The Rise of Silas Lapham* and Dreiser's *Sister Carrie* as the American influences, the pity and calm impartiality of Tolstoy and Chekhov as the Russian realist influence, and the self-identification of Cahan with his Jewish characters as the Yiddish influence. (p. x) In *The Jew in the American*

Novel, Fiedler finds the European Naturalist novel to be Cahan's source and the American novel to be his aspiration.

19. An analysis of the religious significance of *The Rise of David Levinsky* is made by Nathan Glazer in *American Judaism,* pp. 68–69. The religion of the Eastern European Jews emphasized ritual observances at the expense of a theology, which might have helped them resist the challenges to their practices. Like Levinsky, they shed these customs as soon as they escaped the *shtetl.*

20. *David Levinsky,* ed. Higham, p. 61.

21. *Adventure in Freedom* (New York: McGraw-Hill Book Co., Inc., 1954), pp. 125–126.

22. The arrival at Castle Garden or Ellis Island is seen as an image of rebirth by autobiographers as well as education novelists. See Mary Antin, *The Promised Land* (1917), and Joseph Freeman, *An American Testament* (1936).

23. *David Levinsky,* p. 110.

24. The choice of Spencer by the Jewish novelists is not wholly due to their taste for Darwinism. The intellectuality of ghetto children won the admiration of Police Commissioner McAdoo: "Think of it! Herbert Spencer preferred to a fairy story by boys and girls." Rischin, *Promised City,* p. 209.

25. *Aaron Traum,* p. 316.

26. *Ibid.,* p. 92.

27. In *Autobiographies of American Jews,* ed. Harold U. Ribalow (Philadelphia: The Jewish Publication Society of America, 1965), p. 79.

28. Jewish groups had founded the Aguilar Free Library Society. Its East Broadway unit was "the most assiduously used in the city." Rischin, *Promised City,* p. 209.

29. Rischin, p. 141; Joseph Gollomb, *Unquiet* (New York: Dodd, Mead and Co., 1935), pp. 400-401.

30. *Aaron Traum,* p. 284.

31. Rideout, *Radical Novel,* p. 118, finds the book to mirror the spirit of the Twenties in its "unconventional form and its enveloping irony" and conjectures that *The Rise of David Levinsky* was the probable source of the narrative device of a scoundrel revealing all. (See chapter V for the rogue-hero.)

32. Rideout, p. 119.

33. *Haunch, Paunch and Jowl,* p. 63.

34. *Ibid.,* pp. 198 ff.

35. *Ibid.,* p. 200.

36. *Bride of the Sabbath,* p. 203.

37. *Ibid.,* p. 120.

38. *Ibid.,* p. 410.

39. Stanley Kauffmann, in a review of Irving Malin's *Jews and Americans,* conjectured about the literary dominance of the Russian Jews over the German Jews. Less able to assimilate, the Russian Jews turned inward. Their Jewishness became an "enforced and . . . cherished ambi-

ence." Their sense of powerlessness and suffering gave them the same theme that was the great one of Yiddish literature. Stanley Kauffmann, "Our New Cultural Heroes—American-Jewish Writers," *Chicago Tribune Books Today,* May 30, 1965, p. 7.

40. J. Mellquist and L. Wiese, eds., *Paul Rosenfeld: Voyager in the Arts* (New York: Creative Age Press, 1948).

In conversation with the present author, Harold U. Ribalow stated the interest of one academic publisher in a critical biography of Lewisohn. The bibliography alone for this task would be an extensive undertaking.

3

Second Generation:
The Child of the Depression

THE EDUCATION NOVEL IN THE DEPRESSION

With the coming of age of the second generation of
American Jews, the education novel advanced in technique and talent. Except for *The Rise of David Levinsky*,
the European-born group had not contributed memor-
ably to the American Realist novel, the category under
which their work must be subsumed. None of the novels
of the first group has been reprinted recently except
Cahan's; all of the novels in the second-generation group
have been, except Schneider's.[1] The second generation
drew upon recent experiments in the English and American novel. (*A Portrait of the Artist as a Young Man*
was ideally suited to the requirements of the education
novel, although their favorite prototype continued to

be the Dreiserian novel.) In the figures of Henry Roth and Daniel Fuchs, the second generation produced writers of considerable accomplishment, although both must be included among the many one-book novelists of Jewish-American writing.

The maturation of the second generation coincided with the years of the Great Depression, with which their novels continue to be closely associated. Writing directly within the conventions of Marxist protest were Michael Gold, *Jews without Money* (1930) and Isidor Schneider, *From the Kingdom of Necessity* (1935).[2] Transcending the Left in their novels, although ambivalently linked to it personally, were Daniel Fuchs, *Summer in Williamsburg* (1934); Henry Roth, *Call It Sleep* (1934); and Meyer Levin, *The Old Bunch* (1937).[3]

The Marxist second-generation novelist had an economic thesis which he hoped to illustrate by means of fictional Realism, but the injection of doctrine proved to be inimical to art. The precursors of the Depression novelists were able to produce works which recreated their worlds genuinely and without hysteria. Those Depression novelists who did not view art solely as a weapon in the class struggle were similarly successful. Henry Roth was able to draw upon his own complex psyche, Meyer Levin upon Naturalism, and Albert Halper upon his spontaneous compassion for his stories of a Chicago Jewish boyhood, *On the Shore* (1934). But when Halper attempted to enlarge his scope in *The Chute* (1937) to include all the processes of a large commercial enterprise—that is, to implement Marxist novelistic theory—his work became tendentious and dull. His efforts to unite the various strands of the plot with the binding narrative viewpoint of an education novel protagonist failed because so much of the action occurred beyond the purview of a single character.

The Depression novelist who stepped to the type-

writer as if to the barricade found himself cut off from
the resources of his art. The sympathetic attitude toward
the Jewish ethos of the first-generation novelist no longer
obtained. The second-generation writer was the American-bred product of public schools and the *heder*. A
Jewish writer might escape his heritage by facing those
elements in his past which he found hateful. He might
create art from this confrontation and flight; but not if
he explained away the repellent features of his past by
a simplistic economic analysis. At best, the second-generation writer had a subtle and complex attitude toward his
Jewishness, e.g., Roth in *Call It Sleep;* at worst, he un-
feelingly dismissed his past as a reactionary phase of
capitalism, e.g., Schneider in *From the Kingdom of
Necessity*.

Despite his acquaintance with poverty, the Jewish
writer did not fulfill the requirements of the proletarian
writer. He was not, himself, a true proletarian. The socialist writer of the Twenties, with his sure knowledge
of the garment industry and of the needle trades worker,
was closer to the proletariat than was his Depression
successor. Michael Gold's father followed a trade employing large numbers of Jews, house painting. But Gold
himself was too flamboyantly and self-consciously Whit-
manesque to be convincing in the role of proletarian,
despite his early years as a laborer. Meyer Levin was
the son of a tailor and Albert Halper the son of a grocer.
The Jewish writer never escaped very far from *petit
bourgeois* occupations. If the father was a skilled laborer,
then the mother harbored higher ambitions or the uncle
was a small businessman. The trades at which Jews were
skilled were modest ones, often in enterprises owned and
operated by fellow Jews with whom an intimate relationship was customary. In any event, the children were
expected to rise to the professions, particularly if they
had intellectual capabilities. A classic scene was the con-

frontation of the Party member son, devoted to the
cause of art upon the barricades, and the disappointed
parent—an image significantly different from that of
the young laborer turning to art in the class struggle.[4]

THE MARXIST EDUCATION NOVEL

Two of the fundamental precepts of the Marxist
education novel are that the class struggle dominates
every human relationship and that Judaism is an opiate
of the masses. The novels of Mike Gold and Isidore
Schneider explicate these precepts with insistent didacticism.

The two men and their novels have been linked. Gold
and Schneider were fellow journalists on the *New Masses*
and *Liberator* and were among the editors of *Proletarian
Literature: An Anthology* (1935). Gold's *Jews without
Money* and Schneider's *From the Kingdom of Necessity*
are classified together as "conversion novels" by Rideout,
that is, as novels which begin with the protagonist's initiation into life under capitalism and which end with his
embrace of Marxism. Both books are also listed by
Rideout as "Bottom Dogs" novels. Yet another link
between the two books is noted by Blanche Gelfant in
The American City Novel, where *Jews without Money,
From the Kingdom of Necessity,* Gollomb's *Unquiet*
(another Marxist education novel of 1935), and *The
Old Bunch* are grouped as "ecological novels," works
examining a section of the city as a spatial unit.[5] The
two books will be examined here as illustrations of the
communist novel.

Jews without Money

Mike Gold was born Irwin Granich on New York's
Lower East Side. As the first author of an education

novel to be born in the United States, he marks the beginning of the second stage of the education novel.

The name of the narrator-protagonist of *Jews without Money* is Mike Gold, the name by which the author was known to the public. The name of the narrator-protagonist of *From the Kingdom of Necessity* is Isaac, the English derivative of Isidore Schneider's Jewish name, Yitzchok. The names of the characters suggest that the education novel of the Thirties like its predecessors was autobiographically based.

The Thirties brought a degree of recognition to Gold. The sketches which form *Jews without Money* had previously been published in *The American Mercury, The Menorah Journal,* and his own *New Masses.* By the time the book was published, Gold was already prominent as a leading journalist of the radical Left of the Twenties, contributing poetry and book reviews to the *Liberator* and editing the *New Masses.*[6] Perhaps fortuitously, *Jews without Money* was published in 1930, just after the stock market crash. By the mid-Thirties, it was in its fifteenth printing in the Liveright edition. (Along with other "proletarian" writers such as Albert Halper and Jack Conroy, Gold also enjoyed a large Soviet readership under the aegis of government-controlled publishers.)

As the decade progressed, the Communist writer could evoke the anti-Fascist spirit as well as the anti-capitalist one. In the introduction to the 1935 edition, Gold brings the ideological posture of *Jews without Money* up to date from 1930 by describing the Nazi reaction to the book and expressing the hope that the book's many translations will help dispel anti-Semitism. He refers to his mother as the heroine of *Jews without Money,* a "brave and beautiful proletarian woman" and "the best answer to the fascist liars I know."[7] Even farther from 1930 in time and even more remote in spirit is Diana Trilling's

"The Other Night at Columbia." Michael Gold's mother is recalled in quite different terms from Gold's 1935 introduction. Now his mother is seen as part of the Depression era, when the Jew was at his "funniest, shrewdest best," as she ingenuously asks, "did her boy have to write books the whole world should know she had bedbugs."[8]

The bedbugs of Mike Gold's mother are broadcast by her son with the pride of the flannel-shirted proletarian writer in full-throated cry: "There are enough pleasant superficial liars writing in America. I will write a truthful book of poverty; I will mention bedbugs.[9] To Harlan Hatcher in *Creating the Modern Novel,* Gold's indispensable bedbugs are the condensation in a symbol of the entire proletarian novel.[10] Gold's statement indicates the intent of the book as well as its tone: to indict an economic system which compels human beings to dwell among stinks and vermin, nursing the hope of escaping individually, not collectively. But the world is a small one, hardly the world of the giant industries. The distance, after all, between oppressor and oppressed, between slumdwelling worker and landlord or factory owner, was only a matter of the three hundred dollars which would have enabled Gold's feckless father to start a business.

Gold's world is that simple. The characters in his novel are either victims or victimizers. The whores that fill the doorways of the Lower East Side are victims. Consequently they are pathetic: "Simple people . . . like peasants who had been drafted into the army."[11] They represent one result of the exploitation of the proletariat. Their exploiters are types like Kid Louie and Harry the Pimp, who pass on the secret of success in this "wonderful country": learn English. As a model of success, Harry is second in prestige only to Jake Wolfe, the saloonkeeper with "pull" in Tammany Hall; Jake speaks perfect English. The landlord, Mr. Zunzer, of course, is another of the exploiters. He prefers to rent to prostitutes at exorbitant prices, ignoring the complaints of his other tenants. As a pawnbroker, he takes what each has to offer—from the pious, a prayer book and prayer shawl. But at the same time, he is a victim, a miser who writhes in agony at night, fearing the theft of his money. Even the neighborhood doctors can be divided into hare and hound. Portly old Dr. Axelrod dispenses bitter-tasting but inefficacious medicines and refuses to call after a third unpaid visit. Gaunt young Dr. Solow is a puzzle to the East Siders with his humility and his curious remedy for consumption: join a labor union and work of the abolition of the sweat shop.

Young Mike's father is fated to be a victim. A gregarious Rumanian, he finds his talent for laughter and friendship exploited by a partner who robs him of a share in the suspender business that the two have built on the father's sales ability. As a house painter, again he is exploited by the boss. It is apparent that the latter is a victimizer from the depiction of his stout wife reclining in discomfort from overeating.

The book's characters are drawn with a real gusto invariably marred by the narrow limits of the Marxist viewpoint. The restaurant of Moscowitz, a proprietor and cymbalon player, perfectly expresses the mix of Jewish-Americanism of the times: on the wall hangs both a chromo of Theodore Roosevelt charging up San Juan Hill and a crayon portrait of Theodor Herzl, the Zionist leader. The proof of Moscowitz' genuineness as a musical artist is the fact that he has not saved any money after twenty years of making music "with his heart."

Gold's simplistic view of life is evident in the style of *Jews without Money*. The paragraphs and sentences are short, the vocabulary virile. The aphorisms are unsubtle but pithy: "Kindness is a form of suicide in a world based on the law of competition."[12] The hammering tempo gives the novel a driving power which has not disappeared completely. The author's ebullient, Rumanian-Jewish spirit remains vivid, but the Marxist ideology which inspired Gold seems as irretrievable as the East Side ghetto which his book described.

Gold apparently had his own novel in mind when he outlined in 1930, the same year as its publication, a new literary form which he called "Proletarian Realism." Many of the precepts can be applied to *Jews without Money*, e.g., No. 5, "Proletarians should write about what they know best . . . we must write about our own mud-puddle"; No. 7, "the manure heap is the hope of the future"; and No. 6, especially applicable to the style of his novel, "Swift action, clear form, the direct line, cinema in words; this seems to be one of the principles of proletarian realism."[13]

From the Kingdom of Necessity

Jews without Money can be compared to *From the Kingdom of Necessity*, another specimen of proletarian realism. Like Gold, Isidor Schneider was an active figure of the literary Left, an avowed proletarian writer. Unlike Gold, however, he was born in Eastern Europe in Horodenke (Horodemal in the novel) and was brought to the United States at the age of five—young enough for his consciousness to be formed here. (*Call It Sleep* and *From the Kingdom of Necessity* describe the arrival of the protagonist as a child from the Old World, as did most of the early-model education novels.)

The Marxist commentary in *From the Kingdom of Necessity* takes the form of exhortations and even a dramatized historical scene in which Lenin, with steady eyes and a faith founded in a "creative study of history," confronts a shifty, wildly gesturing Kerensky.

Lenin prevails because he "gives peace, bread and power to the masses." At times, the novel is sheer slogan. A minor character Mendel, occasionally takes over the narrator's task of interpreting historical events from a dialectical perspective, (a device of Zola in *Germinal* which Frank Norris was to copy in *The Octopus*). Mendel is only eighteen, but his bitter experiences in Russia have cleared his eyes and made of him a Socialist capable of explaining away the pretenses of the world powers: "The Capitalists of each nation need profits."[14]

The book closes with a family gathering. It is Passover (second only to the Sabbath as a religious set-piece in the Jewish novel). The narrator substitutes for the street-corner speaker who customarily closes conversion novels. In Marxist prose, he predicts a future when Isaac will learn, after the fitful boom, that he cannot escape the kingdom of necessity by leaving his class. "With it, he would march, taking his place in the irresistible movement of the masses of mankind."[15]

The Marxist View of the Immigrant

To Gold and Schneider, *die goldene medineh* (the golden country—America) of the immigrant's imagination turned out to be *Amerika ganif* (America, the thief). They fervently repeated the earlier immigrant curse, *A klug tzu Kolumbusn* (Woe to Columbus), insisting that the "bosses" were responsible for the despoliation of the promised land. Schneider's novel bears an epigraph from Friedrich Engels to clarify the Marxist theme: [Socialism] is the ascent of man from the kingdom of necessity to the kingdom of freedom." The chapter titles continue the Marxist terminology. The first chapter is entitled "The Machine Age Comes to Horodemal." It demonstrates how the *shtetl* is corrupted by the Singer sewing machine, the symbol of international

business. The second chapter is "To Golden America";
the father reluctantly goes to America with its unbearable, speeded-up tempo. To Mike Gold's father, too,
America is a "Land of Hurry-Up" where no gold is to
be dug up in the streets. The same sequence was repeated
by the leftist editor, Joseph Freeman, in his autobiography, *An American Testament:* Chapter I is "A
Vanished Village"; Chapter II is "The Golden Realm."

Like their predecessors in the early models of the
education novel, the fathers of both novels learn through
their failures at business that America is a thief. All that
was necessary for the Depression writer was to make
even more explicit the Marxist reason for the fathers'
lack of business acumen. Both fathers are anti-collectivist;
each insists that he can rise to wealth independently and
refuses to be held back by his class. In their imagination,
penniless as they are, they see a "lazy" socialist union
organizer coming to demand their hard-earned fortune.
Mike's father is cheated out of one business by a *landsman* (countryman); as a house painter, he falls from a
scaffold, crushing his feet. Isaac's father is forced out
of his candy store by a bigger competitor. He manages to
trick "two honest, dull, doomed workers" into buying
his worthless store, only to open a tailor shop which
promptly fails. In America, it would seem, business can
be conducted only in an atmosphere of deceit and imminent failure. Only the landlord and the saloonkeeper,
appearing in the same fraternizing combination in both
novels, flourish, because they are exploiters, a bond
which they realize transcends their nominal differences
as Jew and Irishman.

Religion in the Marxist Novel

The kingdom of necessity might be America the thief,
but the kingdom of freedom is not to be reached through

religion. Gold and Schneider reject Judaism far more uncompromisingly than did their precursors, the socialist education novelists. They indict Judaism for the Old World supersition and New World hypocrisy of its practitioners.

In *Jews without Money,* religion in the Old World was represented by magic rabbis, whose advice must be bought with money or a live fish. These frauds counsel anxious parents to hang an earth-and-spider's-web amulet about their ailing child's neck and to dress him all in white. In the New World, religion is a "fervent affair" of fanatics who persecute one another. Mike is subjected to the inevitable fictional beating by no less than fifty Italian boys who call him "Christ-Killer." His father has the last word on God, however: God answers the prayers of the rich man because he asks for things so rarely.

The most touching of the stories which make up *Jews without Money* is "The Saint of the Umbrella Store." Reb Samuel is a *Hasid* (a member of a pious Jewish sect). As the most devout character in the novel, he is defeated and broken by an America which reached "into his synagogue, and struck at his God."[16] Shocked at the apostasy of his fellow Jews, Reb Samuel devotes his time to building a synagogue to counter secularism. Following ghetto custom, the *Hasidim* import a famous rabbi.[17] But young Mike instantly perceives the gluttony and greed of the man. The rabbi quickly becomes Americanized, demanding costly comforts, siding with the beard-depilating faction of the synagogue, and finally abandoning the congregation entirely for a wealthier one. Mike is not surprised, but Reb Samuel is struck down by paralysis. Even in the synagogue in America are to be found the exploiter and the victim.

To Schneider, the effect of capitalistic America upon religion is to distort its moral values. Isaac is appalled when his father claims that he has the favor of God

who has answered his prayers by shifting the burden of
his failing business onto another. Both parties to the
business transaction prayed side by side on Yom Kippur
(the Day of Atonement), each against the other, both
trailing off into Yiddish in genuine fervor. The sale took
place on that day, a profound sin; but to Isaac, the sin
is not against God, but against man. Isaac rejects this
"lesson" to the Epikorises (apostates) and turns to his
"atheistic" books, estranged from his parents.

The general tenor of Schneider's treatment of Judaism
is deprecatory. To describe the *melamed* as a figure inspiring terror is standard practice in the Jewish novel;
but to say that terror is taken by the pious as the condition of obedience is to overgeneralize. To describe
humash (Bible study) as the "most arrogantly national-
istic education offered anywhere in the world"[18] is gratuitous and inaccurate. The effect of a strict Marxism upon
the novel is, finally, the destruction of truth.

Call It Sleep As a Depression Novel

Mike Gold's East Side world is the same as that of
Henry Roth in *Call It Sleep,* published four years after
Jews without Money. The worlds are remarkably similar
in their vile and oppressive sexuality. Like young Mike,
the boy David in *Call It Sleep* links the hideous sight
witnessed through a keyhole with the sex act. Both protagonists are about five years old at the beginning of
the novel, both learn of sex as the dirty act of the street-
walkers, and, with a sense of betrayal and revulsion,
both promptly associate this act with their mothers. But
Mike recovers quickly, affirms that sex can be good, and
strikes back at the companion who insulted his mother.
He runs with his gang, surviving his environment, one
suspects, by means of his natural strength and spirit,
rather than by virtue of his later-learned ideology.

Neither vitality nor ideology was available to the auto-biographical hero of *Call It Sleep*.

If an author committed to ideology is illustrated by Gold's and Schneider's books, the writer's equivocal relation to the Left can be seen in Henry Roth's *Call It Sleep*, the "underground classic" of the education novel. Although Rideout includes the book in his study of the radical novel, it really belongs in the looser category of social-protest literature, with its generalized cry against injustice. True, the streetcorner Socialist is heard in the babble of voices which surround the young protagonist at the climax of the novel. But this scene is not the typical conversion ending of the radical novel. The refrain adds to the novel's religious and psychological symbolism rather than its collectivist doctrine. To create such a carefully wrought, thoroughly Freudian novel in the period before the education novel had passed from the autobiographical into the psychological stage, and at a time when ideological imperatives were at their strongest, was itself a confession of doubt which, according to Irving Howe, baffled the "politically radical critics then dominating the New York literary scene."[19]

The novel must be considered in the context of the times. Roth was personally indebted to the Left in the figure of Eda Lou Walton, a poet and professor at New York University who had befriended him. The dedication of the novel to Miss Walton apparently was an inadequate endorsement of the Left; the content of the book violated the dogma of the day.[20] The rejection of the novel by *New Masses* critics and by "official" spokesmen of the Jewish community, and its neglect by the non-leftist critics and the public, are seen by Leslie Fiedler as causes of Roth's inability to write after the publication of *Call It Sleep*.[21]

Roth himself has commented upon that long silence. About the time of the revival of *Call It Sleep* by Pageant

Books in 1960, he published two short pieces in *Commentary*. The first, "At Times in Flight; A Parable," describes the danger of getting too close to a horse race. An editorial note takes the horse race of Roth's parable as a symbol of life; it interprets Roth's writing block as the classic response of a martyr protesting the difficulty of writing and living in a society such as ours. In "The Dun Dakotas," Roth, pondering the loss of his creative powers, refers to the "ruinous" quality of the Thirties, a "kind of revolutionary age, or one of rapid transition."[22] The failure to find a sufficient or approving audience for a novel into which he had poured so much energy and skill might have been reason enough for Roth to quit writing at twenty-seven. It is possible as well that Roth was unable to continue drawing upon his emotional life for his art. A breakdown of the kind suffered by David in *Call It Sleep* seems to have occurred.

It has been suggested that Roth avoided the ideological struggle of the Thirties by turning to childhood and to the past for *Call It Sleep*. Unquestionably, the materials of the novel are those of the education novel: the sentient six-year-old and the teeming ghetto replete with Jewish gangs to corrupt and gentile ones to ambuscade. The mother is kindly rather than shrewish, the father fearsome rather than diffident; the son, an only child, completes an orderly Oedipal triangle. Sex and metaphysics render the theme: the awakening of youth to the meaning of life, quotidian and transcendent. The repudiation of Marxist dogma is clearest in the novel's basic situation which pits the father against the mother and son in acts of raging irrationality unrelated to economic conditions. Dogma is also repudiated in the denouement, which implies a better future for the family—not because of their adoption of revolutionary ideology, but because the father finds a job better suited to his temperament and comes to some realization of the folly of his behavior toward his family.

Although *Call It Sleep* is memorable as a novel of the ghetto and a novel of religion, its center is the portrait of David Schearl's mind as he passes through the transfiguring experiences of his childhood years in Brownsville and the Lower East Side. The narrative is focused on David's perception of reality. The technique of expressing David's thoughs not only divulges their nearness to the subconscious, but reproduces the structure and tempo of their language. David speaks three languages, each a thread in the fabric of his mind; together they trace the tensions of the life of the immigrant ghetto child.

The Language of David's Mind

The first, the language of David's thoughts, appears in the novel after the reader has become acquainted with David's different worlds. His thoughts are so closely interwoven with the narration that no quotation marks are necessary; they can be recognized by the shift in rhythm and diction. David thinks:

Box. Yesterday. God it said and holier than Jew-light with the coal. So who cares? But that fish, why was that fish? Couldn't read all the little letters. Wish I could. . . . And that funny dream I had when he gave me it. How? Forgetting it already. Roof we were with a ladder. And he climbs up on the sun—zip one two three. Round ball. Round ball shining—Where did I say, see? Round ball and he busted it off with a cobble and puts it in the pail. And I ate it then. Better than sponge cake. Better than I ever ate. Wonder what it's made of—Nothing, dope! Dreams. Just was dreaming—[23]

These interior monologues, with their abrupt and fragmentary quality, disclose the influence of Joyce.

The novel also draws an Naturalism to the extent that it deals with the brutality of life among the lower classes, which is to say, to a very great degree. The "refrain of the rails" section of *Call It Sleep* can be laid beside Presley's summation at the end of *The Octopus* to indicate the parallelism in style. Roth works several meanings into his image of the power that lies in the rails, and one of them assuredly matches Norris' deterministic one: that an indifferent power moves the earth.

Power! Power like a paw, titanic power . . . Power! Incredible barbaric power! A blast, a siren of light within him . . . (*Call It Sleep*)

FORCE only existed—FORCE that brought men into the world, FORCE that crowded them out of it to make way for the succeeding generation. (*The Octopus*)[24]

But *Call It Sleep* ultimately rejects deterministic theory. The force actually operative upon the Shearls is not chance, nor is it poverty. Rather it is the psychological infirmity of the father visited upon the son, who in turn verges upon morbidity.

David's Street Speech

The second language of David, his spoken one, follows an older literary tradition than that of the first, Joyecean language: the realistic recording of vernacular speech by means of phonetic spelling. In this case, the speech is the lower-class street speech of New York intermingled with traces of a Yiddish accent. This is a speech that lends itself to comic effects—perhaps too readily—but Roth's purpose is not solely comedy. An excerpt indicates the humor, accuracy, and expressiveness in his use of this language:

My ticher calls id Xmas, bod de kids call id Chrizmas. Id's a

goyish holiday anyways. Wunst I hanged op a stockin' in Brooklyn. Bod mine fodder pud in a eggshells wid terlit paper an' a
piece f'om a ol' kendle. So he leffed w'en he seen me. Id ain'
no Sendy Klaws, didja know?[25]

Nonetheless, the transcription does become fatiguing, so
extensively is it used.

David's third speech is the original contribution of the
novel: Yiddish translated into English. The Jewish-
American comic writer records the private conversations
of the immigrant family in the broken English which is
the outer aspect of their lives. In this novel, too, the
efforts of the recent immigrant have the same risible
effect that Arthur Kober and Nate Gross exploited, e.g.,
Aunt Bertha in her candy store: "End a liddle suddeh
vuddeh?" Such is the spoken voice of the difficult, new
language. But these new Americans actually speak Yiddish in the privacy of their railroad flats, and it is the
spirit of this language, unique in its rhythms, idioms, and
even poetry, that Roth captures in English. A fellow
Jew enters Aunt Bertha's store: "How fares a Jew?" is
given for *Was macht a Yid?* and "Where is the prayer?"
(the son who prays) for *Wo is der Kaddish?* Spoken
Yiddish lends itself to this technique readily because it
has so many idiomatic expressions. These rather awk-
ward examples of translated Yiddish recall Hemingway's
obtrusive efforts to capture Spanish in *For Whom the
Bell Tolls.* For the most part, however, Roth's rendering is a supple, formal English rich in proverbs, e.g.,
David's father: "The angel of Fate strikes always on
the side you never guard. I thought that before that dog
saw the last of me, I'd make him writhe. And I would
have!"[26]

That immigrants possessed a culture and a tongue
capable of expressing it is frequently overlooked by the
second-generation writer. *Call It Sleep* demonstrates the
existence of such life and language. Spirited yet dignified,

suffused with memories yet impossible to preserve. Available to the immigrant parents only for limited use and incapable of transmission to the children, the Yiddish of *der heim* (the home), *der momme loschen* (mother tongue), was to disappear, despite the efforts of the Yiddishists. And always mocking the immigrant was the gutter talk of their children and their own, irrepressibly comic attempts to speak the new language: "Stimm hitt!"

The Symbolism of Call It Sleep

Surrounding the three languages of David is the prose of the narration. Rich, allusive, and rhythmic, it softens the dissonances of the other tongues, muting their cacophony. The imagery of this prose is carefully designed to develop the theme of the novel: that the revelation of the meaning of existence comes through terror brought to an unbearable pitch. An aggregate of images duplicates the painful shocks to the nervous system of young David as he undergoes the initiation experience. Rack, comb, barrow, shearing, scraping—these are the words for the daily terrors which assault him. Walls and banks —these are the words for the elliptical, baffling ways in which knowledge comes to the child.

To the fearful child the enclosing warmth of the kitchen and the softness of his mother's bosom are weak refuges against the chilling revelations of the streets. To young David, who shares the hysteria of a sick father, the hearse and coffin and the mystery of a hole in wet cement which hardens into a casing are frightening auguries of a threatening, uncontainable world. Although these terrors are the sign that David is both a small child and the son of his father, they also may be the sign that he is a Jew. The "nervousness" of the Jew is accepted as a group characteristic attributable to centuries of living in perpetual dread in *golus* (exile).[27]

The novel moves inexorably toward the climax, the memorable scene in which David, seeking an explanation for the series of mysteries and traumas which threaten him, thrusts a milk ladle into the open streetcar tracks and is shocked unconscious. The passages leading to this scene quicken in tempo, thrusting at the reader a quick succession of images. These images disclose the chief influence of the book: Freudianism. Earlier in the novel, David has come upon his mother in post-coital repose and is puzzled, deeply disturbed. He senses some connection between his father in the role of husband and the whip his father fiercely and punishingly wields as a milkwagon driver and parent. The connection is suddenly bridged by the bull's-horn trophy which his father sets on the wall. Although he is not aware of the reason, the horns somehow pose a threat.

It is the series of phallic images at the end of the novel which makes the Freudian theme particularly apparent. Escaping the upraised whip of his father, David flees into the street, finds the milk dipper, and sees some children playing a game of "Wolf, are you ready?" (In that period, "wolf" was a slang term for pederast.) Passing a saloon, he is surrounded by the rough voices of the city summer night, by a bartender pointing a bar comb, by a hunchback on crutches, by a coalheaver with "bright eye-balls," by barroom talk of sex, of "coozies" and the accompanying words. The overt sexuality of the saloon intensifies as a patron recalls his sexual advice to a forge worker who stood with "wrench in his han'" and another recalls a degrading incident of her youth involving a pun on the word "cut." As David moves beyond earshot of the saloon, he hears more talk of sex, couched in street terminology and coarse puns. References to pipes and knives, and the voice of the soap-box speaker, who suggests escape from enslavement when the red cock crows, further add to the sexual meanings. David reaches

the tracks and "the wavering point of the dipper's handle
[finds] the long, dark, grinning lips, scraped, and like
a sword in a scabbard—."[28] The street talk continues,
increasing in sexual explicitness, until at last David is
transfixed by a surge of electric power.

Religion in Call It Sleep

To consider the novel as purely a psychological work,
fraught with rather obvious symbolism, is to underesti-
mate its complexity and allusiveness. The milk dipper has
another symbolic meaning to David. It is also the fiery
coal which cleansed the lips of Isaiah. The novel has
many familiar religious symbols, such as the fish and the
name of God on the box of forbidden rosary beads David
covets as a possible answer to his religious quest, the
transcendent level of his search for life's meaning. Addi-
tional religious symbols are to be found. The crowing-
cock reference of the streetcorner speaker is juxtaposed
against the voice of a cockney sailor recalling fish and
chips: "Christ knows how many chaps can be fed off one
bloody cod—."[29] Christianity, however, is one more
source of guilt to the chronically terrified David. The
church represents to him the organist whom his mother
recalls as the real love of her life. The broken rosary
beads for which David has pandered are to his father
the sign of David's bastardy as the supposed son of the
organist.

It is Judaism which supplies David with sublimity.
Judaism, transmitted by his parents as a habit, is avidly
received by David. His *melamed*, despairing of his inat-
tentive charges, is delighted to find in David an "iron
head" at last. But the reb (a polite form of address)
is unequipped to initiate the youth into theological Judaism. The man rarely has the opportunity to pass beyond
teaching rote pronunciation of the Hebrew characters

to translation of the Bible, let alone to interpreting God to a child.

The *heder* of the novel in the Thirties is even more horrendous than in that of the Twenties. The one in *Call It Sleep* is a prime specimen. The Talmud Torah, a religious-school movement which employed modern instructional methods and far surpassed the *heder* in enrollment by the Thirties, makes little appearance in the Jewish novel. The *heder melamed* was a tyrannical incompetent by all accounts, but it is as a stereotypical figure of the inefficacy of religion that he is indispensable to the novelist.

The incongruousness of the *heder,* with its jarring elements of the sublime, the mean, and the comic, is conveyed by juxtaposing passages as they occur in Reb Yidel Pankower's gaslit, backyard *heder*:

Izzy Pissy! Cock-eye Mulligan! Mah nishtanah halilaw hazeh [Why is this night different—from the Passover service. BAS]— Wanna play me Yonk? . . . Where was it? Yea. Page sixty-eight . . . you were saying that man saw God. And a light— How many? I god more den you. Shebchol haleylos onu ochlim—[30]

The same poetic technique for much the same purposes appears in Bellow's *Herzog* (1964) in the chapter describing the ghetto life of the child Herzog on Napoleon Street:

O'Brien
Lo mir trinken a glesele vi-ine
Al tastir ponecho mimeni [Do not hide thy
countenance from me. BAS]
I'm broke without a penny
Vich nobody can deny.[31]

Thus presented, the divinity of the Jew, springing from his abjectivity, provides novelistic tensions and a subject for both *Herzog* and *Call It Sleep*. In his review of *Call*

It Sleep, Irving Howe cites the G. M. Doughty epigram which has been found so expressive of the Jewish condition: "The Semites are like to a man sitting in a cloaca to the eyes, and whose brow touches heaven."[32]

The Old Bunch AS A NATURALIST NOVEL

Meyer Levin provides another instance of the author attracted by communism but finally resisting it. Although Meyer Levin's earlier book, *The New Bridge* (1933) is included by Rideout in his appendix list of "American Radical Novels" and although he labels the Levin of the Thirties a "half-Marxist," Levin's novel of 1937, *The Old Bunch,* is not so listed. The theory which engendered *The Old Bunch* is not communism. Levin resisted the strong pull toward the Communist Party which powerfully attracted Jewish intellectuals in the Thirties. He did not object to Marxist theory (he had lived under a collectivist system in the Twenties—the Palestinian kibbutz), but he opposed the party's stand against Zionism. In *Yehuda* (1930) Levin had written the first novel in English about kibbutz life in Palestine.[33] Levin searched for the meaning of his Jewish identity for much of his lifetime; he subsumed collectivism under cultural Judaism. The contradictory strains of Levin's life—Zionism, Marxism, the heritage of European *shtetl* culture, and the ambitions of his career—were not brought into a congruent pattern in his mind until many years after the composition of *The Old Bunch.* In that novel the contradictions were mitigated by his Naturalistic theory of the novel.

A Naturalistic novel, *The Old Bunch* can be compared to the earlier efforts of Naturalist novelists to describe modern society, dispassionately dissecting the components and then reconstituting them into a work of art. Zola's *Germinal,* Norris' *The Octopus,* and especially

Farrell's *Studs Lonigan* trilogy and Dos Passos' *USA* are the precursors of Levin's study of Jewish "flappers and jellybeans" growing up on Chicago's West Side. The consciousness of a single adolescent provided too narrow a scope for the ambitious project that Levin envisioned. The sociological theory sustaining his conception demanded a wide-ranging, inclusive form: the group novel.[34] The coming of age of a group of coevals acting upon one another parallels the education novel in theme if not in structure.

In his autobiography, *In Search,* Levin explains his theory:

I felt that I had a fundamental observation to make on a form of society in our time in America. While novelists emphasized the individual in the family unit as the determining human relationship, I saw the surrounding group, the bunch, as perhaps even more important than the family in the formative years. Particularly in the children of immigrants, the life-values were determined largely through these group relationships.[35]

Levin's purpose, aside from taking a major step in his development as a Naturalist novelist, was to justify to himself his own relation to his past, to Jewish life in America, particularly to the central situation of the conflict of generations. He wanted to demonstrate with the power of a thousand-page statement how family life and traditions were destroyed in the New World. But the materials of Jewish life were not only important to him as essential components of realistic fiction; they also provided a worthy theme.

Levin does not believe his book fulfills all of the tenets of Naturalism. He has denied that it takes a pessimistic view of Jewish life. In the Darwinian terms of the Naturalist, he admits that his intent was to anatomize an organism, but one which was only partly in decay; the ability to renew itself remained. Farrell's books of lower-middle-class Chicago life seem closest in subject and intent to his own, Levin has claimed, denying that he wrote of the seamy side of life.[36] *The Old Bunch* does describe sex graphically; but sex is integral to the theme, exemplifying the effect of urban values upon the most intimate and central of human activities. Another tenet of Naturalism is fulfilled only partially. The characters are molded by their environment and their occupations; but they are only coarsened, not brutalized; and the process is not inevitable—some escape.

A progenitor as influential in the book as Farrell is John Dos Passos. Traces of his group novels, the *USA* trilogy, can be seen in the texture of *The Old Bunch*. The narrative is composed of very brief, discrete scenes which trace the lives of the several members of "the Bunch." The pace is that of the seemingly haphazard scenes of *USA*. The biographies and facsimile newspaper fragments of *USA* are absent, but Levin does separate the briefer scenes by snatches of popular songs and injects a heavy sprinkling of names from the news. Levin does not attribute influence to Dos Passos in his discussion of the novel in *In Search,* but in *The Old Bunch,* he mentions *Three Soldiers* as an influence upon one of the idealistic characters.

In "Some American Jewish Novelists," Brom Weber compares Levin to Dos Passos for his interplay of themes and trends, but finds that Levin fails to create situations whose "emotional and intellectual significance vary in tension and emphasis."[37] *The Old Bunch* does bring the stories of the characters to denouements resolving their individual problems. But Levin is totally lacking in humor, and his characters are not differentiated by anything but the various ideas they represent. Perhaps a set of the rich, nervous Reginald Marsh illustrations which enlivened some editions of USA might have made up some of the difference.

The group novel is particularly useful for the depiction of the manners of a society, a chief purpose of Levin. He essays the theme of conflict of generations in terms of the differing manners of the three generations of Jews in the Chicago of 1921 to 1934. These generations can be located along a sliding scale of value. At one extreme is the Orthodox grandfather, who brings his own dishes and food to dinner at his daughter's home because he cannot trust the purity of her observance of *kashruth* (the ritual preparation of food). At the other extreme are "the Bunch" and their girls, who derive their values from each other and from the city about them. The parents in between are powerless to transmit even the trappings of their faith because a compulsion stronger than that of religion drives both generations. The foremost task of parents and children in their new world is to succeed. Only the grandparents can afford such idiosyncracies as beards, long hours at prayer and the study of the Talmud, and a binding ethical system. The tragedy of immigrant life was that the children were the experts in American behavior and that the parents had to acquiesce in the rapid abandonment of a faith that seemed lifeless because it was irrelevant.

Jewish Life in The Old Bunch

The novel of social manners usually does not take in the levels of society below the aristocracy of, say, Chicago's North Shore. In *The Old Bunch,* Levin demonstrates that the social differences between a buttonmaker and a smalltime *"real estatenik"* not only are discernible, but can be dramatized for the traditional purposes of the realistic novel. Minute social distinctions among upward-striving groups are essential. They are the benchmarks to inform members of a group who have started from the same point where they stand in relation to each other.

By the Twenties, the era of *The Old Bunch,* the Jews
of urban America had climbed out of the ghetto into the
area of second settlement, the neighborhood. The "greenhorn" and his female counterpart, "*die greeneh cousineh*"
(green cousin), were disappearing. New social types appeared: "the *lodgenik,* or joiner; the *radikalkeh,* or
emancipated woman . . . and the *Ototot,* the almost
emancipated person who clings to a little beard."[38] These
new types are Levin's *dramatis personae*—the West Siders who have escaped from the original Chicago ghetto
of the Near West Side and who are already uneasily
repairing to the next outward ring of the city in order
to keep out of reach of pursuing immigrant groups.

Levin frames the relationships of the multiple figures
of the neighborhood in terms of the succession of generations. An ennobling refrain underlies the footless in-
terrelations of the first and second generations as they
pull at each other, the parents shamefacedly realizing
that they have nothing instructive to offer, the children
guiltily rejecting the folkways of the elders. Some of the
members of "the Bunch" feel deep longing for their irretrievable heritage. They are aware of the emptiness of
their lives, and a very few demand something more edifying.

The Search for Fulfillment as a Jew

As they haltingly fulfill their destinies, the Bunch forms
a paradigm of society. Law, commerce, sports, science,
and the arts are represented.

The sculptor, Joe Freedman, trained on the Midway
of the University of Chicago by a character reminiscent
of the American sculptor Lorado Taft, seems closest in
identity to Levin. Repeating Levin's odyssey, Joe goes
to Palestine, where he joins a communal settlement; but
he cannot bring himself to accept the idea of the Jewish

national home as a state. Levin describes himself in the
Twenties as just such a "cultural Zionist."[39] Like Levin,
Joe leaves the kibbutz to return to America, somehow
satisfied that he is approaching an answer to his longing for a Jewish identity. Joe next wanders to Paris
where he meets Aaron Polansky, a sculptor who helps
him to accept his Judaism, although Polansky is himself
a convert to Catholicism. Levin had been introduced to
Hasidic tales in Paris by Marek Szwarc, and this discovery of Jewish folklore was an important turning point
in his life. Of the members of the group, it is Joe who
realizes that the parents were not merely refugees come
to raise geniuses in a golden land. The parents' tales of
escape from Russia bring him to see that they, too, were
once idealistic "freethinkers."

   At the close of the novel, Joe brings his connection
with Marxism into perspective. Like the Marxist novelist, he sees humanity as a dualism of the unworthy, the
"lumps of human flesh," and the worthy, those aware of
the "streams of human life." But Joe rejects agitation
for a new order. Acting in "harmony with the long historical wave toward the revolution," he will be ready to
welcome a communal society, but only as an observer.
Anticlimactically, he cites Franklin Roosevelt as his
model for the kind of evolutionary struggler who proceeds at a pace which Joe finds consonant with his own
integrity. Such is the end-of-the-novel economic message
of Levin, a plea which stops well short of the rousing
streetcorner speech of the conversation novel.

   Identification with the common Jewish destiny through
the Zion of the future and the folklore of the past is a
legitimate solution to the need for fulfillment. Joe accepts this solution. The attempts of the Bunch to evolve
an acceptable pattern of self-expression through organized religion are less effective. A number of rabbis appear in the novel, but always in contemptible roles, as

officiators at gaudy weddings, for example. At the University of Illinois, a young Reform rabbi has come to establish a "Jewish Foundation" under the auspices of the B'nai Brith. The smooth-faced, pipe-smoking rabbi deftly convinces Joe that the idealistic stand he has taken against compulsory R.O.T.C. is not really worthwhile. It was probably this character as much as the general treatment of Jews in the novel which brought Levin before the Anti-Defamation League, another arm of the B'nai Brith.

Chicago in The Old Bunch

Turning back to the novels written during the Depression, one half expects to find dreary descriptions of dreary lives—not very attractive reading. In reportage of the period, such matter is found. Chicago's endless square miles of poverty perfectly expressed the grayness and boredom of that time. Edmund Wilson's account of the Depression, reprinted in *The American Earthquake,* pictures Chicago with all the sad and sordid details of misfortune. Chicago is seen by Wilson in the images of dark masses stamped out of fog and of a forge starting up.[40] Although his approach is more ponderous and sentimental than Wilson's, Levin does not dwell in *The Old Bunch* on the gray privations of the very poor. Rather, he presents the small-time businessman trying to overcome labor troubles and his son trying to find some way to stay in college.

The city is the force which motivates the Bunch. "Build Chicago" is a suitable motto for their acceptance of the competitive society whose highest expressions are the ornate motion-picture theaters. The Bunch is awed by the greatest of these, with its eight-story electric-bulb sign, "CHICAGO." Was this not, after all, the product of men who had started as humbly as they on the West

Side of Chicago? The culmination of this spirit is the
World's Fair of 1932-3. "A Century of Progress," a
"bright scar" on a consumptive body. The novel ends on
a Naturalistic note. The city stretches out from the
World's Fair; the Loop is its "bludgeon stone-head,"
the semicircle of slums its inner corruption. And always
there are the people, seeking to escape the contamination,
swarming outward, but always in groups ranged in an
ascending order which is changeless.

THE MARKET FOR JEWISH NOVELS

The career of Meyer Levin, the longest of any Jewish-American writer, exemplifies the problems facing the
writer of Jewish novels earlier in the century.
Few mid-Thirties Jewish writers could count on the
small benefits that accrued from the label "proletarian
writer." *Jews without Money* sold well. *Call It Sleep,*
lacking that label, sold only four thousand copies. The
sale of Daniel Fuchs's three novels was even lower: 400,
400, 1,200.[41] All of Nathanael West's novels were sales
failures, and each was brought out by a different publisher. At any rate, the phenomenon of the proletarian
novel was a transitory one. By the time a collection was
issued in 1935, *Proletarian Literature in the United
States: An Anthology,* the school had reached its peak.
The Jewish writer's problem—acquiring a public and
publishers—was not different in the Thirties from what
it was in the decades that preceded and followed; it was
only more difficult, as it was then for other writers, because of the straitened circumstances of the industry.
The topic of Jewish books and publishers is treated
by Meyer Levin in a number of articles and at length in
his autobiography, *In Search.* Not yet in his twenties in
the 1920's, Levin learned that popular magazines refused
Jewish stories. He began to use names from the "none-

such" category for his characters. Elliott Cohen, who later became the editor of *Commentary*, published some of Levin's early West Side sketches in *The Menorah Journal*. Both magazines specialized in Jewish material. Levin had a great many problems as a writer of Jewish themes. His *Yehuda* (1930), a novel of modern Palestine, bore an unsaleable title, salesmen reported back from the road.

Levin's major novel, *The Old Bunch,* further illustrates the publishing problem. It was rejected by the first publisher, Reynal and Hitchcock, despite an advance contract, because the publisher objected to the Jewish identity of the characters. The novel was brought out by Simon and Schuster (who are accorded a pseudonym in *In Search*) ; its publicity muted the Jewish label. Nonetheless, the book was rather widely condemned from the pulpit and in the Jewish press.[42] *In Search* itself was rejected by a dozen publishers because it was "too Jewish." Levin published the book himself in Paris and took to selling copies on lecture tours in the United States. Finally, after some difficulty with the copyright laws, The Horizon Press sold its ten thousand copies plus Levin's remaining five thousand. By 1961 a popular paperback edition was published.

Levin is now an established literary figure (as a bestselling author) whose novels are assured of serious attention. He is perhaps the only Jewish novelist remaining from the pre-World War II days of whom this can be said. Nonetheless, Levin has suffered an unusual amount of sheer bad luck. In addition to the above-mentioned difficulties, he has endured the publication of one novel on the first day of the Roosevelt bank holiday, the suppression of a Federal Theater play through backstairs censorship, law suits against *Reporter* (1919) and *Compulsion* (1956), difficulties in distributing the films he produced, and persistent troubles over *The Diary of*

Anne Frank. But his experiences do illustrate the want of enthusiasm for novels with Jewish subjects during a good part of this century. Levin contends that the careers of writers who devoted themselves to Jewish themes, such as Ludwig Lewisohn, Maurice Samuel, Irving Fineman, and Daniel Fuchs, have suffered accordingly. (Lewisohn himself, although he was certainly a prolific writer, complained in *The American Jew* of the lack of an audience for Jewish writing and the hesitation of publishing houses to bring out Jewish books.)[43]

Some of the authors in this study describe their dealings with publishers. Fear of being stigmatized as a Jewish house caused one firm to reject a Yuri Suhl manuscript. He charges publishers and editors with stifling Jewish-American culture by treating the "Jewish theme as a second-class citizen in the community of literature."[44] However, Albert Halper, whose career as a writer of Jewish and non-Jewish books spans thirty years, emphatically denies the existence of a publishers' blacklist, stating that all "worthwhile books are marketable."[45] In contrast, a third writer, Arthur Granit, author of *The Time of the Peaches*, finds the market for Jewish material to be limited by the profit factor.[46] It would seem, then, that the testimony of the writer does not provide a definitive answer. The truth of the matter seems to be that, prior to the late 1950's, novels of Jewish life were not enthusiastically received, although several hundred were published. It is doubtful that a superior novel lies unpublished, since so many inferior ones have managed to find an outlet. In recent years, a number of Jewish novels of quality have been widely read and have been critically well-received. Indeed, the modishness of Jewish novels in the mid-Sixties is by now a critical cliché. The most obvious cause for this popularity is simply the quality of such writers as Bellow, Malamud, Philip Roth, and I. B. Singer. A second cause can be adduced from the

following by Ihab Hassan: "The two most active cen-
ters of contemporary fiction in America are situated in
the Gentile rural South . . . and the Jewish urban North.
. . . It may very well be that the Southern novelist and
the Jewish writer have both emerged from the tragic
underground of our culture as the true spokesman of mid-
century America."[47] The Jew in the diaspora has long
represented the shocks and terrors of life at the end of
its tether; his appearance in post-war American fiction is
now taken to signalize the condition of all men.

Summer in Williamsburg

New York's Williamsburg, like Chicago's West Side,
was a zone of second settlement, populated by Jews seeking to escape the confines of the lower East Side. Daniel
Fuchs's *Summer in Williamsburg* is a tale of the second
generation like *The Old Bunch*. Fuchs's first novel, it was
published in 1934, three years before Levin's. *The Old
Bunch* looks back to the tradition of the Naturalist novel
and clearly belongs to a closed chapter in literary history.
Fuchs's book on the other hand, anticipates the ironic
novel and is contemporaneous in spirit. Fuchs represents
the refusal to sink into self-pity and hysteria. His irresistible urge toward sad comedy creates such contrasts as
that between Cohen, the posturing unfortunate, and
Sussman, the gas-inhaling suicide. Fuchs's acrid humor,
akin to that of his contemporary Nathanael West, looks
forward out of the dreary solemnity of Albert Maltz
and Farrell to the tense serio-comedy of Malamud and
Bellow.

Fuchs is a prototype for Bellow less in his prose style
—he is addicted to mock-simple irony—than in his antic
treatment of Naturalistic materials. The materials of
both writers are much the same: grotesque gangsters,
outlandishly named characters, the more disorderly

reaches of the city in the febrile summer. Specifically echoed in *The Adventures of Augie March* are the following, drawn from *Summer in Williamsburg:* a dignified father figure with white moustaches and panama hat; criminal types who instruct the developing protagonist, urging him to give in to life; and racy, ring-wearing, cigar-smoking Jews.

Fuchs runs two motifs through *Summer in Williamsburg*. The first is "Collect," the watchword of Philip, the twenty-year-old narrator-protagonist. This is the Naturalist's cry, echoing from Zola with his notebooks at hand to record the factual details of the life he had vowed to dissect as a scientist. "Collect and then analyze," says Philip, intending to include all the fragments of Williamsburg in his attempt to find an explanation of the senseless suicide of a neighbor. The novel does not pretend to survey the whole of Williamsburg. It offers instead a selectively high-keyed, artificially designed image of that society. The novel is particular and prosaic in its presentation of the city during the Depression, but is universal in its detached and ironic vision of the world.

Fuchs has described *Summer in Williamsburg* as a groping first novel of adolescence, written in a "state of sheer terror." He compares his struggle to find a design for the book to his need to find a plan for the life he had witnessed in Williamsburg. Fuchs (as the experienced scenarist writing the 1961 preface to his three youthful novels) now realizes that what he was searching for in the novel was fantasy rather than meaning.[48] "Collect" is the first motif of the novel, fantasy is the second.

Summer in Williamsburg as a Surreal Work

The elements of fantasy in *Summer in Williamsburg* were to be more marked in Fuchs's two later novels,

Homage to Blenholt and *Low Company* (1937). But already the intermittent screams of frustration and rage in *Summer* suggest the brutal howls heard by the Naturalists less than the nightmare cries heard by the Surrealists. A woman screams and Philip, the central consciousness of the novel, visualizes "The creased expression of her face, the jutting jaw, her teeth revealed like an alarm"[49]—an anticipation of Picasso's "Guernica." At its climatic points, the novel reaches horrifying peaks; in its pattern of flow, it follows the serene urban vision of Edward Hopper: "Williamsburg becomes for the day like a bright painting in its motionlessness, and somehow this creates an atmosphere in which you may like to bathe sleepily."[50]

Fuchs is a painterly novelist, but ultimately his visual sense is less that of Picasso and Hopper than it is that of Hollywood. Fuchs has a sharp eye for the cinematic effects of life and for the visual presentation of scene in the manner of the film. The subject of *Summer in Williamsburg* is that of the gangster film of the Thirties (*Low Company* eventually was translated into a modest-budget crime film called *The Gangster,* and Fuchs became a scenarist of gangster films). The plot of *Summer in Williamsburg* pits the possibility for Philip of a career as a minor gangster against the example of ineffectual honesty presented by his father. Uncle Papravel, a specimen of the Americanized "all-rightnik," emulates the style of the movie gangster (as did Runt Plotkin of *The Old Bunch*). With cool authority and dapper clothes, he strides into a rival's bus station, representing himself as the agent for the "Williamsburg Business Board," the equivalent of the movie gangster's "Businessmen's Protective Association." His henchmen proceed to smash the station of the uncooperative businessman with that coolly professional violence that marks the movie gangster. Such is the cinematic vision of life in the Thirties.

That vision is the codex of values in the world of Williamsburg. Motion picture "palaces" are plentiful, and it is not only the small-time gangster who studies suitable comportment there. Even little Davey, whose childish adventures are a counterpart to the more momentous deeds of the adults, longs for the day when he will exhibit the adroitness of an Adolph Menjou. Philip's girlfriend orders her life to match the romanticized life on the screen, and Philip himself is captured by the beauty of the movie star. Unintentionally, all fall into the postures they have seen on the screen.

Philip's friend Cohen, in rented dinner jacket, cannot resist the temptation to glide elegantly down the street with the nonchalance of the movie hero; but he cannot sustain the pose. His clumsiness brings him, drenched with pickled herring, to a Chaplinesque grief. The true genesis of the unfortunate Cohen is the *shlimazel,* the puny Jew who moves through Yiddish literature with the dark cloud of his ineptness hovering above him, discomposing his ill-assorted features and dispelling the clarity of his vision.[51] Cohen also satirizes the petty intellectual, the educated fool who consumes high-level culture and tries to impress his friends with his subtle and profound insights.

Jewishness in Summer in Williamsburg

Williamsburg was a Jewish enclave, and Philip and his collected specimens are Jewish. As in most education novels, anti-Semitism is not directly an important subject. The Jewish identity of most of the characters is one of the reasons for this; the characters deal with one another, having little contact with non-Jews. This last indirectly indicates the insularity of the group, an evidence of restriction, whether imposed internally or from without, but little is made of it. In the Depression novel, the enemy was not religious prejudice; it was the economic system. The social-protest novel of anti-Semitism was to come in the 1940's, but not in the form of the education novel. In such a sophisticated work as *Summer in Williamsburg,* the appearance of anti-Semitism as a "problem" would be discordant.

A Sabbath table scene gives Philip a chance to reflect on the familiar pleasures of Jewish cooking and to test the strength of the family's hold upon him—the traditional use of a traditional scene in the Jewish novel. But Fuchs characteristically adds a twist. A note of outrageous humor is injected at this serious moment: Philip clowns over the meal, pretending he is poisoned, an old family joke which strikes the reader with a shock of incongruity.

Fuchs is a masterful dialect humorist with an accurate ear for the idiosyncracies of English flavored by Yiddish idioms. A bystander, attempting to prevent violence as the gangsters prepare to demolish the bus station, addresses their leader: "Listen, my friend. I don't like to go where I don't belong, but let me tell you something. What I say is that a man can't be successful unless he's got a warm heart and is willing to give another fellow a chance."[52] The rhythms of Yiddish-accented English lend a wry flavor to the insensate destructiveness of the scene. Fuchs, as a comic ironist, records the gangster's speech of thanksgiving to his men: "And it is only a beginning, because, remember, there is still a God over America."[53] The line is a brilliant variant of the *goldeneh medinah-Amerika gonef* equation.

The Jewish material is handled with a far more sophisticated humor, fraught as it is with irony, than that of the popular comic novelist, but the same tricks are used. The novel is narrated by a mock-simple, omniscient voice which makes the undignified scramblings of the characters seem even more trivial and ant-like—they are a low company indeed. Among the most empty are the old men in the synagogue poring over the Talmud. Their voices, endless sounds in the dusty air, are repeated more for their effect as incantation than for their revelation. "Rabbi ben Onz said this to mean this, Rabbi ben Twos . . . said it is to mean that. . . ."[54]

Fuchs's city contains more than Jews. The Communist Party is also subjected to satire. Cohen turns to the Party after hearing a speaker in Union Square. But there is no offering of absolution, no surcease of pain. The diffi-dent, half-mad Cohen is taken to the cell meeting-place: "A heavy girl with loose face and big lips came up to him wielding a cigarette. 'My name is SHURA,' she said pointblank and with dreadful solemnity. 'Who are you?' "[55] Cohen enlists in the Party to serve in the "agit-prop" section, but he does little more than talk about a one-act play which somehow will hold within its confines the standard plot of the conversion novel with all the wanderings and discoveries of the hero. The Party fails Cohen as he fails it. Shura bluntly informs him that she will not provide the sex which is his real need. Rejecting Orthodoxy and Marxism, Fuchs, the existential ironist, stays clear of all eschatological theories.

The oblique perspective and the wry turning away from the easy answer are the marks of Jewish literary intelli-gence at its best. Henry Roth and Meyer Levin had their own, more solemn, reasons for doubting the Marx-ist solution. For Daniel Fuchs the rejection of the Party sprang from his persistent sense of the incongruity and absurdity of life.

NOTES TO CHAPTER 3

1. The first-generation novelists can be brought into the context of the more radical years of the Thirties. Turning further left, Samuel Ornitz and Lester Cohen played more than a minor role as Marxist-inclined literary figures during these years. In 1931 they joined Theodore Dreiser in a committee sent by the Communist-organized National Committee for the Defense of Political Prisoners to "investigate conditions" in the Harlan County coal fields, according to Daniel Aaron. In 1932, along with Isidore Schneider (see below) and fifty others, they were signatories of the pamphlet "Culture and Crisis: An Open Letter to the Writers, Artists, Teachers, Physicians, Engineers, Scientists and Other Professional Workers of America." The signers included "self-proclaimed converts to Communism and others who would soon become prominent in the Left movement," to quote Aaron. In 1933 they were the object of a sharply ironic attack by T. S. Eliot, who wrote in the January number of *The Criterion* that the young Communist intellectuals in New York were turning to the "arduous study of Ernest Hemingway and John Dos Passos; and the end of their precipitous ascent will be an appreciation of the accomplishments of Sam Ornitz, Lester Cohen, and Granville Hicks." (Daniel Aaron, *Writers on the Left* [New York: Harcourt, Brace & World, Inc., 1961], *passim*.) In contrast, Cahan and John Cournos, author of *The Mask,* were not involved in any leftist activity significant enough to gain them a place in the index of Aaron's thorough study. Cournos, in a tandem review of several mid-Thirties education novels, claimed that Communist propagandizing weakened Schneider's *From the Kingdom of Necessity,* the most doctrinaire of the novels. (John Cournos, "Truth and Fiction," *The Menorah Journal,* XXIV, No. 2 [April-June 1936], 151-153.) Joseph Freeman, describing the radical scene in the mid-Twenties, condemned Cahan's *Daily Forward* for being controlled by anti-Soviet Socialists and trade-union bureaucrats. (Joseph Freeman, *An American Testament* [New York: Farrar & Rinehart, Inc., 1936], p. 248.)

2. Michael Gold, *Jews without Money* (New York: Liveright Publishing Corp., 1930); Isidore Schneider, *From the Kingdom of Necessity* (New York: G. P. Putnam's Sons, 1935). Daniel Aaron has conjectured about the appeal of the Party in "Communism and the Jewish Writer," *Salmagundi,* I, No. 1 (Fall 1965), 23-36.

3. Daniel Fuchs, *Three Novels* (New York: Basic Books, 1961); Henry Roth *Call It Sleep* (New York: Pageant Books, 1960); Meyer Levin, *The Old Bunch* (New York: Simon and Schuster, 1937.)

4. Joseph Freeman describes such a scene from his own life in *An American Testament.* His autobiography frequently repeats the situations of the education novel.

5. Walter Rideout, *The Radical Novel in the United States* (Cam-

bridge; Harvard University Press, 1956), p. 313; Blanche Gelfant, *The American City Novel,* (Norman, Okla.: University of Oklahoma Press, 1954), pp. 12-13.

6. Freeman, *American Testament,* pp. 250-251.

7. Gold, *Jews without Money,* Intro., n.p.

8. Diana Trilling, *Claremont Essays* (New York: Harcourt, Brace & World, Inc., 1964), pp. 159-160.

9. *Jews without Money,* p. 71.

10. Harlan Hatcher, *Creating the Modern Novel* (New York: Farrar and Rinehart, 1935), p. 267.

11. *Jews without Money,* p. 30.

12. *Ibid.,* p. 243.

13. Quoted in Aaron, *Writers on the Left,* p. 209.

14. Schneider, *From the Kingdom of Necessity,* p. 196.

15. *Ibid.,* p. 450.

16. *Jews without Money,* p. 191.

17. The most famous of these was Rabbi Jacob Joseph of Vilna, who was made Chief Rabbi of New York in 1888: Nathan Glazer, *American Judaism.* (Chicago: University of Chicago Press, 1957), p. 70.

18. *From the Kingdom of Necessity,* p. 17.

19. Irving Howe, "Life Never Let Up," *The New York Times Book Review,* Oct. 25, 1964, p. 1.

20. Roth, *Call It Sleep,* p. xxiv; Marie Syrkin, "Revival of a Classic," *Midstream,* VII, No. 1 (Winter 1961), 89-92.

21. Leslie Fiedler, "Henry Roth's Neglected Masterpiece," *Commentary,* XXX, No. 2 (Aug. 1960), 102-107. (Fiedler overlooks the laudatory Cournos *Menorah Journal* review.)

22. Henry Roth, "At Times in Flight," *Commentary,* XXIX, No. 1 (July 1959), 51-54; "The Dun Dakotas," *Commentary,* XXX, No. 2 (Aug. 1960), 107-109.

23. *Call It Sleep,* p. 447.

24. *Ibid.,* p. 569; Frank Norris, *The Octopus* (New York: Doubleday, Page & Co., 1901), p. 634.

25. *Call It Sleep,* p. 183.

26. *Ibid.,* p. 175.

27. Louis Wirth, *The Ghetto* (Chicago: University of Chicago Press, 1956), p. 69.

28. *Call It Sleep,* p. 562.

29. *Ibid.,* p. 567.

30. *Ibid.,* p. 308.

31. Saul Bellow, *Herzog* (New York: The Viking Press, 1964), p. 136.

32. Howe, "Life Never Lets Up," p. 1.

33. Harold U. Ribalow, ed., *Treasury of American Jewish Stories* (New York: Thomas Yoseloff, 1958), p. 186.

34. In this same year, Howard Fast published his first novel, *The Children* (New York: Duell, Sloan & Pearce, 1937), a tale of slum life with a group hero. One of the four children of the book is a Jew.

35. Levin, *In Search* (New York: The Horizon Press, 1950), pp. 75-76.

36. *Ibid.*, pp. 95 ff.

37. Brom Weber, "Some American Jewish Novelists," *Chicago Jewish Forum*, IV, No. 3 (Spring 1946), 179.

38. Wirth, *The Ghetto*, p. 250.

39. Levin, *In Search*, p. 52.

40. Edmund Wilson, *The American Earthquake* (New York: Anchor Books, 1964), p. 449.

41. *Call It Sleep*, p. xxviii; and *Three Novels*, p. vii.

42. Benjamin Weintroub, the editor of the *Chicago Jewish Forum*, encountered some difficulty in publishing an early, favorable review of the book. (In conversation with the present author.) Harold U. Ribalow, "A Note on Meyer Levin," *Chicago Jewish Forum*, IX, No. 1 (Fall 1950), 9-11; Meyer Levin, "When I Was a Book Peddler," *Congress Bi-Weekly*, XXVIII, No. 19 (Dec. 15, 1961), 6-8.

43. Ludwig Lewisohn, *The American Jew* (New York: Farrar, Straus & Co., 1950), p. 153.

44. In *Mid-Century*, ed. Harold V. Ribalow (New York: The Beechhurst Press, Inc., 1955), p. 320.

45. Letter to the present author.

46. Letter to the present author.

47. Ihab Hassan, "The Character of Post-War Fiction in America," *On Contemporary Literature*, ed. Richard Kostelanetz (New York: Avon Books, 1964), p. 38.

48. Fuchs, *Three Novels*, p. vii.

49. *Ibid.*, p. 4.

50. *Ibid.*, p. 44.

51. Cohen is seen as the ridiculous "alter-ego" of Philip by Irving Howe in an interpretation of *Summer in Williamsburg* which emphasizes the economic base of the book, calling it a "naturalistic genre novel." "Daniel Fuchs: Escape From Williamsburg: The Fate of Talent in America," *Commentary*, VI, No. 1 (July 1948), p. 29-34.

52. *Three Novels*, p. 18.

53. *Ibid.*, p. 380.

54. *Ibid.*, p. 50.

55. *Ibid.*, p. 210.

4

Getting Older:
The Time of Alienation

THE ALIENATION EDUCATION NOVEL

In the 1940's an old theme appeared in Jewish-American letters in a sophisticated guise. A number of young Jews shook off the economic motifs and the Naturalistic model of the Depression novel to adopt a new metaphysics expressed in a new style. "Alienation," the key term of this movement, was the major concern of the education novel of this period.[1] The names associated with the school of alienation are Isaac Rosenfeld (the *meister* of the group), Saul Bellow, Delmore Schwartz, Paul Goodman, and Clement Greenberg, to use Daniel Bell's list.[2] *Commentary* magazine (formerly the *Contemporary Jewish Record*) and the *Partisan Review,* then moving into its post-Marxist phase, are the magazines associated most

111

closely with the work of these men, although they also wrote for the academic quarterlies. They and their literary heirs must be counted as critics as well as fiction writers, for they have produced a body of criticism equal in quantity to their fiction. Much of this criticism has escaped the fate of occasional writing. It can be found in volumes of collected reviews under the names of Isaac Rosenfeld, Paul Goodman, Alfred Kazin, Leslie Fiedler, Harvey Swados, Robert Warshow, Irving Howe, and Norman Podhoretz. While they are not a group, they have been ironically dubbed "The New Reviewers" by Renata Adler.[3]

Alienation as a literary style using the plot of the education novel will be illustrated by Isaac Rosenfeld's novel *Passage from Home* (1946) and by Alfred Kazin's fictionalized autobiography *A Walker in the City* (1951). Saul Bellow's *The Adventures of Augie March* (1953) will be examined as the novel which brought Jewish fiction out of alienation into what has been called "affirmation" and "accommodation."[4]

The Nazi-Soviet non-aggression pact of 1939 is a commonly accepted point to mark the disenchantment of American intellectuals with the Communist Party.[5] The rupture was temporarily repaired. The "Popular Front" position carried some of the intellectuals through the war years. (In response to questions about the influence of their Jewish heritage upon their work, Ben Field, Albert Halper, and Delmore Schwartz noted, ironically, that the Nazi regime was responsible for arousing an awareness of their Jewish identity.[6]) But the publication in 1944 of Saul Bellow's *Dangling Man,* the story of the disenchanted ex-Communist searching for a posture and unable to accept "Doctor-Win-the-War," indicated the ambivalence among intellectuals. The earlier visions of Kafka and Dadaism began to seem more prescient than the collectivist dreams of the Thirties. And then the cataclysmic end of World War II, with its revelations of the extent of the "final solution," and the Cold War came as assaults upon the sensibilities of the intellectuals.

Jewish life in the United States seemed hardly more inspiring than politics as a subject. In these years, the popular novelist was provided with the themes of anti-Semitism and Zionism. But the series of novels in which the cruelties of the country club were exposed or a neurotic reluctantly was converted to the joys of the kibbutz seemed too programmatic and obvious to the serious writer.

It seemed clear, though, that the attempt to achieve wholeness by entering the dominant American culture and abandoning the family and Judaism had failed. The concept of marginality was clarified in this period by the Gestalt psychologist, Kurt Lewin, in *Resolving Social Conflicts* (1948), and by Daniel Bell, a critic who spoke more directly to the intellectuals. The Jew's marginal position in society now seemed to be a reflection of the insecurity and dread of the Western World. As a long-time expert in alienation, the Jew presumably could provide insights that now had a universal application. A theme had been found. Ironically, the Jew gained admittance as an outsider.

In February of 1944, the *Contemporary Jewish Record* published a symposium which was to cause "distress" and "strong reaction," in the words used by Samuel Dinin in summarizing the year's "Cultural Activities" in *The American Jewish Yearbook* (Vol. XLVI). Proudly citing the accomplishments in literature of the children of the Jewish immigrants, the editors of the *Contemporary Jewish Record* presented the responses of eleven young intellectuals to questions designed to determine whether there was a conscious or unconscious influence of Judaism upon them; whether their work could be distinguished from that of non-Jews by themes or manner of response to themes; and whether the "revival" of anti-Semitism had modified their position as artists. The article was called "Under Forty: A Symposium on American Literature and the Younger Generation of American Jews."

The cause for the alarm which followed the article was the disavowal by the respondents, not of being Jews, but of Judaism. The articulate voice of the children was clearly heard to deny any central influence by organized religion, cultural Judaism, or the official Jewry of the organizations. The young men felt indebted to the seventeenth-century English religious poets and the *New Masses,* but not the Rambam or *Pirke Abot.*

Equally unsettling was the claim made for the Jewish identity which all but three of the eleven maintained had a significant influence upon their work. Delmore Schwartz and Clement Greenberg asserted that the negative feelings and the marginal position in American culture which they suffered as Jews had heightened their awareness and sharpened their perspicacity. As Rosenfeld put it: The Jew is a "specialist in alienation (the one international banking system the Jews actually control)."[7]

A definite pride was taken in the sharing of this unhappy state, and a claim was made for its wider application in modern life than to the Jews alone. The perspective of Jewishness, it was asserted, opened a vista that made the Jew privy to the mysterious, destructive forces which now threaten human life and culture. After reviewing the provincial life available to him as the child of immigrants in New York City, Delmore Schwartz applauds the clarity which his estrangement grants him: "I understood my own personal squint at experience; and the fact of being a Jew became available to me as a central symbol of alienation, bias, point of view, and certain other characteristics which are the peculiar marks of modern life, and as I think now, the essential ones."[8]

The above passage suggests the strategy available to the Jewish writer: to continue to depict the strains and dislocations of Jewish family life from the point of view of the sensitive son. It was not that the Jewish intellectual had changed. (Greenberg still saw socialism as the solution for the lack of integration of the Jewish writer.) It was the reader who would find in this same fiction, now informed by Kafka, Joyce, and Max Weber rather than Zola, Dreiser, and Farrell, insight into his own situation.[9]

In yet another symposium, this time in *Partisan Review,* "Our Country and Our Culture," Irving Howe, a notable proponent of the conception of alienation, and Delmore Schwartz, an acute practitioner of the literary style of alienation in poetry and story, addressed themselves to the question of the dissociated state of culture of the time. Their responses were similar: that this is indeed a time of groping, that non-conformism must be maintained, and that alienation is a useful stance for the writer. Inevitably, given the limitations of symposia, their ideas were barely developed; better articulations of their conception of alienation are contained in Howe's essay "The Lost Young Intellectual" and Schwartz's novella *The World Is a Wedding.*[10]

ISAAC ROSENFELD

A central and representative figure of this school is Isaac Rosenfeld. He seems to have been a man whose life was as inspiring as his work. Despite the slender *ouevre* he left—one novel, one collection of short stories, another of reviews, and a second, still unpublished, novel —he continues to be remembered. Before his death, his stories and reviews appeared in a number of serious publications; since his death, his work continues to be anthologized. The critic Theodore Solotaroff returned to the University of Chicago on the rumor that he was teaching there. Saul Bellow, a friend since high school years, shared some of his stylistic qualities and has continued to champion him. Alfred Kazin lent his name to a dust-jacket encomium on the occasion of the republication of *Passage from Home*: "I am very glad—and more than a little moved."[11] Seymour Krim, in *Views of a Nearsighted Cannoneer,* recalls the stimulation of belonging in the early Forties to the Greenwich Village literary circle composed of Isaac Rosenfeld (whose name is given first), Dave Bazelon, Manny Farber *et al.,* and their occasional *confrères* Saul Bellow, Delmore Schwartz, and Alfred Kazin. Krim conjectures that the intense pressure of the group's high intellectual standards may have contributed to the early deaths of Rosenfeld, Robert Warshow, and Elliot Cohen and the suicides of Weldon Kees and Willie Poster. Krim's book offers evidence of the group's extraordinary devotion to literature and its profound involvement with the modern literary masters of the Western world.[12]

Five critics well equipped to assess the structures and implications of alienation fiction turned to *Passage from Home* as a prototypical example. Harvey Swados and Irving Sanes in "Certain Jewish Writers" used the novel and the family chronicles of Delmore Schwartz to explicate their disapproval of the new stereotype of "Alienated Americans," because it overlooked the obvious solution to the American problem, i.e., Socialism.[13] Irving Howe saw the "new social type," the unsuccessful intellectual, as a latter-day version of *luftmensch* in "The Lost Young Intellectual."[14] Daniel Bell, in "A Parable of Alienation" applauded alienation as a new theme and explored one of its roots, the bureaucratic age as seen by Kafka, Toller, Max Weber, *et al.*[15] The bulk of Bell's article, a study of alienation as a *Weltanschauung,* is devoted to *Passage from Home,* which, he declared, made Rosenfeld "a major interpreter of the perceptions and emotions of the young Jewish intellectual." Theodore Solotaroff, like Bell, called the book autobiographical, particularly at "the points of emphasis where character and theme intersect." That is to say, Rosenfeld had lost his mother early, and the depiction of the effect of such a loss on Bernard's character can be read as autobiography. The alienation reading of the novel is supported: Bernard's vision of the separateness of human beings is a sign of the primary concern of Rosenfeld "as a Jew as well as a writer" with the problem of self-integration. Not quite accepting Bell's interpretation of the ending as a parable of race experience, Solotaroff sees it, rather, as a paradigm of Rosenfeld's own life, foretelling the continuing wavering between Jewish life and "a type of Reichian-method Bohemianism" which Rosenfeld was to follow.[16]

Passage from Home

The problem of inventing situations and a prose style for the education novel in its new, more intellectually sophisticated form is brilliantly solved in *Passage from Home*. Symbols and philosophical ideas are solidly anchored to events and realistic effects, and all is related to a single theme: the coming to maturity of an adolescent "sensitive as a burn," to single out a favorite phrase of the critics. Rosenfeld's method as a critic was the simple one of focusing on the depiction of human life.[17] In Rosenfeld's one published piece of sustained fiction, he likewise concentrated on the texture of living experience. The constant attention to the perceptional process of the protagonist to the exclusion of external message, sociological comment, and other preoccupations makes the book a model fictional exploration of the adolescent mind.

"An unhappy childhood is a writer's gold mine," wrote Rosenfeld in a 1949 review.[18] The raw materials for *Passage from Home* are the familiar ones of the Jewish family novel: the ebullient relatives, the uncommunicative father, the acute son. Rosenfeld successfully refurbishes these, as well as the unaccepted stepmother and the snuffling grandfather, making the dry bones dance. In part, the vitality of the novel comes from the precision and humor with which the Jewish materials are treated. The group scenes provide realism and a foil to the extended solitary musings of the first-person narrator. The holiday gathering, with its flash of diamonds and vapor of cigars, is shown in telling detail: "We stuffed ourselves, got up from the table to dance—or merely to wander grinning about the house and shout 'Hoo! Haa!'—came back and drank. . . ."[19] This is not Breughel the Elder; the pleasure is too transitory, the shadows too imminent—Hieronymus Bosch, perhaps.

The center of the novel does not lie in the accuracy and conciseness of the family scenes, however. To reach it one must unravel a pattern of symbolism, setting, and theory of perception. One system of symbols is based on the sterile observance of Judaism by Bernard's family. Another set, more artifically devised, marks the Oedipal struggles of Bernard with his Aunt Minna who, estranged from the family, has departed the Jewish neighborhood on the Northwest side of Chicago for a lakefront Bohemian one. These contrasting neighborhoods form polar colonies; Bernard's incomplete understanding of the life style in each gives the plots its tensions. Each of the two colonies must be examined as a set of symbols; their polar relationship expresses the alienation theme of the novel.

Judaism as a Symbol in Passage from Home

The Judaism of Bernard's family has become diluted. This vitiation is symbolized by the preparations of the stepmother (she is always so called by the narrator) for the *shabbes*. The orthodox rituals have been reduced to the compulsive cleanliness which is by now part of the stereotype of the Jewish matronly personality.

We, however, had none of the usual concomitants of an orthodox Sabbath. My stepmother baked no *chalah,* traditional woven loaves, billowy or braided like wigs and covered with a glossy patina of egg; nor, covering her head and cupping her hands, did she light candles after sundown. All this was left to my grandmother. Step-mother's tabernacle was the toilet, and the tub was *mikvah* enough. She braided her hair in place of dough, and as for the gleaming of candles, she found an equivalent in cold cream which when applied to her nose in particular, was as good a substitute as you could want.[20]

The stepmother, complex like Bernard and his father, senses the inadequacy of these preparations. Another note, the Oedipal one, has been introduced, adding to the infelicity of the moment. Bemoaning Bernard's lost Jewish education, she suggests he read Aleichem, Peretz, Mendele—or at least have his father read them aloud. Finally, she proposes a visit to Grandfather. The West Side of Chicago has the older, therefore less corrupted, settlement of Jews.

The humiliation and exaltation of Jewish life are compressed into a walk with Grandfather who, like other grandfathers of Jewish-American fiction, contains the essence of Jewish life in a purer form than the father, who has not been freed by age from the corrupting demands of making a living. Grandfather's abasement occurs at his former grocery store, lost through his feeble business methods. The new proprietor is a success; his white apron, clean-shaven face, and derbyless head, the fashionable window display and the up-to-date equipment, contrast to Grandfather's old country air and ways. The grocery store is a common setting in Jewish fiction. Albert Halper's stories of boyhood as a grocer's son are set in the same Near Northwest and West Side neighborhoods that Rosenfeld depicts. Malamud resuscitates the bare-shelved Depression grocery in *The Assistant*. In *Passage from Home,* the grocery store embodies the theme of unappealing squalor in Jewish life and permits the use of realistic detail to anchor the more abstract parts of the novel.

Jewish life has a dimension other than the abject, however. After debasing himself before his successor by asking for a candling job and, in general, behaving foolishly, Grandfather proceeds with Bernard to visit the home of the Reb Feldman. The Reb reclines in state, surrounded by a respectful assemblage who, in a scene out of a woodcut, discuss some close Talmudic point, interrupting one another but deferring instantly to Reb Feldman. They are *Hasidim,* members of an especially devout and unassimilating sect. To complete the vignette, the men suddenly spring into a hand-clapping and bent-knee *Hasidic* dance. Hardly understanding why, Bernard shares with his Grandfather the ecstacy of the moment; but he is distressed by the old man's incongruous mixture of moods as they proceed on this odd journey.

The choice of a *Hasidic* household is suitable. The nineteenth-century garb of the men, an inviolable feature of their lives, strikes the eye of the Americanized Jew with an aspect embarrassing and, at the same time, admonitory. The gaberdine (the long, shiny frock coat), the *shtreimel* (fur-brimmed hat), and the untrimmed beard and *payos* (curls at the temples)—these are the symbols of their intransigence, of their fervid espousal of Judaism as a mystical faith, composed of emotionality

as well as law. Their spirited behavior, so unlike that
of the inhibited American Jews, is in itself a mixture of
the embarrassing and the sublime which is Bernard's
image of Jewish life.[21]

Setting as Symbol

Bernard's ambivalence toward his Jewish heritage is
set against the appealing life that his Aunt Minna leads
in the city's Bohemian center on the Near North Side.
This setting has a symbolic function. Aunt Minna's free
life is rendered by the open images of lake and park,
while the closed society of Bernard's Jewish world is
symbolized by its flat, dry pavements and bricks, separated from the lake by endless rides on the street car.
Bernard's parents walk the streets of a Sunday in search
of rest; but his Uncle Willie happily lolls in the park on
weekdays, collar undone, a beatific smile on his face. In
an essay written some years later, "Life in Chicago,"
Rosenfeld expanded this dual symbol into a theory of
urban life: the "beach-head" of high culture is but a
mile deep and beyond it lies a wasteland, parched, ignorant, and fearful.[22]

Bernard lives in a Jewish wasteland. As a minor motif
in the novel, the inhibited life of the Jews is symbolized
by the imitation-log, gas-vent fireplaces in their apartments. From these, Bernard had imagined that fire was
religiously proscribed: "Fire was the image of that
raging, destructive spirit, found also in drunkenness,
bloody meat not salted or soaked, life without prayer,
the freedom of the world without God, against which
we locked our doors."[23] Minna's apartment, of course,
has a fireplace which is used even in the summer months.

Minna and the Oedipal Theme

The Oedipal theme, prefigured faintly by Bernard's stepmother, receives a sharper statement in Minna. Bernard's efforts to achieve a relationship with Minna having failed, he introduces her to Cousin Willie Harpsmith, a gentile whose wife had died. The wife's name, Martha Vogel (bird), suggests the ethereal nature of the departed one. Bernard senses that it had been his intention to do this from the beginning; he is compelled to work out the terms of the Oedipal theme.

As Minna is a surrogate mother (rumor has it that she kidnapped Bernard after being rejected by his widowed father), so Willie is a father, one who can display affection freely. After Bernard has run away from home to live with Willie and Minna, he explicitly speaks of Willie's paternal sympathy, as opposed to the prudence and severity which have been his portion as a son.

The two fathers are rivals, then. Willie is indolent, morally lax, free of responsibilities. Tall, slim, and White Anglo-Saxon Protestant, he is the opposite in every way of Bernard's father. Over the *seder* table at Passover Willie and the father conduct a contest. Harry presides, alternating a patriarchal tone with an assumed, uneasy affability; Willie clowns, losing his skullcap, finally wins, leading the gathering in a rendition of "That Old-time Religion." The divison in Bernard's life is further underlined.

The appeal of a free life is mixed. Willie reveals the nature of Minna's life. She has "lived a woman's life," although she is unmarried. This knowledge, the first peek behind the attractive veil of *La vie de Bohème,* is received with characteristically ambivalent emotions by Bernard. He resolves to learn the truth as his *rite de passage* (a phrase suggested by the novel's title). "By instincts not yet awakened . . . or by a common knowledge not yet accumulated," he will see as clearly as a man and thus become one. But the flash of insight is to come as a revulsion from Minna's disordered, roach- and grease-filled kitchen. "The moment of nausea was in the nature of a perception."[24] The fastidious youth, anxious to abandon the excessive cleanliness of one home, is not yet ready for the squalor of the other.

Adolescent Perception as a Theme

The theme of enlarging perception is expressed by Bernard's slowly deepening insight into the taut relationships in Minna's *ménage*. Before the climactic events that focus his understanding, however, the theme of perception is traced through several abstract passages. With adolescent self-absorption, Bernard falls into a kind of trance on the elevated train, seeing himself from afar, sensing his life as a vacancy. In another incident, he prides himself on his intellect, insisting that a friend stand beside him in the cold night as he identifies constellations, taking the shivering friend's abandonment of him as one more proof of his uniqueness. At thirteen, not really grasping their complexities, he has read Schopenhauer and Nietzsche and, like the true hero of an education novel, Spencer's *First Principles*.

Bernard's self-absorption is penetrated partially by the parables which Minna and Willie tell him. (It is this explicit adoption of a Kafkaesque technique, more than the atmosphere—drab, but not fantastic—which reveals the effect of that influence upon Rosenfeld.) Minna tells a tale about her dressmaker's mannequin. It was a doll, her companion, until she had to strip off its limbs to provide for her little sister, Bernard's dead mother. Thus obliquely is rendered the emotional self-portrait of Minna, who feels that her sister had the womanly fulfillment of husband and child denied her. Willie's tale is out of Mark Twain rather than Kafka. He recalls the year he ran away from home. He was fourteen, the same age as Bernard, who has also run away from home. But Willie's odyssey is a success, carried out in the solace of the great woods, the humans encountered all friends or kin. Like Huck Finn, he gives false names, steals a boat, drifts beneath the stars, and gets lost. And unlike Bernard, he is greeted as a man with sympathy and understanding by his father upon his return home.

In the end it is Bernard, perhaps only because he is one-third the age of Willie, who is to enjoy the possibilities of an open life, whose passage from home is to lead him back home where he can start again in mature estate. Human gesture and symbolic action are the medium for expressing this. Rosenfeld, in a review for the *New Republic* written about the time he was composing the novel, started his simple, even obvious, view of character: "The structure of character, its emotional pattern . . . should serve as the fundamental means of psychological identification" and "the will's deep commitment to struggle" should be expressed as "the simple feelings of the inner life."[25] Rosenfeld achieves this kind of structuring more in his development of the motivations of the characters than in the sometimes labored symbolism. An example of realistic character development: Bernard fails to reform Willie, to teach him to dress properly; but an improvement in Willie's appearance follows upon his affair with Minna. The attempts to indicate personality through symbolic gesture vary in success, e.g., in a YMCA room, Bernard turns to the window, gazing toward the lights and activity; Willie stares at the instruction card on the door and at the Bible. This scene comes off better than some of the extraneous Freudian invention, e.g., in the basement getting a cot, Bernard crawls through a buggy frame, whereas Willie is too large: Bernard is young enough to achieve a rebirth, but Willie is too far into adulthood.

Although Bernard returns home at the close of the novel, it is clear that the world outside will draw him out again. Probably it will be that intellectual world represented by Minna's Bohemian life. Bernard is clearly Rosenfeld as a youth; the sensitive protagonist of the education novel invariably prefigures the novelist who is to create him in an ultimate act of introspection. In Rosenfeld's life we have yet another example of that familiar figure, the urban Jewish intellectual—Bernard grown to manhood. The socialism implicit in Minna's talk of bourgeois manners was, for a time, Rosenfeld's path. (Rosenfeld recalls in "Life in Chicago" the excitement of politics, Trotskyite and otherwise, on the University of Chicago campus in the Thirties.) *Passage from Home* is an artistic statement of the loss of direction suffered by the post-Marxist intellectual; the changes of direction and psychological dislocations of Rosenfeld's life, perhaps, are the result of the same process. Rosenfeld came to his sad end, suffering a heart attack at thirty-eight in a lonely room on Chicago's Near North Side, not far from where Minna's fictional apartment would have been.

A WALKER IN THE CITY AS A NOVEL OF ALIENATION

In 1959, in an article in *Harper's Magazine,* "The Alone Generation," Alfred Kazin deplored the super-abundance of current American fiction dealing with lonely characters, generally children or adolescents, psychologically portrayed: stories of "the self and its detractors."[26] In 1951, Kazin had published *A Walker in the City,* an autobiographical account of a lonely adolescent—an internal examination of the dynamics of environment acting upon a sensitive youth. The form of the book is reminiscence. Action is suppressed. Denied an active part in the plot, the vibrant grotesques melt into the background much in the way that Kazin was to decry in 1959. In another article written in 1948, "The Mindless Young Militants," Kazin had deplored the use, without real understanding, of the set materials of Jewish fiction by such writers as Irwin Shaw: "the dramatic seasoning of Jewish family bitterness, the Jewish joke, the classic *j'accuse!* of Jewish experience throughout the ages. . . ."[27] *A Walker in the City,* includes, if not a bitter family, one which knows permanent poverty. It includes the divisive relationship of a pious mother and a free-thinking father, the inventory of candy store and delicatessen, and the complete *shabbes* menu.

Some of Kazin's reviewers regarded the book as the kind that he, himself, had denigrated. Morris Freedman, reviewing *A Walker in the City,* found a dry, sociological detachment in its tone and a vagueness about the narrator.[28]

But if the premise of alienation as a posture is accepted by the reader, he finds a dimension added. Leslie Fiedler, reviewing the book in 1952 for *Partisan Review,* did see it in the tradition of alienation, saying that the image of the young Jewish intellectual on his lonely walks gives the book another dimension because he is the "very symbol of our urbanization . . . central to our plight." He tells us that Kazin, through his serious, religious tone, escapes the pitfalls of this kind of book, with its "Joycean prototype": "sentimentality, local color, and finally the impulse to become just another 'first novel,' the pseudo-fictional confession which is a bore before it is told." (The education novel author never received much encouragement.) By the time Fielder came to refer to the novel in 1959, he had lost some of his enthusiasm, classifying it along with *Passage from Home* and Sam Astrachan's *An End to Dying* as "up from the ghetto" fiction, an unredeemable pattern, "nostalgic and vestigial."[29]

The book can be called beautiful. Kazin makes a searching attempt to stretch his materials to their metaphysical reaches. He essays an intense portrait of the state of mind of a bright young Jew moving out of the Brownsville scene away from the orthodoxy of the ramshackle *shul,* the streetcorner socialism, the camaraderie of Odessa tea room, the whirr of the Singer sewing machine in the kitchen. The spiritual journey of Alfred in late Twenties and early Thirties covers much the same ground as that of Bernard in *Passage from Home,* going from the enclosed Jewish family to the larger secular world. But Alfred makes it across the bridge, his vehicle the open but encapsulating culture of museum paintings, Modern Library reprints, and that preoccupation of the New York intellectual, the movies.

In 1944, Kazin, like Rosenfeld, had been a contributor to the "Under Forty" symposium which had indicated that others had experienced the process of acculturation to the intellectual world. While Kazin expresses in the symposium an admiration for Sholom Aleichem (again like Rosenfeld), for the Bundist Socialists and "the texture of a genuine and received Hebrew culture," he admits that their influence upon him as a writer has acted in ways hard to determine and states that Jewish-American culture has nothing to recommend it. Jewish-American writers are singled out in particular for their inability to ground their experience in the life they reject —the life Kazin rejects but reproduces gracefully in *A Walker in the City. The* writing of Jews which touches him is that of the scholars and critics rather than the "popular novelists" (i.e., Trilling, Rosenfeld, Greenberg and Schwartz, rather than Ben Field and Albert Halper, to mention just symposium participants). The deepest influences upon Kazin are Melville, Emerson, the English poets, and the Russian novelists; like other Americans, he has had to create his own culture. Implicit in Kazin's intellectual progress is the disavowal of the Left as one more of the strands of Brownsville life.[30]

Rejecting Marxism and the Brownsville culture, then, in *A Walker in the City* Kazin combines the drab setting of city streets with the image of the lonely, intellectual youth to create an essay in alienation, managing through a suggestive prose to infuse the sterile streets he describes with a sense of vitality. He manages the difficult trick of writing entertainingly about the depressing matter of poverty.

Two Cultures of Brownsville

In 1956, for *The American Scholar,* Kazin chose *Call It Sleep* as the most neglected novel of the past twenty-five years, admiring its authenticity as a psychological portrait.[31] It is a psychological portrait that Kazin attempts in *A Walker in the City*—a portrait of the soul of an innocent as a battleground for conflicting cultures.

The strongest expression of the tensions inherent in living between two cultures is found as the first-person narrator recalls the time he doffed his phylacteries and prayer shawl to find in the lefthand pages of his Bible, in the English translation, the deepest worship of God. This shock of recognition (the book has many—all springing from Alfred's immersion in the culture beyond Brownsville) sets him to examining his Jewish life. He realizes that the spiritual life available to him only through *melamed* and synagogue has, in reality, denied him the "grandness and austerity" of being a Jew. He searches among the self-satisfied, joyless worshippers for a *Hasid,* the embodiment of joy in the Lord, only to have the men shrug away the thought of such a *meshuggener* (madman).

At the opposite pole from religion in Brownsville is socialism, more various in its manifestations than is the still pure Orthodox Judaism. Young Alfred found mitigation of his loneliness in a pale band of Socialists who were not quite up to the conviction of the Communists then dominating the soap boxes. The shibboleth to separate the two groups is "Negro"; the Communists are able to bring a respectiful warmth to the word denied to Socialists. The necessities of the theory of alienation are satisfied in Kazin's treatment of the Party. The Communists are obsessed with international "sellouts"; their appeal to the crowd is vitiated by the formalism of their slogans. The real life goes on at the back of the crowd in the dialectic among workers oblivious of the speaker.

The plot, then, is that of the education novel worked out in the terms of the Jewish-American novelist: departure and arrival, the quest and the discovery, the rejection of Brownsville and the acceptance of Washington Heights. Novelistic technique, implicit in the handsome if self-conscious prose, makes the theme manifest. Unable to sustain this extended piece with simple plot and rich prose, Kazin introduces symbolism. A brick wall inscribed DAZZY DAZZY DAZZY, echoing the Eliotic cry of SHANTIH SHANTIH SHANTIH of Alfred's poetry-drunk friend, is continually assaulted with a rubber ball by Alfred trying to beat down the entombing walls of the ghetto.

Fictional Technique

The details of Kazin's life history in *A Walker in the City* may be factual, but their appearance in his book are demonstrably fictional in impact. The chief device is symbolism, pictorially employed. The scene Kazin limns is reminiscent of the airy, featureless cityscapes of di Chirico, a touch more unreal and strained in their barrenness than the scenes of Hopper, which only border on the fantastic. The guilt and anxiety of the alienated are worked into the texture, for instance, in the scene recalling a silent motion picture. The sight of Monte Blue being locked into an iron maiden intensifies the guilt that young Alfred suffers whenever he sits in a darkened theater during daylight hours—an adult emotion, really. The very shaft of sunlight falling across the screen as the door opens is, arbitrarily, "hostile" and "ominous."

More satisfying, because it ascribes a more credible emotion to young Alfred, is a scene equally symbolic and and visual: a drugstore placard showing "THE HUMAN FACTORY," a chart of the digestive system drawn in mechanical form. The sign recalls to Alfred the speech clinic at the Board of Education, which he has just left, singled out for embarrassing special treatment because of his stuttering. Another image is matched to the dehumanized "HUMAN FACTORY." Alfred drops his lunch bag; the stale food seems to be turning "stiff with death." The despair that he feels at that moment is caused by the mechanistic, bureaucratic, Anglo-Saxon public school system.

The technique seems plain: to recall to the reader some ugly remnant of popular culture and to link it to a subjective state of the protagonist. In the movie theater, the emotion evoked is terror; in the street, it is the depersonalization of city life. The "HUMAN FACTORY" could serve quite suitably as a subject for "Pop" art. The use to the artist, whether in words or paint, is the same: to demonstrate the dehumanization of modern life. In a later manifestation, the popular culture of the Thirties, with its store of inescapable, universally recognized images, becomes a literary game which the author plays with the reader, omitting the subjective experience which the symbol suggests for Kazin—"Pop" art again. Marion Magid sees this use of the artifacts of the Thirties and Forties as a "kind of instant comic iconography," which needs only the mention of some familiar object to provoke a laughing response among the cognoscenti.[32] Although Kazin works up his remnants of culture with real craft, he is using a device.

Character, too, thickens the texture of the novel. Far more vivid than the mother, a dim figure sewing into the night, are the cousin and her emancipated friends. Their Bohemianism recalls that of Minna, the cousin in *Passage from Home*. Refusing to marry without love— a form of madness to Alfred's parents, who have sublimated such individualized emotions in their conception of family—the friends spend their evenings in a Russian ambience of tea and Victrola music.[33] Lacking a function in the plot, they vanish without a word of their fate, leaving a faint cloud of powder. Slightly more substantial is Alfred's friend, David, a Marxist who shares Alfred's love of literature. He has a destiny: the Civil War in Spain. Fifteen pages are devoted to the Soloveys, working out their fated failure, he as a bankrupt, she as a suicide.

A Walker in the City and "The Bitter 30's"

One can only wonder at the closeness with which life mirrors art as Kazin's reminiscences are compared to the education novel. Only the inevitable older sister of the education novel is missing, but the cousin takes her place. That these are facts, selected and rearranged to maintain the integrity of the narrative, cannot be doubted. Kazin, after all, has told even more in "The Bitter 30's," a "personal history" published in 1962 in *The Atlantic*[34] and expanded into *Starting Out in the Thirties* in 1965. The unmarried Bohemian cousin reappears, Russian blouses and all; her name is Sophie, it seems. Even the picture of Psyche in her room is now identified as George

F. Watts's "Hope." Actual figures also appear: Malcolm Cowley, William Saroyan, *et al.*

Looking back at the bitter Thirties from the perspective of the Sixties, Kazin recalls the pride of the Jews in that period. Their very poverty and oppression made them feel that they were at the center of things: "History was preparing, in and through us, some tremendous deliverance and revelation. For this reason I hugged my aloneness, our apartness, our poverty, our Jewishness, as a mystical sign that pointed to our power to create the future."[35] Alienation is again claimed as a sign of special favor, of being chosen, but it is not here also a theory of composition. Kazin is attempting instead to examine the later period of his life with an objectivity that is more controlled.

Comparing the two works, one sees that providing a fate for Sophie hasn't made fiction of the later piece. (After waiting bitterly for the man owed her by life, like Laura in Schwartz's *The World Is a Wedding,* she ends her days in a Midwestern insane asylum.) The Sophie section, the affair with Nora, and the dinner party for Ferguson (a description, from the point of view of the Jewish student, of the Abe Jones-Eugene Gant dinner in *Of Time and the River*) in "The Bitter 30's" are handled in a poetic style; but the more detailed accounting of incident and character and the carefully wrought time scheme place the work as a whole in the category of factual writing. The looser time sequence, vaguer attention to fact, and especially the more aesthetic intentions of *A Walker in the City* place that work in an infrequently used category, fictionalized fact.[36]

THE ADVENTURES OF AUGIE MARCH

Alienation as an outlook on life in the twentieth century continues; alienation as a literary style, at least in its Jewish-American novel phase, has run its course. The movement away from alienation as both an outlook and a literary style can be traced in the work of Saul Bellow. A novelist highly conscious of the ideological implications of his work, Bellow has recognized this. In an interview with David Boroff upon the publication of *Herzog,* Bellow identified himself as one of the former "chieftains" of the school of "victim literature." He considered *Herzog* to be a break from that tradition. In the interview, he stated his own brief definition of the spirit of alienation with a hint that he regards his work since *The Adventures of Augie March* (1953) to bear its marks.

Victim literature purports to show the impotence of the ordinary man. In writing *Herzog* I felt that I was completing a certain development, coming to the end of a literary sensibility. This sensibility implies a certain attitude towards civilization—anomaly, estrangement, the outsider, the collapse of humanism. What I'm against is a novel of purely literary derivation—accepting the canon of Joyce and Kafka. With Dostoevsky, at least, his eyes are turned freshly to the human scene.[37]

The alienation posture is not easily transformed. The charge of excessive passivity, of being a victim—applicable to all of Bellow's heroes—has been made against even Moses Herzog.

Nonetheless, the book that marks a sudden leap beyond the spirit of alienation is *The Adventures of Augie March.* Bellow's first book, *Dangling Man* (1944), had described, as the title suggests, one typical exercise in marginality: waiting for induction into the army. The style of the narration exemplifies the literary doctrine of alienation. The setting is a gloomy rooming-house neighborhood in Chicago. The protagonist is utterly dissociated. Joseph (who recalls a Kafka anti-hero in more than name) is in limbo, an unperson to the Communist Party, attempting to discern a "common humanity" in the jumbled particles of facts and people in the city, despairing of finding "a colony of the spirit." The ending is ironically ambiguous, as Joseph submits himself to military regimentation, hardly hoping to find there the connections he seeks. The Jewish identity of Joseph (like that of Joseph K) is veiled. Charles Eisinger takes Joseph's quest for self-knowledge to be that of a Jewish protagonist but calls the main tradition of the novel alienation.[38]

The second Bellow novel, *The Victim* (1947), repeats the grim tones of *Dangling Man*. The theme is the mutuality of guilt and dependency in the relationship of Jew and gentile. The resolution is brighter. The protagonist (for once not an intellectual) grabs for happiness, although ambiguity vitiates his attempt. Symbolism similar to that of *Passage from Home* elaborates the theme: the ending of the novel finds the protagonist caught in the darkness of a theater, needing an usher to help him to his seat.

Bellow and Rosenfeld shared a long personal and literary association in which mutual influence is evident. In a reminiscence, Bellow has recalled the brilliance of young Isaac in the debating club of Chicago's Tuley High School, when he already evidenced a talent for philosophical speculation of the kind which was to appear in his fiction and Bellow's as well. Each has translated Yiddish stories, and their literary enthusiasms overlap: the late nineteenth-century Yiddish masters and the major modern European novelists. Seymour Krim, a disciple for a time of Rosenfeld, listed the modern masters as Eliot, Yeats, Proust, and Joyce.[39]

The streets of Chicago and the small Jewish enclave around Humboldt Park are the setting for the all but inevitable autobiographical novel of each. Rosenfeld, attempting to move into new, more allegorical material for his second novel, was unable to find a publisher; only portions of the work have appeared in academic magazines. Bellow avoided the first novel trap by waiting until his third novel to draw on his boyhood material, as Richard Chase has pointed out.[40]

Augie March as an Education Novel

As much as any American novel of the Fifties, *The Adventures of Augie March* enters a world dynamic, various, and unrestrained. The title (an obvious echo of Twain) signifies the form and the theme—not just a passage from home, but an encyclopedic journey through a world whose nature is clarified by the rogues encountered along the way. The education of Augie March, an alternative title, takes the protagonist beyond the Jewish world of boyhood (here a far from delimited one, to be sure) to a society richer in possibilities than the airless one of Minna's flat in *Passage from Home*.

Kazin has stated that all of Bellow's novels are *Bildungsromaner*.[41] But the novel which takes up the theme of youth's initiation into experience most directly is *The Adventures of Augie March*. As education novel, it traces the education of Augie from the age of twelve in the post-World War I era until the end of World War II, when he is in his late thirties. This time span does not quite recall the biographical plot of the early model education novels, although, like those authors, Bellow's first language was Yiddish. For one thing, the socialism of those early models has vanished, except for the flirtation with the Party by Simon, Augie's older brother, and the despairing communism of a minor character or two. Even the later Trotskyism of Rosenfeld is gone. Economics is not at the heart of the novel. Even as a labor organizer, Augie finds himself making love as he hides from strikebreaking thugs. As Marcus Klein has it,

"Alienation, the sense of separate and unconciliating identity" has developed, if not into Klein's accommodation, then at least into affirmation.[42]

Some facets of Augie's character resemble those of the typical protagonist of the Jewish novel of youth, the ones that permit the novel to register the effects of life: the core of intelligence which makes of him a reader and student, and the impressionability—here not just a by-product of youth, but the center of his nature. A third resemblance, a sound one for a hero, is his goodness. He is capable, like the foundling Tom Jones whom he resembles, of consummating a lust or of telling a lie or two, but never of meanness or ignobility. The resemblance to Tom Jones is evoked as Augie's girl guesses that his father "must have been some aristocratic bastard."

Edmund Bergler, subjecting Augie to "psychoanalysis," finds that Augie is not well realized, that he is too passive to have had such adventures.[43] It would not be entirely a mistake to take Augie's passivity as a vestige of Bellow's previous alienated heroes. The later reappearance of the passive actor, Herzog, suggests that this character type is basic in Bellow's work. But one must note Einhorn's discovery of opposition in Augie and Augie's refusal to be adopted by Mrs. Renling. His pliability is really a necessary subterfuge, given his orphaned state and his need for patrons; but, also, the pose is that of the good listener silently drawing out his teachers. The complexity implied by this pose is supported by some sentences Bellow wrote in the year in which *The Adventures of Augie March* was published.

Society does not do much to help the American to come of age. It provides no effective form. That which churches or orders of chivalry or systems of education did in the past individuals now try to do independently. When the boy becomes a man in an American story we are asked to believe that his experience of the

change was crucial and final; no further confirmation is necessary.[44]

When the novel is read as the independent attempt at
an American education, a *Bildungsroman,* the function
of Augie's passivity becomes more apparent.

Life among the Machiavellians

The mentors of Augie's life—the book can be read as
an education novel by tracing their teachings—are a
gallery of "thirty-odd Machiavellians." Marcus Klein
relates them, particularly William Einhorn, to the phi-
losopher-king figure who is to reappear in later novels as
Tamkin in *Seize the Day* and King Dahfu in *Henderson,
the Rain King.* (The original title of *Augie March* was
"Life among the Machiavellians.")[45]

The closest to Augie of these instructors is his older
brother Simon. Simon had an earlier incarnation as Amos,
the older brother in *Dangling Man* who chose the unex-
amined life of a stock broker, and he has a later resusci-
tation as Will in *Herzog.* Like Amos, Simon has taken
a rich wife and suggests that his younger brother do the
same. Augie, capable of love in a way denied to alienated
Joseph, is strongly attached to Simon; agreeable as ever,
until he reaches the limit of opposition deep within him,
he pursues another Magnus daughter, but cannot bring
himself to consummate the affair. His goodness has asserted itself. Simon's instructional methods are precept
and threat. Not a progressive educator, he alternately
offers the carrot of an affluent life and the stick of with-
drawn funds. In the end, aware that his own masquerade
as one of the self-possessed, overbearing rich has failed,
Simon is mastered by his wife, a true daughter of Magnus.

The lesson of the rich is better taught by those more

naturally heir to wealth than Simon or, at least, those
unburdened by Simon's suicidal tendencies and not dominated by his early model, the English gentlemen of boys'
books (an enthusiasm of Bernard in *Passage from
Home*). Mrs. Renling, an aristocrat *manqueé,* teaches
Augie the grace of fine tweeds and foulards. She wishes
to formalize their relationship, a quasi-Oedipal one, by
adopting Augie, who balks. He senses that the answer
to his life's search does not lie here: "Why should I
turn into one of these people who didn't know who they
themselves were?"[46] Thus Augie's education is furthered
step by step.

Augie March as a Jewish Novel

It is clear, then, that *The Adventures of Augie March*
is an education novel; but is it a Jewish novel, going so
far afield as it does? R. W. B. Lewis finds the book to
fuse Yiddish traditions with the Anglo-American literary ones of *picaro* and pilgrim. Yiddish folklore supplies
a model for Augie: the *shlimazel,* the "comic victim of a
series of misadventures." Lewis postulates that the novel
creates a "sense of positive purpose through the very
force of repeated negation."[47] This last idea very much
suggests the Jewish people as an historical entity; the
sufferings of the past are evoked continually, indicating
that they possess an inspiring quality. The wedding ceremony ritual of stamping on a wine glass is now the reminder not only of the destruction of the Temple in the
past, but also of the destruction of European Jewry in
this century.

As for Augie the *shlimazel,* Howe and Greenberg, in
the introduction to *Treasury of Yiddish Stories,* call the
"sainted fool" a favorite theme in Yiddish literature,
finding it not only in folklore but in I. B. Singer's "Gim-
pel the Fool" and I. L. Peretz' "Bontsha the Silent."[48]

Both stories are in Bellow's anthology, *Great Jewish Stories* (1963). The phrase perfectly describes Augie, whose foolishness is not a lack of intelligence, but a quality of his life impelling him toward the irrational acquiescences that somehow result in his epiphanies.

The overtly Jewish elements of the novel can be appraised. Augie was born a Jew and raised in a Jewish neighborhood. When asked his identity, *"Jehudim?"* [*sic*], he pauses introspectively and, always Augie, does the good thing, but confusedly: "Yes, I guess."[49] The Jewishness of the characters in the first third of the book is attested to incidentally by a casually spoken Yiddish phrase or an indifferently followed custom, such as the rents in Einhorn's vest which symbolize a state of mourning. Even more muted are the references to the Wells Street charitable agency and the Arthington Street home for the blind. Neither is identified as a Jewish institution; they represent officialdom like the police or W.P.A.; all must be treated with guile and dissembling. But the Jewish quality of this novel must have more than a nominal expression.

In the process of anatomizing the Jewish quality of the stories he chose for an anthology, Bellow abstracts the following, loosely-drawn characteristics: (*a*) "the kind of oddly tilted perspective that permits a dog to accompany an angel on a great mission"; (*b*) "the over-humanizing of everything, of making too much of a case for us, for mankind, and of investing externals with too many meanings"; and (*c*) the curious mingling of laughter and trembling. He decries the tendency of Jewish writers to idealize the slums and ghettos, to conceal their truth in sentimental trappings: "for sadness the Kaddish, for amusement the schnorrer, for admiration the bearded scholar." Distinguishing between art and public relations, he finds the Jewish slums of his Montreal boyhood to be filled with an extraordinary life calling for realistic depiction. He makes one final point, offering a very brief philosophy of composition: a piece of fiction must be "inexplicably absorbing."[50] Why inexplicably? How frustrating to the critic who would explicate. Bellow, as critic of Jewish literature, finds in Jewish humor an ineffable mystery and elusiveness.

Mystery suggests the supernatural and one may say that in Jewish writing are also to be found echoes of the divine, of the immediacy of the God whom Sholom Aleichem's Tevye addresses with such familiarity. Bellow achieved this quality of supernatural suggestiveness in *Henderson, the Rain King* (1959). The echoes are raised in that novel by extending the natural exoticism of the African locale beyond the bounds of the real through strange and wondrous incidents. The characters and action serve as portents of the wonderful. In all the novels preceding *Henderson, the Rain King* there is the sense of the "inexplicably absorbing"—but not arising from such calculated means. Bellow's list of the characteristics of Jewish fiction can be freely applied to *The Adventures of Augie March* in the hope of determining if the absorbing quality of that novel is, at least partly, the result of the kind of Jewish literary spirit that Bellow defined.

Bellow, like Philip Roth whom he has defended, has been condemned for his unfavorable portrait of Jews. The religious observance of Grandma Lausch is "kitchen religion," more pagan than holy in spirit. (Although she eats pork, she is not an atheist like the junk man, Anticol, who lost his faith observing a pogrom.) Of the same superstitious order is the hewing to custom by Mrs. Einhorn, who covers the mirrors after a death. The Jewish (and religious) center of the novel is not to be found at this level.

Augie is singled out as a "Christ-killer" by the Division Street Poles, but Bellow understands them much as does Nelson Algren. Augie suffers the customary attack of a gentile gang but doesn't brood over it; he has a Pole named Stashu for a friend instead. Bellow thus rejects the *tallis-and-hot-pastrami* decor. He approaches metaphysical questions instead, expressing them indirectly through the structure of the novel, rather than in the direct confrontation of Jews as Jews, theological, sociological, historical.

It can be said that Bellow invests much in externals. He has the Naturalist's love for the catalogue of city artifacts, the "thinginess" that thickens the texture of the urban novelist. Like Thomas Wolfe, he seeks to render the precise look and sound of familiar objects. People are surrounded by things and can be identified or measured by them. The poolroom spender is known by his "rings, cigars, quality of socks, newness of panamas"; his rank can be so ascertained. Is he a "giver of scrolls to the synagogue, a protector of Polish relatives"? Rosenfeld used the same device in his Chicago essay, recreating the straw seats and ozone smell of the trolley car; Bellow presents the brain-deadening quality of long rides with the sun reflecting off the windows. Like Dreiser, he felt the dehumanizing quality of the sheer mass of asphalt and bricks of the endless Chicago wards—a perception readily available to the Chicago writer.

The ambience of Bellow's Chicago is lighter than that of Dreiser and Farrell. The multitude of names, people, and objects in *The Adventures of Augie March* is infused with life. The cumulative effect of the surrounding objects is vibrant, rather than deadening. People and things flash by with the airiness they possess in a Chagall painting.

Eisinger calls the enthusiastic but disorderly spirit of the novel a *Hasidic* one.[51] Rather than being confined by the law of the Torah, the *Hasidim* rejoiced in it, affirming life with song and dance, releasing their emotionality. Eisinger's comparison is apt if fanciful. Irving Howe and Eliezer Greenberg divide Yiddish literature into four strains: *Haskalah,* the secular enlightenment; Zionism; Socialism; and *Hasidism.*[52] A son of *Haskalah,* as are all assimilated Jewish intellectuals, Bellow also writes in the *Hasidic* tradition: his dominant note is joyful love and the acceptance of life.

Augie, despite his blond handsomeness, is a Jew. His story is very much again the young Jew's quest for definition. The transcendental reverberations of the quest are signified by the name of the hero: August March. Augie is a *talmid* (permanent student) and this is a prime characteristic of a Jew. In a comment expressing the low estate of the scholar in the mind of the American *prosteh Yid* (vulgar Jew), Uncle Charlie Magnus (the rich uncle type, not the socialist hero of the early model) says: "Goddammit the schools. There's schoolboys now until gray hair. So what are you studying for, a lawyer?"[53] There is no vocational goal to Augie's studies. In part, they are in the spirit of the autodidact; he is intoxicated with books, falling to reading those he steals instead of filling the illegal orders. A backless volume found in a Mexican trash pile—a closely printed, odd anthology of Machiavelli, Saint-Simon, Comte, Marx, and Engels—dazes him with its intimations of a world to be grasped by speculation.

To sit at the feet of a sage is very much the act of a Jew. The succession of men who counsel Augie, generally at the metaphysical level, are rabbis, if we take the word in its true meaning—teacher. Even a thieving friend and his whores offer Augie some knowledge which, he conjectures, may be transcendent. The incongruity of Augie's Macchiavellians as teachers and their appearance one after the other give the book its picaresque quality. The employment of such wretches as metaphysical speculators suggests what Bellow has described as the tilted perspective of the Jews; they are the dogs accompanying the angel on his sublime mission.

William Einhorn, Augie's first "superior man," commingles the noble—his refusal to be prostrated although he is paralyzed in legs and arms—with the ignoble—his lusts for food and women. His projects mirror his bifurcated nature. He enlists Augie in the classification of an edition of Shakespeare to be indexed like the Gideon Bible. A peculiar combination of businessman and classical scholar, "realtor" and philosopher, he categorizes Shakespeare under the headings: "Slack Business, Bad Weather, Difficult Customers, Stuck with Big Inventory of Last Year's Models, Women, Marriage, Partners."[54] Like Bellow, Augie is able to see the humanity in Einhorn and the other odd characters of the novel.

The humor as Jewish humor is harder to approach. One can imagine Rosenfeld, like Kafka, reading over the day's work and laughing. There is much that is Jewish in the scene in *Passage from Home* in which Willie leaps over as if to embrace Minna when the two learn at first meeting that they are aunt and cousin to Bernard; or in the scene in *Amerika* where Karl Rossman is set upon by his friends of the road. Still, each novel is melancholy more than it is comic. Bellow's humor is based on the unmitigated expression of human personality, seen, for example, in the expansiveness of Uncle Charle Magnus as he dismisses Augie with his "Fo-kay!" while the family laughs indulgently. For Uncle Charlie, Augie's "book business" (stealing books to-order for students) raises the specter of "starving Pentateuch peddlers with beards full of Polish lice and feet wrapped in sacking."[55] Another such touch is the image of the Commissioner, lying abed in splendor, gazing at Dingbat, his son, in National Guard khakis: "Ee-*dyot!*"[56]

The portrait of the Einhorn and Magnus dynasties is only peripherally in the tradition of criticism of *bourgeois*

Jews. The families are accorded *yikhus* (high status) for their power, their ease with deeds, lots, and wills. In America this is enough to earn them good repute. Their religious observance has atrophied. Friday night is still a traditional time for the family to gather, but no mention is made of *Shabbes*. At an unbuttoned ease with their identity and the few remnants of custom in their lives, they are too secure in their wealth to practice hypocrisy. David Daiches, assessing Jewish-American literature, admitted the sociological and psychological accuracy of the portrait of the Einhorn family but denied that it added up to a "real Jewish insight"; that is, the determination of what Daiches calls the "Jewish consciousness" in Bellow's work is a more complex question than the accuracy of his social commentary.[57] The creation of a sound psychological and social portrait is not a small accomplishment; but it is, to be sure, not the sum of art. The definition of Bellow's Jewish art must be found, more tangentially, in the web of metaphysical filiations and novelistic technique.

Augie finally comes to his own expression of the meaning of this life. His answer to the Jew's "Who am I?" is the universal one that Daiches has called for from Jewish-American writing, one that illuminates the general condition. Misled for a time by ambitions, but always seeking, Augie has gained knowledge. The "axial lines of life" bring man to true joy. They are to be found in human connections. These lines connect man to man despite the "big social jokes and hoaxes." (David Cort's phrase is apropos: "social astonishments.") "Death will not be terrible to him if life is not. The embrace of other true people will take away his dread of fast change and short life."[58] The emphasis on a loving life, on a present life, is quintessentially Jewish. The phrase used by Zborowski and Herzog as the title for their book on the culture of the *shtetl* affirms the idea: "Life is with People."

The episode of Basteshaw, one of the last of Augie's rabbis, but a false prophet, dramatizes this idea. Cast adrift on a sea rich in Melvillean possibilities, the last two survivors of an American destroyer recognize each other as just a couple of West Side Jewish boys. Hyman, the true son of Aaron Basteshaw, "the Soupngreens King," has a diabolic identity behind his nominal one. Sitting "heavy as foundry brass," dominating Augie, he proposes that they elude their rescuers and drift to internment in the Canary Islands where they can continue Hymie's experiments in biochemistry together. Basteshaw has already created protoplasm, discovering the secret of life. That night, Augie confirms his own secret in a dream. In it he gives a West Side crone coins in a magical order. Touching her head, he senses a thrill— it is angel hair. " 'Why shouldn't I have,' she says gently, 'like other daughters of men?' "[59] Augie fights Basteshaw, refusing his offer; he wants only to rejoin his wife to make children. The fate which joins him to humanity is the answer to his quest, not tampering with the atoms.

NOTES TO CHAPTER 4

1. According to Irving Howe, the term has been expanded from its original Marxist meaning (workers are alienated from their capacities) to include intellectuals estranged from bourgeois society. Irving Howe, "Our Country and Our Culture," *Partisan Review*, XIX, No. 5 (Sept.-Oct. 1952), 575n.

2. Daniel Bell, "A Parable of Alienation," in *Mid-Century*, ed. Harold U. Ribalow (New York: The Beechhurst Press, Inc., 1955), p. 148 n.

3. Renata Adler, "The New Reviewers," *The New Yorker*, XL, No. 20 (July 4, 1964), 60-80.

4. Isaac Rosenfeld, *Passage from Home* (New York: The Dial Press, 1946); Alfred Kazin, *A Walker in the City* (New York: Harcourt, Brace and Co., 1951); Saul Bellow, *The Adventures of Augie March* (New York: The Viking Press, 1953).

5. Alfred Kazin describes the shock of the announcement of the treaty in "The Bitter 30's," *Atlantic Monthly*, CCIX, No. 5 (May 1962), 99.

6. "Under Forty: American Literature and the Younger Generation of American Jews," *Contemporary Jewish Record*, VII, No. 1 (Feb. 1944), pp. 17-20, 23-25, 12-14.

7. *Ibid.*, p. 36.

8. *Ibid.*, p. 14.

9. Charles Glicksberg, in "The Theme of Alienation in the American Jewish Novel," lists Kierkegaard and Kafka as progenitors and uses Jo Sinclair's *Wasteland* (1946), Schwartz's *The World Is a Wedding*, Bellow's *The Victim*, and Rosenfeld's *Passage from Home* as his examples. (*The Reconstructionist*, XXIII, No. 13 [Nov. 1, 1957], 8-13.)

10. Howe, "Our Country and Our Culture," pp. 575-580 and 593-597; Howe, "The Lost Young Intellectuals," in *Mid-Century*, ed. Ribalow, pp. 152-163; Schwartz, *The World Is a Wedding* (Norfolk, Conn.: New Directions, 1948).

11. The Meridian edition of *Passage from Home* in 1961.

12. Seymour Krim, *Views of a Nearsighted Cannoneer* (New York: Excelsior Press, 1961), p. 11.

13. Harvey Swados, *A Radical's America* (Boston: Little, Brown & Co., 1962), pp. 158-64.

14. I. Howe, "The Lost Young Intellectuals," in *Mid-Century*, ed. Ribalow, pp. 152-167.

15. Daniel Bell, "A Parable of Alienation," in *Ibid.*, pp. 133-151.

16. Introduction by Theodore Solotaroff to Isaac Rosenfeld, *An Age of Enormity*, Cleveland: World Publishing Co., 1962), p. 20.

17. Rosenfeld, *An Age of Enormity*, Intro., p. 17.

18. Isaac Rosenfeld, review of Graham Greene's *Nineteen Stories*, in *Partisan Review*, XVI, No. 7 (July 1949), 754.

19. Rosenfeld, *Passage from Home*, p. 159.

20. *Ibid.*, p. 78.

21. Philip Roth used *Hasidic* characters for much the same purpose in "Eli, the Fanatic." *Goodbye, Columbus* (Boston: Houghton Mifflin Co., 1959), pp. 247-298.

22. Rosenfeld, *Age of Enormity*, pp. 323-325.

23. *Passage from Home*, p. 22.

24. *Ibid.*, p. 171.

25. *Age of Enormity*, pp. 56-57.

26. Alfred Kazin, "The Alone Generation" in *Recent American Fiction: Some Critical Views*, ed. Joseph J. Waldmeir, (Boston: Houghton Mifflin Co., 1963), p. 18.

27. Alfred Kazin, "The Mindless Young Militants," *Contemporaries* (Boston: Little, Brown & Co., 1962), p. 501.

28. Morris Freedman, "The Jewish Artist as Young American," *Chicago Jewish Forum*, X, No. 3 (Spring 1952), 213.

29. Leslie Fiedler, "The City and the Writer," *Partisan Review*, XIX, No. 2 (March-April 1952), 240-241; and Fiedler, *The Jew in the Ameri-*

can Novel, (New York: Herzl Institute Pamphlet No. 10, 1959), pp. 42-43.

30. "Under Forty," pp. 9 ff.

36. Alfred Kazin, "The Most Neglected Books of the Past Twenty Five Years," *The American Scholar,* XXV, No. 5 (Autumn 1956), 486.

32. Marion Magid, "Mocking Heroics," *Commentary,* XXXVII, No. 5 (Nov. 1964), 81.

33. Harry Golden, recalling his boyhood, maintains that physical love was not commonly displayed by the parents in the Jewish home. *Five Boyhoods,* ed. Martin Levin (Garden City, N. Y.: Doubletday & Co., Inc., 1962), p. 59.

34. Kazin, "The Bitter 30's," pp. 82-99.

35. *Ibid.,* p. 92.

36. William Manners, in *Father and the Angels,* (New York: E. P. Dutton, 1947), an account of his father's humorous experiences as a small town rabbi, has done somewhat the same thing on a less serious level.

37. David Boroff, "The Author," *The Saturday Review,* XLVII, No. 38 (Sept. 19, 1964), 77.

38. Charles Eisinger, *Fiction of the Forties* (Chicago: University of Chicago Press, 1963), p. 346. The characteristics of the alienated Jew are well caught by Bellow in *Dangling Man,* according to Ihab Hassan, who summarizes them in *Radical Innocence; Studies in the Contemporary American Novel* (Princeton, N.J.: Princeton University Press, 1961), p. 297:

> To begin with, Joseph is a Jew, and a city Jew. He manifests certain qualities of abrasive intelligence, knowledge of—even an urge for—suffering and humiliation, and an attitude toward enforced social norms, of which the war is a major symbol, that are relevant to his particular situation. Furthermore, his ambivalence toward friends and relatives within a recognizable ethnic community underscores the failure of family and tradition to provide an adequate buffer against the contemporary forces of chaos.

For a reading of *Dangling Man* and *The Victim* as novels of alienation, see Norman Podhoretz, *Doings and Undoings* (New York: The Noonday Press, 1964), pp. 206-215.

39. Saul Bellow, "Isaac Rosenfeld," *Partisan Review,* XXIII, No. 4 (Fall 1956), 565; Krim, *Views,* p. 22.

40. Richard Chase, "The Adventures of Saul Bellow," *Commentary,* XXVII, No. 4 (April 1959), 324.

41. Alfred Kazin, "My Friend, Saul Bellow," *Atlantic Monthly,* CCXV, No. 1 (Jan. 1964), 53.

42. Marcus Klein, "A Discipline of Nobility: Saul Bellow's Fiction," in *Recent American Fiction: Some Critical Views,*" p. 121.

43. Quoted in *Ibid.,* p. 277.

44. Saul Bellow, "Hemingway and the Image of Man," *Partisan Review*, XX, No. 3 (May-June 1953), 342.

45. Klein, "A Discipline of Nobility," in Waldmeir, pp. 121-138; Saul Bellow, "From the Life of Augie March," *Partisan Review*, XVI, No. 11 (Nov. 1949), 1077.

46. Bellow, *Augie March*, p. 151.

47. R. W. B. Lewis, "Recent Fiction: *Picaro* and Pilgrim," *A Time of Harvest*, ed. R. E. Spiller (New York: Hill and Wang, 1962), pp. 148-150.

48. Irving Howe and Eliezer Greenberg, eds., *A Treasury of Yiddish Stories* (New York: Meridian Books, Inc., 1958), p. 40.

49. *Augie March*, p. 129.

50. Introduction, *Great Jewish Short Stories*, ed. Saul Bellow (New York: Dell Publishing Co., 1963).

51. Eisinger, *Fiction of the Forties*, p. 345.

52. *A Treasury of Yiddish Stories*, ed. Howe and Greenberg, pp. 17-19.

53. *Augie March*, p. 221.

54. *Ibid.*, p. 70.

55. *Ibid.*, p. 221.

56. *Ibid.*, p. 87.

57. David Daiches, "Breakthrough?" *Commentary*, XXXVIII, No. 2 (Aug. 1964), 63.

58. *Augie March*, p. 455.

59. *Ibid.*, p. 507.

5

Bemused Again:
The Dream of Success

FROM TEMPORAL TO SUBJECT CATEGORY

In the years following the periods of the Depression and alienation, the education novel continued to appear, but it can no longer be grouped exclusively by generations. Generally, Jewish-American novels continued to be the work of the second generation. In the Sixties, the voice of the third generation was sounded as black comedy. This school will be taken up in the last chapter of this study. The two intervening chapters will treat the education novels written after World War II and before the Black Comedy novels. These books fall into two groups. The first of these repeats an old theme in the Jewish-American novel—the struggle for material success. The second approaches the ghetto past from a new perspective, nostalgia.

The decision to shift from temporal category to subject category is somewhat arbitrary. The novels of Fuchs, Levin, and Bellow previously treated could be viewed again from the perspective of the dream of success, as could those of Blechman, which, instead, will be examined in the last chapter. The scope of this chapter is based, not upon chronological principles of classification, but upon more imprecise ones. Our exposition has reached a point where parallel developments are apparent, a time when writers either were sustaining an old literary style or taking some individual bypath. For example, Sam Ross exemplifies the Depression Realist out of his time, and Philip Roth represents a new voice. The shift from period to subject study is made on the grounds that it makes a more illuminating treatment possible.

THE SUCCESS MYTH INTERPRETED

In *The Dream of Success,* a study of Dreiser, London, and other early twentieth-century American novelists, Kenneth S. Lynn sees the Horatio Alger waif as the archetype of the American dream of success.[1] During the time when Alger's stories of the rise from rags to riches were popular, serious novelists offered their own version of American life. One reading of American fiction of the last century might see it as a grappling with the terms of life in a money-dominated society. Such a reading is an essential component of the study of Jewish-American fiction, although not the only one—the Jewish character and social relations peculiar to the Jews carry their own complications. The fantasies of American life are a catalyst to Jewish character, exacerbating it, not forming it.

The dilemmas of life in a commercial culture are, of course, still with us. Mark Harris, sensing the relevancy

of the Alger myth, entitled his autobiographical account
of the California gubernatorial campaign of 1962, *Mark,
The Glove Boy*.[2] The book's conflict is based on the
irreconcilable views of life inevitably held by Harris, a
Jewish college professor, and Richard Nixon, Republican
candidate for governor, each of whom has assiduously
pursued his own path to success. The book assumes that
each possesses a different heritage; this and the fact that
these differences act in subtle ways to prevent easy communication between the two, indicates the existence of
special circumstances in Jewish-American life that can
be explored under the rubric of the dream of success.

The basis of American dream is the idea that the good
life is reached by the possession of riches and the power
and standing which accrue to wealth. Anyone may achieve
this wealth, no matter how humble his origins. Indeed, a
lowly beginning is part of the pattern, but the failure to
rise is a sign of some grave deficiency. (The Calvinist
influence becomes apparent here.) The struggle upward,
conceived also in Darwinian terms, is furthered by drive
and chance but need not be accompanied by scruple or
native talent.

The struggle may be advanced by the beneficence of a
philanthropic millionaire, a Dickensian touch, also to be
found in the Alger stories. The *Adventures of Augie
March* fulfills the terms of the Alger tale as well as the
picaro tradition. Augie is an orphan, a barrow boy; the
grace of his person attracts the good offices of the
wealthy; he retains his pure spirit despite his worldly experiences.

Another significant variation of the basic mythic pattern shows the successful hero who is unfulfilled by his
riches and longs for his lost boyhood. The 1941 film,
Citizen Kane, developed this tried idea into a two-hour
mystery, concealing its obviousness with cinematics. It is

precisely this aspect of the myth that *The Rise of David Levinsky* used, gaining its novelty from the use of the Jewish ethos.

Such are the outlines of the American myth; what are the special elements which the Jew brings to it?

Immigration to the United States was undertaken by the Jews to obtain freedom of opportunity for their children as much as for themselves. Among Jewish immigrants there were proportionately two and one-half times more children than in other groups.[3] The parents could be satisfied that their expectations for their children had been fulfilled even at the cost of the uncertain and onerous life that they had experienced as Americans. The terms of success in America are given thus a peculiarly Jewish meaning: "living through the children."

For Jews in America, the main routes to success are easily identifiable: retail trade, the arts, and the professions. When opportunity was circumscribed, the Jews joined the procession of upward-striving Americans on the more taxing paths. Professional boxing formerly was one of the routes to success open to minority groups. As late as the 1940's, the film *Body and Soul* could still depict a Jewish boxer on the "golden boy" model to dramatize the dream of success. By the 1950's, it was necessary to update the television version of *Body and Soul* by changing the characters to Puerto Ricans. But the expression of the dream of success in real life was in the less flamboyant terms of shop counter or "C.P.A."

The bent of the dream-of-success protagonists is similar to that of Colonel Sellers and Frank Cowperwood, but their dimensions are more those of Clyde Griffiths. Just as the businesses in the Jewish-American novel have been limited to the garment industry and retail trade, so the ambitions explored in the novels of this chapter are limited to the comparatively modest ones of Jewish-Americans. A 1936 *Fortune* survey of the economic standing, the sources of wealth, and the businesses dominated by Jews in America revealed that Jewish economic power was limited in industry to garment manufacturing, junk metals, and motion pictures. In retail trade a better showing was made, in banking and heavy industry, a much worse one.[4] Surveying Jewish life in America at mid-century more optimistically, Howard M. Sachar finds, in *The Course of Modern Jewish History*, economic importance still in scrap metals, in clothing manufacture, in tobacco buying (cigars, not cigarettes), in liquor, furs, and motion pictures. The proportion of Jews in skilled trades had declined markedly, the probable reason for the disappearance of the garment worker as a character in fiction. The percentage of Jews in professions and retail trades had increased.[5]

The businesses which appear in the novels in this chapter are modest ones, those in which Jews have figured prominently or, at least, to a degree: small-scale manufacturing, services, retail sales, real estate, also on a small scale. Their involvement in the motion-picture industry, on the other hand, has been far less limited, and they figure prominently in Hollywood novels.

THE DREAM-OF-SUCCESS NOVEL

American Jews have been as committed as any other group to life in terms of upward movement through individual achievement, and this faith is the basis for the dream of success novel.

Yet these are not really business novels. When the hero of Seymour Epstein's *The Successor* (1961) tricks his way into a first job at "Joli Creations," he does not even know what the creations are.[6] What is important is his ability to sell himself through cleverness and brashness. The mechanics of business fail to appear in the novel. The conception of commerce is rudimentary compared to that in the earlier *Rise of David Levinsky* and does not show the same interest in financial manipulations that Dreiser's Cowperwood trilogy did. In *Someday, Boy* (1948), Sam Ross's grasp of the details and the psychology of the real estate boom of the 1920's does not equal Wolfe's in *You Can't Go Home Again* (1940). As a Hollywood novel, Budd Schulberg's *What Makes Sammy Run?* (1941) is inferior to West's *The Day of the Locust* (1939) and Fitzgerald's *The Last Tycoon* (1940). For an esoteric study of the operations of industry, one must turn elsewhere than to the education novel. An organic limitation of the education novel lies in the premise that it deals with the psychological states of a *naïf*. As soon as the protagonist reaches the estate of wisdom, his story is over.

The protagonist most successful in business, Sammy Glick in *What Makes Sammy Run?*, shams talent and becomes a movie studio power by exploiting others. The other protagonists of these novels also lack the ability or technical dexterity which might grant them some degree of fulfillment. Their mode of operation is that of the salesman—depending for success on the power of "personality," expending their store of energy for good will; but they find that theirs is the tough New England territory of Willy Loman. The refusal of the author to confer genuine business skill upon his dream-of-success protagonist characterizes the novelist in one of his favorite roles, the social critic. The apocryphal story of Sherwood Anderson stalking out of the paint factory fits the image of the American novelist much better than do the business activities of Mark Twain. The flirtation of the artist with the money society is a love-hate relationship for both partners.

Dreiser's massive novel of 1925 suggests an alternative title for this chapter: American tragedies. That novel, with its monumental study of a plebeian broken by his vulgar ambitions, could serve as a prototype for these novels. Just as Dreiser, in *An American Tragedy*, maintains a severe objectivity but nevertheless communicates a deep sympathy, the education novelists see their protagonists with the detachment hitherto reserved for the rogue-hero. Their young men are the true descendants of Clyde Griffiths, sharing his ill-formed conception of a grander life beyond his drab streets.

The Depression mood of the novelist was not dispelled by the prosperity that came to American Jews in the years following the Thirties. However, the entry of the Jews as a group into the middle class and their achievement of a degree of prosperity caused the novelist to turn from denouncing the controllers of the means of production to excoriating the system's agents and consumers. As the novel moves into mid-century, the shift from left-wing social criticism in the novel to what Irving Howe has described as the "recoil from experience" becomes apparent. With the maturation of writers whose consciousness developed after World War II, such as Philip Roth and Mordecai Richler, the education novel was freed at last of the Marxist frame of reference, but not from the obligation to decry materialism.

The Rogue and the Innocent Again

Two kinds of protagonists are discernible in these novels: the rogue-hero and the innocent. The *lazaron* or rogue tradition began in the Jewish novel with *The Rise of David Levinsky*. It can be traced through *Haunch, Paunch and Jowl* to Jerome Weidman's *I Can Get It for You Wholesale* (1937) and Schulberg's *What Makes Sammy Run?* Neither of these two is a true developmental novel because their protagonists undergo no change. Born rascals, they remain so, unquestioningly committed to the money society, undergoing no transformation. The knave was revived once more, overtly, by a Canadian novelist writing in the traditions of the Jewish-American novel, Mordecai Richler. *The Apprenticeship of Duddy Kravitz* (1959), the most skillful of its type since Cahan, mitigates the villainy of the protagonist, striving for a psychological rather than a sociological portrait.

A variation of the rogue in the dream-of-success novel is the gangster, more accurately described by Meyer Levin's term, the "East Side Gangsters of the Paperbacks." Levin's specimens are drawn from Harold Robbins' *A Stone for Danny Fisher* (1951) and the Irving Shulman trilogy, *The Amboy Dukes* (1946), *Cry Tough* (1949), and *The Big Brokers*. To the list could be added the somewhat more skillful *Life and Death of a Tough Guy* (1955) by Benjamin Appel. Such books will be ignored here because of their sub-literary quality, but Levin's article fixes their place in the category of the education novel. He anatomizes the type: the first-person narrator, the sordid boyhood, the clash of generations. These are the constituents of the education novel but are used here only as trappings. Levin denies the verisimilitude of these books, making his point with *The Amboy Dukes,* which was reprinted in paperback with the Jewish references expunged. The overtly Jewish elements are in no way integral to the novel. He calls these novels a distortion of reality, since no kind of Jew other than gangsters appears in the novels. (In actuality, other depictions of Jews do appear: parents, social workers, etc.)[7]

The standard format for these novels, however, presents the clean-cut youth, forfeit to destiny and born to be a victim. Benny Gordon in Sam Ross's *Someday, Boy* will serve as the model.[8] The older brother of the earlier education novels has now been moved to the center of the stage. Athletic, not too bright, he accepts unquestion-

ingly the business mystique. In his next novel, *The Sidewalks Are Free* (1951), Ross reverted to the more typical protagonist, shifting the lust for material success to
the parents.[9] Philip Roth's *Goodbye, Columbus* (1959)[10]
takes the protagonist out of the neighborhood into the
suburbs. The analysis of the novels of the dream of success will begin with the standard hero of Ross (both the
extroverted Benny and the introverted Hershy) and Roth
and conclude with the rogue-hero of Weidman, Schulberg, and Richler.

SOMEDAY, BOY

A sustained attempt to depict the psyche of the young
victim of the dream of success is found in Sam Ross's
Someday, Boy. Benny Gordon is followed through his
eighteenth year, which coincides with the last upward
surge of the stock market and the crash of October 1929
—the novel's climax. Ross is not a subtle writer. His
fictional means are those of the Naturalist. As such,
Ross calls to mind those other Chicago Naturalists, Meyer Levin and Albert Halper. However, the intricate plotting, the creation of the neighborhood ambience and of
credible characters, the informed grasp of the commercial and Jewish worlds of Chicago, all to be found in
The Old Bunch, are not to be found in *Someday, Boy*,
nor is the utter simplicity and warmth of Albert Halper's
Chicago stories in *On the Shore* (1934) and *The Golden
Watch* (1953). (The latter qualities are apparent, however, in *The Sidewalks Are Free*.) And the minute examination of the simple-minded does not lend itself to the
fine psychological effect. The excellence of the novel lies
in the doggedness with which Benny's mind is explored
and in its close, devoted exposition of the dream-of-
success theme.

The plot of *Someday, Boy* is simple: in Book One,
"The River Swim," Benny's fate is prefigured by his fail-

ure in a long-distance swim; in Book Two, "The Money,"
Benny starts his climb to success as a salesman in a du-
bious real-estate firm and as suitor to an ex-bootlegger's
daughter; in Book Three, "The System," Benny's funds
are lost in the crash.

The Characters of Someday, Boy

The characters other than Benny require only a cur-
sory look; their function as symbols suppresses any vitality they might have shown. Benny's parents and older
brother are not his antagonists; they are too tired and
resigned to life to do more than utter feeble warnings.
(As a point of curiosity, there is no sister in the family,
a rarity in education novels.) Recognizing in Benny's
energy and optimism the buoyancy of the potential success, they concede that "It's his America." The line, ironically used, states the theme of the novel.

In contrast to *Someday, Boy,* Epstein's *The Successor*
emphasizes the parents. The protagonist recoils from the
emptiness of their lives without really envisioning an alternative life. His mother's mind is a mixture of cheap
novels and Hollywood movies. As a second-generation
American, she has lost her religion; this is symbolized
by her use of pork and her inability to bake. (The skillful preparation of food is the sign of a true Jewish mother.) Like her husband, she can imagine only a life of material success, but she envisions her son as the bearer of
happiness. The tension of the novel arises over the question of whether or not the son will choose a fate like that
of his parents. The protaganists of *The Successor* and
Someday, Boy have the attractiveness and vigor of youth;
but, lacking a model to demonstrate the rich possibilities
of life, in the end they can only follow the path of their
parents, hoping to achieve more of the same kind of
prosperity.

The girlfriends in *Someday, Boy* have a symbolic function. Benny's crude neighborhood girlfriend, Martha, represents the defeat of accepting what is available. Laura, his newer, wealthier one, represents the unattainable, the prize in the race for success. Similar first girlfriends—brainless, acquiescent, overblown—function to the same purpose in the novels of the rogue-hero. Most of the protagonists rid themselves of the encumbrance, seeking a richer girl, like a Fitzgerald hero, more for what she represents than for her money. Their failure to win these girls prepares the reader for their eventual failure in the money society, or, if they achieve success, signifies that their victory is a hollow one.

Of the other characters of the novel, Canby, the real estate entrepreneur, recalls the financier Samuel Insull, who is often introduced as an offstage figure in Chicago novels treating the boom of the Twenties. Canby, as the symbol of the flimsiness and gaudiness of business practice in boom, has risen from a mysterious background of poverty like Fitzgerald's Jay Gatsby. Canby has convinced even himself of the solidity of the business bubble, perhaps through the several booster speeches he delivers in the novel. These are not striking or authentic enough to convey what the author intends: a compressed revelation of the sham of the business ethic. A parody speech demands the verbal facility, accurate ear, comic sense, and insight into character of a Wolfe or Sinclair Lewis. These are beyond the talents of Ross, a lesser stylist, who has not mastered even the cadences of Jewish idiom in this novel.

Benny

Ross has assigned himself the difficult task of rendering a rather dull youth whose mind is bounded by the gymnasium and the shabbier streets of the Chicago business districts. The question of how astute the boy protagonist credibly may be is relevant in the case of such an intuitive fourteen-year-old as Bernard of *Passage from Home;* with eighteen-year-old Benny, the problem is, rather, how to engage the reader's attention during the inventory of an unremarkable mind.

Benny's soliloquies, like Canby's booster speeches, are inexpressive. "Man, but the grass was growing thick. Man, but he was going to throw a party at the Blackhawk. Man, but he was going to make Laura's eyes pop. . . . Man, oh, Man!"[11] The thoughts are, indeed, monotonous. On a park bench, Benny dreams of glory. As a guest of Mr. Harry Payne Whitney on the lawn at Churchill Downs, he recalls Al Jolson's gracious invitation: " 'Say, Benny, old sock, old kid, having a little party tonight, down by the Swanee shore, like to have you there, oh won't you make it there?' Al sang."[12]

The banality of the protagonist suggests that Farrell's *Studs Lonigan* trilogy has exerted a deleterious influence upon the novel. Some direct parallels are to be found. Like Studs, Benny loses several thousand dollars in the stock-market crash and, hoping to make up the loss, visits a horse betting parlor concealed in the back of a cigar store. Studs is frisked: " 'O.K. Let's have it,' a voice from behind the inside door called, as if in the performance of some strange and mysterious rite." Benny is frisked: " 'All right, let's have it,' a mouth with teeth gripping a cigar bawled out."[13]

Benny is not quite such a nonentity as Studs. He has a talent, long-distance swimming, and the first section of the novel achieves some vividness in the painstaking portrayal of his emotional state as he struggles to win the three-and-a-half-mile race and its prize, a scholarship to Northwestern University, a symbol to Benny of the affluent life. His loss of the contest prefigures his failure in business. The ballyhoo of the race mirrors the showy

fraudulence of the boom. Benny's verve as an athlete
and the purity of his pleasure in his body are described
in an appropriately obsessed way, with more conviction
than the business scenes.

Someday, Boy as a Chicago Novel

Ross uses setting to explicate his theme. In the "Berg-
man Foundation," the Jewish People's Institute, a land-
mark of Chicago's West Side can be recognized. (Meyer
Levin was, for a time, a drama counselor in the Jewish
People's Institute.) The swimming coach, Groucho, calls
to mind a real-life "Bosco," a familiar figure in the boys'
clubs of Chicago's Jewish West Side in the 1930's. The
use of realistic detail resembles that of Defoe in its particularity and verisimilitude. The references to Chicago
function in *Someday, Boy* as local curiosities to intrigue
the few who might recognize them, but such a function
is irrelevant. To describe the real is not to ensure realism
or even credibility. The realistic novelist is not obliged
to guarantee that his work is based on what he has observed, but to create an amalgam of setting, character,
and story which is faithful to truth, that is to his own
aesthetic and moral vision of the way that lives are lived.
Ross's book is accurate but cannot claim literary distinction. It conveys no unique tone, no special depth of
compassion, no power reminiscent of the major Naturalist novelist.

Comparison of Judaism as a theme in *Someday, Boy*
with the Catholicism in the *Studs Lonigan* trilogy discloses the insubstantiality of the former novel. In Farrell's work, the Roman Catholic Church is a potent factor in the life of the South Side Irish, contributing to the
ecological nature of the books, defining the relationship
between institutions and people in the novel. Benny's
Judaism is perfunctorily indicated without being assimi-

lated into the plot. "As he grew older, the great difference in the life on the streets and the foreign atmosphere of the *cheders* and *schules* had sent him adrift. He felt himself without roots, without any emotional tie-up to the long past, and he became content to say, 'I'm a Jew' and to let it go at that."[14] This explanation of the effect of Judaism in Benny's life is inadequate because it is not dramatized, only stated. The absence of a total view of the urban complex in *Someday, Boy* forces the business scenes to account entirely for the character and fate of Benny; and Ross's understanding of the commercial society is not adequate to this task.

The criticism of the money society in *Someday, Boy* is expressed by surface details: the ballyhoo of the swimming race, the pep talk of the business meeting, and the appurtenances of Chicago society—the Oriental rugs and marble of the comfortable apartments, the steam room of the "Lake Shore Athletic Club," the fashionable haberdashery of padded suits with flaring cuffs. The terms that customarily signify affluence in the Jewish novel are clothes, cars, and richly appointed apartments, but seldom the table (compare, say, *Sister Carrie*, where a dinner at Sherry's awakens Carrie to the delights of wealth). The joys of fulsome Jewish *mittel-European* cooking are accorded the protagonists in their improverished days, rather. Wealth is likely to mean a refinement of dining pleasure rather than an enlargement of bounty. Food figures in Jewish novels as a ready device to indicate nostalgia for what is available at home, not what must be sought in the American society without. The only character whose success is symbolized by eating, Meyer Hirsch in *Haunch, Paunch and Jowl*, remains within the culture of the home; his counterpart in the novel, who steps outside the home, dies from his rejection of the Jewish table, in effect.

The strategy of the novel—to demonstrate the effect

of the externals of Chicago society upon an immature
mind—is an adequate one. But the author lacks sufficient
skill as a Chicago novelist. The features of life in Chicago possess a peculiar potency for the novelist. The
quality which this life bears in fiction is so familiar that
it can hardly be expressed in general terms without falling into clichés: raw, powerful, crude, vital. The meaning of American life is very accessible to the Chicago
artist. The great symbol of the twenty-mile-long Po-
temkin village facade of apartment towers which con-
ceals the flat wards from the lakeside, the stockyards
with their odor of death, and the ethnic insularity of the
neighborhood "communities"—all pre-exist as symbols
requiring minimal transformation for fictive purposes.
The roster of Chicago novelists who have employed these
symbols, often to the same effect, is an impressive one:
Herrick, Dreiser, I. K. Freidman, and Upton Sinclair
earlier in the century; then Farrell, Wright, Levin, Zara,
Halper, Algren, Rosenfeld, and, finally, Bellow.

The divine compassion of Dreiser, the monumental
singleness of purpose of Farrell, the colossal verve of
Bellow—these suggest the habitual dimensions of the
Chicago novelist. Ross is unable to make very much of
a novel of *Someday, Boy*. In his next novel, Ross essayed
the same theme, the dream of success, using the same
term, "It's your America," with a slightly darker intona-
tion, but wisely focusing on the narrow confines of the
coal-heated flat, the stress of the family in conflict, and
the familiar sensitive boy of the education novel.

THE SIDEWALKS ARE FREE

The Sidewalks Are Free goes back a decade earlier
in time than *Someday, Boy,* to the beginning of the economic boom. Its protagonist, Hershy Melov, is just ten
years younger than Benny Gordon. But the eight-year-old

Hershy is not yet formed in the image of Benny Gordon and the novel's question is, what will he be? Benny's kind of Americanization is to be seen both in Hershy's older sister, who loves dancing and jazz music, and is involved with a petty gangster, and in Hershy's mother, who lusts for the material comforts that to her are the ultimate goal of life.

Ross, as a true novelist of youth, slowly traces in Hershy the varied sensations of growing up. Hershy is fascinated with sex and uncertain of his values; the conflict between his mother and father over a ten-thousand-dollar insurance benefit (an unlikely device acceptably handled) instructs him in their contrasting value systems.

Gelfant's *American City Novel* theorizes that the experiences of city childhood are "literary conventions" in all novels of urban youth. Using *The Sidewalks Are Free* as example, she cites such conventions as the gang attack on the boy who ventures into an alien neighborhood, the infatuation with the sweet little girl who symbolizes the purity of desire, and the emphasis on the change of seasons. These are also to be found in *Studs Lonigan,* for example.[15] Gelfant offers no explanation for the ubiquity of the conventions. One may attempt some conjectures. In Jewish novels, the gang attack also appears in scenes laid in the Pale of Settlement. The deep-seated Jewish fear of the non-Jew found in such occurrences a microcosmic expression. In America the fear and the incidents persisted, but not the more fatal pogrom, which can be called the adult version of the boys' ambuscade. Of course, ethnic groups other than the Jews attack each other. None of the three conventions is unique to the Jews. The curly-headed girl (albeit in a more mature form) appears in the adolescent novel as the inevitable concomitant of puberty. As for the seasons, Allison Davis in *Social-class Influence upon Learning* describes the lack of heat and light which makes a nightmare of the life of the poor.[16] The city poor live as close to the seasons as country folk.

Apart from his sensitivity, Hershy has little individuality. His sensations as a street gamin are those of all boys: "when he went into a game reluctantly because of some anger or irritation, the magic of the street, through the guys and the game itself, would lift him up and hurl him right into its spirit, completely absorbed."[17]

Jewish lore enriches the dream-of-success theme. Hershy feels the pull of the American success culture, but his father draws him back with a Talmudic anecdote. When that enemy of "foreignism," the Anglo-Saxon public school teacher (another staple of Jewish-American fiction), reads the class an account of Steinmetz in the *American Weekly,* Hershy's father puts a Jewish twist on the matter. Steinmetz, a Jew, is as great a wizard as the rabbi who made the golem, a clay monster who protected the Jews from a pogrom. But even Steinmetz had to go to college—so must Hershy. The struggle between cultures is symbolized musically. The father David loves to play the records of Cantor Yosele Rosenblatt on the phonograph he has built; the sister Rachel adores Al Jolson (who seems to figure prominently in the fantasy life of Ross's characters). The choice is fitting. Jolson, himself the son of a cantor, enacted the story of a cantor's son who abandoned his faith for the stage in the film *The Jazz Singer.*

The Family in The Sidewalks Are Free

The center of Hershy Melov's life is the family—the parents, the uncles and aunts—more substantially than the streets. Their value system, expressed in folk tales and superstitions and even in their brutal quarrels, supplies a richer texture for the novel than did the downtown effects for *Someday, Boy.* Ross has worked up these details thoroughly; his somber touch exerts a degree of force sufficient to the demands of this novel. When Ross departs from the streetboys and the parents, he flounders. For example, dutifully fulfilling the requirements of city childhood fiction, he introduces a blonde, curly-haired, non-Jewish girl as the object of an infatuation. A character straight out of *Tom Sawyer,* she tosses her head and grants Hershy the favor of carrying her books. Big sister Rachel, who is seduced by a neighborhood tough, is a device contrived to enhance plot and symbol. It is the father who brings the book to life.

David Melov's history is recounted in the first chapter. The son of a *soyfer* (a scribe of the Torah scroll), he becomes a carpenter, after the usual religious training. (We are told by Ross again, as in *Someday, Boy,* that the American *heder* fails to bring learning because it must be content with teaching only the phonics of Hebrew, not the meaning of the words.) Following *shtetl* traditions, David's *yikhus* (high status) is sufficient to command Sonya as his wife without regard for her wishes. It is she who will be better adjusted to the American dream of success, and her resultant resentment is to have its consequences.

David is unlike the fathers in Jewish-American fiction in many ways besides having a fully transcribed history. He is not a *luftmensch;* he has dignity; he is articulate; his learning has not spoiled him for a trade; and he has a good sense, grounded in his philosophy of life, of his limitations. Unfortunately, all his qualifications do not spare him from that frequent bane of the Jewish husband in fiction, a nagging wife. Hershy benefits from the counsel of his father, however. In perhaps the same Humboldt Park rowboat in which Bernard of *Passage from Home* failed to communicate with his father, David successfully explains himself to Hershy. The Talmud provides arguments for his contentment with the modest portion of the workingman. "Why is a man born with his hands clenched, but when he dies his hands are wide open? . . . Because on coming into the world man desires to grasp everything, but when leaving it he takes nothing away."[18]

Not every adult is satisfied with as little as David. Hershy's mother, jealous of the luxurious life available west of Humboldt Park, prevails upon David to invest insurance money in a laundry. Her dissatisfaction with the onerous life of a workman's wife is encouraged by a *landsman,* a former suitor who surprised everyone by doing well in America, and by her envy of Uncle Hymie, the "sport," and his wife, the well-dressed "society lady." After all, Uncle Hymie understands money. The discussion of finance galvanizes him, bringing him to his feet infused with energy. He explains the origin of America: "People sailed around the world and discovered new lands in search for [money]; that was how America was born."[19]

The novel reaches a violent climax as Hershy only half-unwittingly destroys the family's laundry and with it the family fortune. The frenzy of those moments brings the family to its senses, to a willingness to settle for the modest dimensions of their previous life. To Hershy it brings a rebirth, a chance to grow to manhood free of the obsessions of the money society.

GOODBYE, COLUMBUS: A CONTROVERSY

In *Goodbye, Columbus,* Philip Roth uses the education novel plot to examine the dream of success as it is envisioned by the suburban generation at mid-century. Alfred Kazin sees the theme of the novel as the frustration in love of a "romantic and credulous youth defeated . . . by a brutally materialistic society," like Fitzgerald's Gatsby.[20] Gatsby is as much a forerunner of the pro-

168 THE INVENTION OF THE JEW

tagonist of these novels as is Clyde Griffiths. Roth's hero
has his Daisy Buchanan and Thea Fenchel in Brenda
Patimkin, the "golden girl" daughter of a plumbing
manufacturer. Neil Klugman, a twenty-three-year-old
former philosophy student, survives the fatal attraction
of the bitch goddess. His name suggests his eventual
ability to see beyond the soul-killing relationship.

Roth's career demonstrates the rewards of the current
literary life; but it also illustrates the continuing re-
sistance of Jewish readers to fiction that portrays Jews
in an unfavorable light. *Goodbye, Columbus,* a novella
published together with five short stories, was a critical
success, the National Book Award winner for 1960. Roth
has been favored by much official recognition: winner of
the O. Henry Award (1958), the Aga Khan prize for
fiction (1958), a Guggenheim Fellowship (1959-60), a
Houghton Mifflin Literary Fellowship, and a Ford Foundation grant in play-writing at Princeton University,
"writer-in-residence" and professorship at the major
universities in "creative writing." Jewish readers have
been less approving. Springing to Roth's defense, Theodore Solotaroff, David Boroff, and Dan Isaac have each
described the negative reactions to Roth's treatment of
the Jews. Roth himself discussed such responses in "Writing about Jews."[21] Appearing as sermons, editorials, reviews, post-lecture remarks, and letters in the Jewish
press, the plaints, in essence, ask, "What will the *goyim*
(gentiles) think?" An example of this kind of reaction
is found in an article by Richard Cohen, " 'Best Novel'—
Worst Award," which appeared in the *Congress-Bi-
Weekly.*[22] Objecting to the choice of *Goodbye, Columbus*
for a National Book Award, the article leveled an ideological charge: that the characters of *Goodbye, Columbus*
are depicted as unpleasant because they are Jews.

Roth's self-defense in "Writing about Jews" not only
answers the complaints of Jewish readers but illuminates

the significance of Jewish fiction, reinforcing the definition which is attempted throughout this study. After re-
futing the notion that the contemporary United States
needs an art which shows how well the Jews live, Roth
affirms the importance to his work of using Jewish characters truthfully, taking advantage of the particular
tensions such characters bring to the story that he has
in mind. To alter the identity of the characters would be
to alter the story. Finally, he identifies his work with
the great tradition of Jewish writing: "to indicate that
moral crisis is something to be hushed up, is not of course,
to take the prophetic line; nor is it a rabbinical point of
view that Jewish life is of no significance to the rest of
mankind."[23] The Israeli novelist, Aharon Megged, has
made the same defense for Roth, placing his writing
within the wider context of world Jewish literature. In
the symposium, "Jewishness and the Creative Present,"
he calls Roth's criticism of the Jewish present the con-
tinuation of the "great tradition of Isaiah."[24]

The Affluent Jew in the Novel

The Patimkin family of *Goodbye, Columbus* can be
taken as Roth's analogue of contemporary middle-class
life; that they happen to be Jews is not, however, in-
significant. Their suburban life-style is a fact of Jewish
existence in America today, just as the ghetto was the
fact of a half century ago.

While the suburban Jew is a new social being and
Roth's portrait has a good deal of freshness, sharp
glances have been directed at moneyed Jews at least as
far back as Edith Wharton's Rosedale in *The House of
Mirth*. (The name, an anglicization of Rosenthal and
therefore a euphemism, is an example of one of the most
familiar and facile methods of satirizing Jewish assimilation. The literary device for exposing the subterfuge is

to follow the anglicized name on the page with a *né,* then
with the original Jewish name, and finally, for ironical
effect, a question mark, setting all in parenthesis, e.g.,
Rosedale [*né* Rosenthal?]. Fictional wealthy Jews have
been depicted in the past as city dwellers. Non-Jewish
authors provide the examples. Thomas Wolfe's vision
of the luxurious Jewish New York theatrical society in
You Can't Go Home Again is expressed in terms of food,
the fleshpots. His fantasy is the underside of the populist
stereotype in which the Jew has usurped the easeful,
bounteous life of the American past. The constituents of
this fantasy as they appear in Wolfe's novel are the dark
exoticism of the women, sensual in a way denied to the
husk-like Christian women; the Oriental, royal barbarity
of the hooknosed men; and the secret exclusiveness of
both, conveyed in their knowing gestures and elliptical
phrases. The populist image of the superior Jew (Behrman in Frank Norris' *The Octopus* is another example)
is the reverse image of the Jew as social climber, e.g.,
Wharton's Rosedale, Fitzgerald's Wolfsheim, Hemingway's Cohn.[25]

Roth's Patimkin family has some of the components
of the Wolfe stereotype. They take an unabashed pleasure in possessions and are unselfconsciously ebullient.
The women are overblown and sensual, the men powerful
and proud, knowledgeable and ruthless in business. What
is changed in Roth's portrait is the scale—the Patimkins
are "comfortable" or "well-off" rather than wealthy.
They are not social climbers. The Patimkins live in what
sociologists have called a gilded ghetto, deriving the satis-
factions of human relationships from their co-religionists.
Willingly taking their place in a rigidly stratified America, they derive their social status from the offices they
hold in temples and Jewish organizations. Unlike the
affluent urban Jews of the non-Jewish authors, the new

suburban Jew has settled comfortably into his position, choosing to remain a distinct entity in the social body.

The Patimkins

The Patimkin family rivals Bellow's Magnus family in their lusty and unthinking enjoyment of the good life. Many of the wealthy families portrayed in Jewish fiction up to mid-century were diffident about their money. Insecure in their social position, they alternated efforts at social climbing with longings for the old life. The progression of an immigrant family by stages from Rosenheimer to Ross in Thyra Samter Winslow's "A Cycle of Manhattan" is typical.[26] The children have become pettish, the mother neurotic, the father bored. The only sign that the Patimkin family is not completely deracinated is their ghost in the attic, the furniture from their former apartment in Newark. The symbols of their unquestioning acceptance of wealth are the "sporting-goods trees," oaks which seem to have dropped various game equipment on the lawn like leaves, and their refrigerator, in which mounds of fruit seem almost to luxuriate.

The language of exaggeration portrays the family. They are epic, Brobdingnagian. The son Ron is a new type: an immense Jewish athlete, a football hero at Ohio State, capable of shaking hands while treading water. In a parody of Neil's situation, Ron, upon attaining the responsibility of a fiancée, promptly drops his vague plans to become a gym teacher and joins the family business.

Mrs. Patimkin represents high culture in the suburban Jewish family. She busies herself with the Ladies' Benevolent Society, Hadassah, and the Orthodox synagogue. It would seem that the old pattern of religious social climb from Orthodox to Reform Judaism no longer obtains. The intellectual depth of her faith is indicated when she tries to place Martin Buber: "Is he orthodox or conservative?"[27] She is pleased that Ron, in another gesture of responsibility, is to join the B'nai B'rith when he marries.

Roth's easy dismissal of Hadassah, the Women's Zionist Organization, brings Jewish fiction a long way from the first appearance of Hadassah as a "potent force" in *The Old Bunch* a quarter century earlier. Meyer Levin—although he was the first writer to introduce Zionism as a theme in Jewish-American fiction in the story, "Maurie Finds His Medium," in the *Menorah Journal* in the late 1920's—has moved in the same direction as Roth. Both condemn the mindless fraternal motive which brings many to Zionist and other Jewish organizations, e.g., in Levin's short story, "After All I Did for Israel," in *Commentary* in 1951. The touchstone to identify genuine Zionism in that story is whether or not the Zionist is willing to send his children to Israel.[28] The destiny of the Ron Patimkins is a place in the family business rather than on the kibbutz. As Mr. Patimkin puts it: "There's no business too big it can't use another head."[29]

Roth's cavalier treatment of the community groups which play such an integral role in Jewish-American life is another example of the rejection of official life made by the Jewish writer, even as he participates in one or another of the forums and symposia that such groups sponsor. In this repudiation, the Jewish writer aligns himself with the intellectuals of Bohemian protest. It was only the first generation of Jewish-American writers who enjoyed the security of an organization which provided both a tradition of protest and communal association. Robert Warshow described this phenomenon in a tribute to his father, "An Old Man Gone." "He belonged to the [Jewish] Socialist movement as one belongs to a certain city or a certain neighborhood: it gave him his friends and it embodied his culture. . . ."[30] More firmly than ever, today's Jewish writer, identifies himself with American culture even though his subject is the Jew.

Ben Patimkin, the father, is the familiar fictional "all-rightnik" who doubles as the prospective father-in-law. Masculine, hairy, a cigar chewer, "a ferocious eater" (though not the equal of Ron), he professes a pure version of the business ethic: one must be a *gonif* (thief) and vigilantly practice "dog eat dog." Even Ron, pure muscle, is an "idealist" in the atmosphere of the shipping room at Patimkin Kitchen and Bathroom Sinks. (Mr. Patimkin seems to be shipping-room foreman rather than plant manager.) The business ideal pervades Patimkin's attitudes toward his family. In a parodic letter to his daughter, he links faith in his children with faith in an equally serious undertaking, business. Brenda's mother, in another such letter, summarizes the responsibilities of parenthood: to provide the best that money can buy. Roth's depiction of the Patimkin family is not uncompromising; one can feel an ambivalent sympathy toward Ben. The novella's severity is further mitigated by the genuinely pathetic scene in the Cathedral and the epigraph, a Yiddish proverb, "The heart is half a prophet."

Goodbye, Columbus as a Novel of Manners

Roth's authority as a novelist of manners was challenged by Jeremy Larner in an article which gave the title of a Roth short story a new meaning.[31] "The Conversion of the Jews" might also stand for the satirist's distortion of Jewish characters beyond artistic truth; the exaggeration of reality allowed the novelist fails to fulfill its function, to reveal the actual world, when it is entirely an artistic device. An example of this (not used by Larner) is the symbolic meaning of Neil Klugman's job, librarian. The meaning—presumably that all those

books stand for the intellectual world of Neil—is unsup-
ported by reality. Although this occupation has served
to denote the aspiring intellectual in Wales or the Mid-
lands for John Braine or Kingsley Amis, it does not
identify the American intellectual. The symbol must be
substantiated by a credible referent.

The more serious charge that Larner levels is that
Roth—despite the testimony to the contrary by Irving
Howe, Alfred Kazin, and Saul Bellow—does not ac-
curately portray the world of the upper middle-class Jew.
These critics do not recognize Roth's inaccuracy because,
Larner says, as "anti-bourgeois intellectuals," they too
are unfamiliar with this life, observing it only through
their students.

The wider question raised by Larner's criticism is,
what is the function of an accurate picture of social manners in the novel of Jewish life? If the novelist cannot
substantiate his insight into the social processes of modern life with a correct picture of the behavioral patterns
through which these processes are enacted, then his insights must be suspect. The realist's imaginative grasp
of life springs from his knowledge of life. Roth, in *Goodbye, Columbus,* is perhaps not an impeccable observer of
social realities, but his talents are sufficiently grounded
in an understanding of the moral implications of Jewish
life as it is lived to make his novel succeed as a work of
art within its own modest terms.

The Dream-of-Success Theme

The central expression of the dream-of-success theme
in *Goodbye, Columbus* occurs in St. Patrick's Cathedral.
Here transcendental implications abound, the protagonist
may seek his "heart's ultimate need" (in the phrase from
Seize the Day), the physical juxtaposition with Rocke-
feller Center reinforces the theme, and the irony is com-

pounded by the prayer of a Jew. The impromptu "little speech" of Neil Klugman is addressed to God:

> What is it I love, Lord? What have I chosen? Who is Brenda? The race is to the swift. Should I have stopped to think? . . . If we meet You at all, God, it's that we're carnal, and acquisitive, and thereby partake of You. . . . Which prize is You? . . . the noise of Fifth Avenue met me with an answer: Which prize do you think, *schmuck?* Gold dinnerware, sporting-goods trees, nectarines, garbage disposals, bumpless noses, Patimkin Sink, Bonwit Teller—[32]

The expression of the theme in these Jewish terms is not essential to the universal meaning of the tale; but the specificity of the terms lends credence and irony.

The theme is expressed again in that favorite device of the modern psychological novelist, the dream. Neil's rejection of the lush society is prefigured by his dream of a tropical island. Accompanied by a little Negro boy whose longing for Gauguin's Tahiti mirrors Neil's own unfulfilled desire for the rich life, he drifts away as the native girls chant, "Goodbye, Columbus . . . goodbye, Columbus." This phrase, combined with the protagonist's name (Klugman), repeats the theme: such is the golden America which the Jewish immigrants discovered. *"A klug zu Columbusn,"* "Woe to Columbus," was the half-ironic cry of the immigrant, cursing his lot in the New World.

THE ROGUE-HERO

The rascally Jewish protagonist is a recurrent figure. Cahan and Ornitz had used the type in the early education novel; Weidman, Schulberg, and Richler used it in the dream-of-success education novel in much the same way. The appearance of the unconscionable rogue in a central position indicates the theme: the nightmare version of the dream of success. The novels follow the pro-

tagonist not merely to the point of sentience of the socialist boy-hero or the alienated anti-hero, but deeper into
the oblivion of a career in the business world. The rise
of David Levinsky is repeated as Meyer Hirsch climbs
the judicial ladder, Harry Bogan cheats his partner to
become a manufacturer, and Sammy Glick races toward
his spiritual death in increasingly costly shoes. David
Boroff assigned a name to the type in a review of *The
Apprenticeship of Duddy Kravitz:* the "rogue-hero."[33]

*I Can Get It for you Wholesale and
What Makes Sammy Run?*

There is but one plot for the rogue-hero novel: The
son of immigrants climbs to the top by exploiting fellow
Jews. In some of its plot specifics, Weidman's *I Can Get
It for You Wholesale*[34] drew very closely indeed upon
its garment-industry predecessor, *The Rise of David
Levinsky.* Like Levinsky, Bogan starts his first shop with
a diffident designer stolen from a successful firm. In both
novels, the designer supplies the capital, has a wife opposed to the partnership, and is quickly dropped from
the new shop.

I Can Get It for You Wholesale also bears similarities
to Schulberg's *What Makes Sammy Run?*[35] The rascality
of Bogan and Glick are attested to in the same way. Each
has, back in the old apartment, a mother to whom he
sends checks, but fails to visit with the requisite weekly
frequency. Weidman uses the mother to provide Bogan's
few soft moments and some Jewish family comedy. She
is not to be taken seriously. Schulberg saves her for his
denouement, as damning evidence of Sammy's past. Man-
heim, the narrator of *What Makes Sammy Run?* who
has followed Sammy's rise from office boy at sixteen to
motion-picture producer at twenty-four, visits the mother's East Side flat. The setting is, by now (ten years

later than Mike Gold's *Jews without Money*), itself a cliché, as are the mother's first words: *"Oi Weh's mir, my little Sammele!* Something has happened to him!"[36] Such a line is in the tradition of the Warner Brothers scenario or dialect comedy.

I Can Get It for You Wholesale is the unpretentious creation of a skillful writer for a popular audience. The wit and intricate scheming of Harry Bogan have not lost their appeal; the novel is still readable in the "good-bad book" tradition of Orwell. Schulberg's novel is another matter. Sammy Glick is of the same stamp as Bogan. Glick's weaker appeal is a clue to Schulberg's more ostentatious purpose: to classify the genus and to fix the origin of all the Sammy Glicks. By enumerating the social and economic forces that create a Sammy Glick, Schulberg intends to dampen the ammunition that *I Can Get It for You Wholesale* gave to the anti-Semites.

The style of *What Makes Sammy Run?* can be called "popular front." Charles E. Eisinger, in *Fiction of the Forties,* holds the book a failure because it reiterates outdated liberal ideas criticizing the "system," for example, condemnation of the slum.[37] It is unfortunate, as well, that these ideas are very crudely developed. Sammy's father, sounding like a parody of Clifford Odets, denounces the bosses in the familiar vein of combined Judaism and Marxism: "Papa Glick's voice was deep and sure as if he were reading from the Bible. 'To be a partner in a sweat shop, such honors I can do without'."[38] The father's death is told in bathetic terms.

The attempt to color in Sammy's background is perfunctory, although none of the correct details is omitted: the idealistic brother; the bully in the playground with his cry of "Christ killer!"; the ineffectual *melamed;* the sordid, premature initiation into sex; and the rogue-hero's street-gang leadership. The mechanical didacticism with which these are presented smacks of the proletarian novel. Schulberg finally falls into deterministic popular-front prose:

> I thought of him as a mangy little puppy in a dog-eat-dog world
> . . . I no longer even hated Rivington Street but the idea of
> Rivington Street, all Rivington Streets of all nationalities allowed
> to pile up in cities like gigantic dung heaps smelling up the world,
> ambitions growing out of filth and crawling away like worms. I
> saw Sammy Glick on a battlefield where every soldier was his
> own cause, his own army and his own flag . . . Sammy was prov-
> ing himself the fittest, the fiercest and the fastest.[39]

Another weakness of the novel is the shallow character of Sammy. David Levinsky and Meyer Hirsch were
aware of the tawdry nature of their "success." They
share in what Robert Warshow called the "characteristic
mental insecurity, a mixture of self-pity and self-con-
tempt" of the second generation who saw no alternative
to the money society.[40] Their self-hatred is unhypocritical
and expressed with a disarming quality which is in the
tradition of Jewish humor. *What Makes Sammy Run?*
has no such humor, only the facile psychological mystery
of its title question and the shoe symbolism—Sammy's
growing affluence finds its highest expression in ever more
flamboyant shoes because he wore cast-off shoes as a child,
although these did not impede him as he started his race
to success.

The Apprenticeship of Duddy Kravitz

Mordecai Richler's *The Apprenticeship of Duddy
Kravitz*[41] is perhaps the best of the rogue-hero novels
since *The Rise of David Levinsky*. Its setting, characters,
protagonist, and the novelistic traditions which inform
it, are superior to those in *What Makes Sammy Run?*
(although it seems likely that Sammy Glick, of all the
rogue-heroes, will be remembered best). *Duddy Kravitz'*
"ticklish" theme, as Alfred Kazin puts it on yet another

of his book-jacket endorsements, is "the desperate striving of a poor Canadian Jewish boy for success, almost at any price." Richler takes up the familiar theme manifestly intending to give a bravura interpretation to a familiar piece; one of his characters calls Duddy "Sammy Glick." This time the dream of success has an explicit embodiment. Duddy's unremitting efforts are directed toward buying a plot of land, in response to his grandfather's adjuration, "A man without land is nobody." His quest is really that of the non-rogue hero: self-definition.

Canada as a Jewish America

The setting of the novel is the Jewish district of Montreal; and it is apparent immediately that the life there is the same as Jewish life in the big cities of the United States. (Richler has been embraced by such reviewers as Stanley Kauffmann and Charles Angoff as being surely in the American tradition.) The characters cover the socio-economic range from the cab driver in the greasy restaurant to the parvenu in the suburb. Present is the conflict of generations with its concomitant hostilities and failures of communication. There is, of course, the goal of material success. The motives nurtured on Montreal's city pavements are carried into the spacious hills and lakes of Canada which are, in the novel, an ignoble summer resort area.

Several Jewish-American writers can be seen as influences upon Richler. The rich texture of Richler's Montreal is partly inspired by a tale of life in another provincial city, *The Adventures of Augie March*. Specific echoes are found in the novel's title; in the series of tawdry and improbable enterprises in which Duddy, like Augie, engages at high tempo (bilking stamp dealers of approvals, selling black-market American comic books, stealing autographed hockey sticks) ; and in the character Dingleman, a paralytic who receives petitions for aid in shady enterprises much as did Einhorn (a paralytic with a brother named Dingbat). Leslie Fiedler calls Richler an "underrated Rothian commentator on the Jewish Canadian scene."[42] To David Boroff, Dingleman, with his fabulous foray into far-off New York and his return with a fortune, recalls Uncle Ben of *Death of a Salesman*.[43] Reinforcing Boroff's comparison is the allusion in the novel to Miller's play, which Duddy sees in New York as Dingleman tries to educate him (as Einhorn does with Augie).

Unlike Augie March, but very like the victim of the dream of success (Studs Lonigan at the bookstore window or Benny Gordon at the Art Institute), Duddy learns nothing from his instruction in high culture. There is a gratuitous touch to this phase of the conventional treatment of the dream's victim. The author seems to be insecure in his demonstration of the acculturation process which has saved him from the fate of the protagonist. The scene is the reverse of that in which the autobiographical hero cites Spencer, Tolstoy and the rest of the enlightening books. In *The Apprenticeship of Duddy Kravitz,* the burden of enlightenment has been shifted from the protagonist to the uncle, the Mencken-and-Dreiser-reading, irreligious Uncle Benjy (not Uncle Ben). A success in business, but not proud of it, Benjy contributes to Communist Party causes, but even there finds foolishness in the dreamy magazine visions of "summer camps where solemn Negroes sang progressive songs."[44]

The uniqueness of Richler's Montreal grants the novel a degree of originality. In Montreal, *épater les bourgeois* means greeting the rabbinical students at the Lubovitcher *yeshiva* with snowballs. It means firing matches into gasoline puddles during an air-raid drill, thus subverting Feinberg's Canadian Provost Corps. This last is in the Yiddish tradition of self-lampooning. Stout Feinberg, in steel helmet and Churchill zipper suit, is pompous and falsely martial, that is, un-Jewish. Chaim "Cuckoo" Kaplan is a *tummeler* (social director in a summer resort). Richler accurately draws the type, exposing the practical jokes, disorderly personal life, and the low ambition—to follow Danny Kaye's path from the Borscht Circuit to Hollywood.

Resort life provides an easy target for the satirist. The microcosm of the summer hotel, where the gorgeous "sports wear," the immense meals, and the clumsily played competitive sports are already a caricature of middle-class life, requires minimal exaggeration. Richler's scenes at Rubin's Hotel Lac de Sables do no more than imply the existence of the life in the public rooms, focusing instead on the backstairs where Duddy evolves from street urchin to the determined eighteen-year-old who pursues adult schemes through the last two-thirds of the novel.

Richler as a Satirist

Parody and mock drama are the media for Richler's satire of middle-class Jewish life. The Reform temple ministered by Rabbi Goldstone, M. A., is described. So secularized has Judaism become that the rabbi gives "sex talks" in the temple's "marriage clinic." The theme of the children's shame of their parents is dramatized. At the high school commencement, the children turn away embarrassedly from the noisy behavior of their parents in the audience. There is a mock scenario in the manner of S. J. Perelman. Duddy's greatest scheme is to produce documentary movies of local *bar mitzvahs* with the aid of a drunken surrealist film producer. Their first production is fully described as a mixture of sight gags, bizarre cinematic juxtapositions, comical left-wing clichés, and vulgar actions of the guests at the post-*bar mitzvah* celebration—the materials, in short, of black humor.

Structural problems and oscillation between a some-times forced burlesque and realistic narration mar the novel, but it is redeemed by the unifying presence of the hero. Duddy's pursuit of success has credible psycholog-ical motives. These are love for his father, a braggart proud of his sobriquet, "Max the Hack"; love mixed with jealousy for his older brother, the scholar of the family; and the absence of any goal other than that of success of the flashiest kind. Duddy suffers from the con-flict of generations: the inability of the New World parents to transmit the inherent dignity of being a Jew to the children. So far removed is Duddy from this knowledge that he is unable to assist his grandfather, Simcha (the blessed one), in upholding his beliefs. Simcha's advice to Duddy to become a man by owning land is nothing more than the memory of dignity. After so many years in the New World, he is fit only to live out his last years in the city, refusing the gift of a house on Duddy's hard-won land. The novel ends on this am-biguous note, with the final commentary on the dream of success suspended and Duddy robbed of his definition of self. *The Apprenticeship of Duddy Kravitz* is the subtlest of the novels on the success theme because, finally, it with-holds a tendentious comment.

NOTES TO CHAPTER 5

1. Kenneth S. Lynn, *The Dream of Success* (Boston: Little Brown & Co., 1955).

2. *Mark, The Glove Boy* (New York: The Macmillan Co., 1964). Harris has published his education novel material as reminiscence, the long preface to a play, *Friedman and Son* (New York: The Macmillan Co., 1963).

3. C. Bezalel Sherman, *The Jew within American Society* (Detroit: Wayne State University Press, 1965), p. 60.

4. "Jews in America," *Fortune*, XIII, No. 2 (Feb. 1936), 79-144.

5. Howard M. Sachar, *The Course of Modern Jewish History* (New York: Dell Publishing Co., 1963), pp. 343-345.

6. Seymour Epstein, *The Successor* (New York: Charles Scribner's Sons, 1961).

7. *"Mid-Century,* ed: Harold U. Ribalow (New York: The Beechhurst Press, Inc., 1955), pp. 350-364.

8. Sam Ross, *Someday, Boy* (New York: Farrar, Straus & Co., 1948).

9. Ross, *The Sidewalks Are Free* (New York: Farrar, Straus & Co., 1951).

10. Philip Roth, *Goodbye, Columbus* (Boston: Houghton Mifflin Co., 1959).

11. *Someday, Boy*, p. 181.

12. *Ibid.*, p. 327.

13. James T. Farrell, *Judgment Day* (New York: The Vanguard Press, Inc., 1935), p. 218; *Someday, Boy*, p. 328.

14. *Someday, Boy*, pp. 200-201.

15. Blanche Gelfant, *The American City Novel*, (Norman, Okla.: University of Oklahoma Press, 1954), pp. 242-243.

16. Allison Davis, *Social-class Influence upon Learning* (Cambridge: Harvard University Press, 1948), pp. 24-27.

17. Ross, *The Sidewalks Are Free*, p. 180.

18. *Ibid.*, p. 134.

19. *Ibid.*, p. 162.

20. Alfred Kazin, *Contemporaries*, (Boston: Little, Brown & Co., 1962), p. 259.

21. Theodore Solotaroff, "Philip Roth and the Jewish Moralists," *Chicago Review*, XIII, No. 1 (Winter 1959), 87-99; David Boroff, "Philip Roth and his Audience," *The Menorah Journal*, XLIX, Nos. 1 and 2 (Autumn-Winter 1962), 156-157; Dan Isaac, "In Defense of Philip Roth," *Chicago Review*, XVII, Nos. 2 and 3 (1964), 84-106.

22. Richard Cohen, " 'Best Novel'—Worst Award," *Congress Bi-Weekly*, XXVII, No. 19 (Dec. 19, 1960), 12-14.

23. Philip Roth, "Writing about Jews," *Commentary*, XXXVI, No. 6 (Dec. 1963), p. 451.

24. "Jewishness and the Creative Present," *Congress Bi-Weekly*, XXX, No. 12 (Sept. 16, 1963).

25. It was apparently the practice of the non-Jewish writer to base his Jewish characters on actual people. Robert Herrick's Simeon Erard in *The Gospel of Freedom* was based on Bernard Berenson; Wolfsheim was inspired by Arnold Rothstein, a New York gambler, (Lynn, *Dream of Success,* pp. 219-220; Andrew Turnbull, *Scott Fitzgerald* [New York: Charles Scribner's Sons, 1962], p. 307.) Two of the most famous fictional Jews, themselves well-known figures, replied at booklength to their portrayal. In *The Journey Down*, Aline Bernstein, the Esther Jack of *The Web and the Rock* and *You Can't Go Home Again,* and in *The*

Way It Was, Harold Loeb, the Robert Cohen of *The Sun Also Rises,* refute the tone of their portraits, but not the lineaments.

26. In *Treasury of American Jewish Stories,* ed. Harold U. Ribalow (New York: Thomas Yoseloff, 1958), pp. 337-397.

27. *Goodbye Columbus,* p. 88.

28. Harold U. Ribalow, "Zion in Contemporary Fiction," *Mid-Century,* ed. Ribalow, pp. 572-573.

29. *Goodbye, Columbus,* p. 109

30. Robert Warshow, *The Immediate Experience* (New York: Anchor Books, 1964), p. 73.

31. Jeremy Larner, "The Conversion of the Jews," *Partisan Review,* XXVII, No. 4 (Fall 1960), 760-768.

32. *Goodbye, Columbus,* p. 100.

33. David Boroff, "An Authentic Rogue-Hero," *Congress Bi-Weekly,* XXI, No. 9 (May 25, 1960), 17.

34. Jerome Weidman, *I Can Get It For You Wholesale* (New York: Random House, Inc., 1937).

35. Budd Schulberg, *What Makes Sammy Run?* (New York: Random House, Inc., 1941).

36. *Ibid.,* p. 221.

37. Charles E. Eisinger, *Fiction of the Forties* (Chicago: University of Chicago Press, 1963), pp. 103–105.

38. *What Makes Sammy Run?,* p. 232.

39. *Ibid.,* p. 249.

40. Warshow, *The Immediate Experience,* p. 30.

41. Mordecai Richler, *The Apprenticeship of Duddy Kravitz* (Boston: Little, Brown & Co., 1959).

42. "Second Dialogue in Israel," *Congress Bi-Weekly,* XXX, No. 12 (Sept. 16, 1963), 69.

43. David Boroff, "An Authentic Rogue-Hero," *Congress Bi-Weekly,* 17.

44. Richler, *Duddy Kravitz,* p. 60.

6

Second Childhood: The Nostalgic Backward Glance

During much of its course, the ghetto novel was the object of critical complaint. In 1929, the young reviewer Lionel Trilling objected in *The Menorah Journal* to the "mean qualities that characterize the best of the genre— the crabbed pathos, the niggling heroics, the stuffiness, grimness, vexatiousness, the something that is almost sordid . . . as soon as the Jewish writer gets his hero to be a Jew, he wraps him up warm in a *talith* and puts him away."[1] Trilling's advice was to supplant the mean qualities with "poetry, passion, a little madness," a prescription that does seem to have been taken by Nathanael West, Henry Roth, Daniel Fuchs, Bernard Malamud, and Saul Bellow—the best of the Jewish writers.

185

More recently, Stephen Longstreet characterized Jewish novels in the same way as did Trilling: "the portable
wailing walls, the dramatic laments, the grin and poverty,
the theater of ghetto and ritual, the painful humor and
the feeble desires to live up to the idea that they are the
Chosen People. In real life I didn't find many such Jews.
I will tell you a secret: Jews are just like other people."[2]
If this be true, then there is sufficient reason to write
about them; the unsensational life offers much insight into
the nature of man. But to recall again the joke that the
Jews are like everybody else, only more so, suggests a
peculiar difficulty and, perhaps, advantage of the Jews
as a subject to the artist who already seeks to heighten
reality. C. Bezalel Sherman theorizes that "where Jews
move in the direction of the country as a whole, they
usually move at a faster pace."[3] As an example, he cites
the post-World War II move to the suburbs which was
carried out most rapidly by the Jews. As New York City
offers a glimpse into the neurotic super-metropolis of
the future, so the Jew reveals a more intense vision of
general social patterns. What is less conjectural than this
is that the Jewish-American ethos is still as clearly
demarcated, still as visible as ever. The Jew enacts the
drama of the socially insecure middle class on a small
stage; his emotional intensity makes that stage a theater-
in-the-round.

A group of novelists writing at mid-century moved
away from the syndrome of Jewish self-pity but along
entirely different lines from those proposed by Trilling.
The same Jewish materials which had been used in the
past for an indictment of society or for "weepy self-
examination" were used by them to evoke what can best
be termed "nostalgia" in a new variation of the education
novel.

Fulfilling the tendency of the Jewish-American novel
to fit into the general schema of the American novel, the

Jewish nostalgic novels coincided with the appearance in the Fifties of the novel of sentiment, an emergent form of the city novel described by Gelfant. She pairs the novel of sentiment with the novel of violence; examples of the latter also are found among education novels, e.g., Shulman's *Cry Havoc* trilogy. The characterization of the city in the novel of sentiment is still negative, but the ending predicts the protagonist's ultimate ascendancy; the theme is summarized in the sentence, "Tomorrow will be better," according to Gelfant. Such "ecological studies of city life" re-create the "manners and tensions of a confined social world" without contrast or sweep. They exploit manners rather than reveal basic truths.[4] This description also fits the Jewish nostalgic novels. The special quality of the Jewish novel is the attitude of the authors toward the particular dynamics of life in the Jewish ethos—a more favorable attitude toward life than is customary in the general class of novels of sentiment. An important structural effect of this difference is that it lends greater congruence to the optimistic ending of the Jewish novels.

There is some evidence that the Jewish authors draw upon a genuine fund of nostalgia for their own boyhoods, although, for the younger ones, these were spent in the Depression decade. David Mark, who plans his novels carefully in advance, found that his boyhood novel, admittedly autobiographical, came to him with a spontaneity and tenderness of viewpoint which surprised him.[5] Herbert Gold felt that he had found a similar release in writing his autobiographical story, "The Heart of the Artichoke": "Oldtime troubles in love suddenly came to life in my head and I found that they were now funny to me; and although no less sad, I could grieve for others because I was now very clearly someone quite different from myself as an adolescent."[6] He further wrote of this same story that it is "my most personally crucial story because, by writing it, I learned to be a writer. I had a sense of mastering my experience. Not just examining, not just using it, but *riding* my world, with full use of my faculties in the open air."[7] Mark and Gold illustrate the motive and the reward for the writer's return to the past: eliciting material from the subconscious.

On the other hand, searching the past for material has been described by Theodore Solotaroff as a serious obstacle to the Jewish artist who seeks access to his subconscious: "Jewish life seems so self-contained and peculiar, so drenched with nearly invariable shades of local color that it can become almost inaccessible to the imagination. The writer simply begins to remember and details of character and milieu come by the bucket."[8] The hack is delighted by the easy recipe for writing fiction implicit in Solotaroff's statement; the serious writer can be permanently baffled.

A touchstone to determine the inhibiting effect on the author of converting his boyhood into fiction is whether or not he can write other kinds of novels subsequently. Both Mark and Gold wrote novels before and after their autobiographical ones. But some writers of the education novel exhausted their vein with one excellent book drawn from their childhood: Isaac Rosenfeld, Henry Roth. Each wrote an unpublishable second novel and no others. Roth described his state during the years he was composing *Call It Sleep* as one of near ecstasy; and the novel unmistakably displays the artist's access to his own psyche, as well as his ability to use the resources of his craft.[9] The education novel, with its demand for an intimate examination of the novelist's soul, apparently does carry certain dangers to the artist who manages to utilize his innermost self and then finds that he has exhausted his material. Such cases are free, in any event, of the kind of uncreative memory work against which Solotaroff cautions.

Generally, the nostalgic education novel makes a more conscious use of materials and has more modest goals than the above suggests. Their usual intent is to please with gentle, inoffensive comedy and the evocation of the sentimental mood. Three novelists will be treated separately. Herbert Gold's *Therefore Be Bold* (1960), Albert Halper's *On the Shore* (1934), and *The Golden Watch* (1953), and the first two novels of Charles Angoff's David Polonsky series, *Journey to the Dawn* (1951) and *In the Morning Light* (1952) deserve individual attention.[10] The remaining nostalgic novels fall into two groups, the comic and the serio-comic, and can be treated together. These offer an opportunity for some generalizations about Jewish-American fiction, about the function of food and religious holidays as fictional materials. Dialect and humor in the Jewish novel will also be examined.

The serio-comic group includes David Mark's *The Neighborhood* (1959), Arthur Granit's *The Time of the Peaches* (1959), and George Mandel's *The Breakwater* (1960).[11] The comic group includes Herman Wouk's *The City Boy* (1948), Yuri Suhl's *One Foot in America* (1951) and *Cowboy on a Wooden Horse* (1953), and S. J. Wilson's *Hurray for Me* (1964).[12] Several collections of short stories were published as nostalgic education novels. In addition to Halper's and Suhl's books of stories, there are Elick Moll's *Memoir of Spring* (1961) and Burton Bernstein's *The Grove* (1961).[13] The episodic nature of the novels in the comic group makes more difficult the problem of defining the novel as an entity separate from the collection of short stories.

SETTING IN THE NOSTALGIC NOVEL

The time and place of the nostalgic novel are clearly defined. The time is that period later in the Great Depression when poverty has become a settled way of life. The first shock of the stock-market crash has subsided and the call for the Marxist solution has become a familiar chant. The father in Wilson's *Hurray for Me,* voted most likely to succeed in high school, is, after fifteen years, a librarian; but his wife accepts this good-humoredly: they can't afford a yacht, but still it's living. The federal job or city sinecure, the school teacher's post obtained after years as a substitute—these served during the long years until entering the professions would again become a realistic ambition. The *mise en scène* is Brownsville, Williamsburg, or the West Side of Chicago, the enclave where drama is played out amidst comfortable familiarity. An aura of timelessness pervades; the neighbors have discovered various means of subsistence; and, even though they are barely surviving, they have some confidence that conditions will not change for the worse in the foreseeable future. Freed of the necessity for thesis-mongering, the author can now examine character for the sake of its coloration.

The slow turn of seasons has the changelessness of childhood. The protagonist of the comic novel is likely to be a child who, although undergoing the transformation requisite to the education novel, is spared the problem of fitting himself into an occupation or committing himself to a doctrine. The most he is called upon to do is observe the play of incident or to take some minor part in it. The protagonist is no longer a sensitive ideologue or nascent poet. He may so develop, but to begin with he is a simple street urchin, eager for a game of baseball. (One sign of later inclinations is the story-telling talent possessed by two of the protagonists.)

The hero of the serio-comic novel is an early adolescent of about fifteen years, possibly because that stage can credibly include the sexual initiation of the protagonist. The serio-comic novel can be distinguished from the comic by the presence in the former of prostitutes and marital difficulties. The protagonist's character is more defined and situation is more closely related to his inner development. In the comic novels, psyche is subordinated to humorous effect.

The nostalgic novel strikes a new note. Urban pleasures mitigate the eternal blistering heat and wintry winds. Halper's grocer's son in *The Golden Watch* escapes the pavements to ice skate and swim in the park lagoons. In Mark's *The Neighborhood,* Arnie Aronson plays baseball, listens to park-bench raconteurs, and distributes handbills as a partisan in a local election.

The inhabitants of this new, more congenial city are somewhat bolder in outline than the didactic figures of the Depression novel or the dream-of-success novel. The sign of this is their names: The Chicken Plucker, Mandelbaum the Tenant, Doodie Diamond, Black Lil, and Knishes. Unrestrained, they are great brawlers and cursers. High-spirited, they resist their fate with rent strikes which may include pummeling the landlord and hurling garbage into the street; even the relief food queue is likely to break into disorder. They rail against their poverty in more disorganized ways than the characters in the Depression novels. Their Rabelaisian behavior is, particularly in the comic novels, rather forced. Non-Jewish characters are common, the neighborhood is less insular, and poverty has obscured ethnic differences.

The comic novels are filled with sunshine. A good deal of affection is evident in them except in the most mechanical examples. In the serio-comic style, blue filters create shadows and the actors are touched up with more garish makeup. Indeed, the setting is more likely to be night; but the season is still open summer when the stream of people on the streets increases human contacts.

THE COMIC NOVELS

The main tradition of the comic novels is a Jewish humor, not of the European gallows variety of Peretz or the folk type of Sholom Aleichem, but of the American nineteenth-century "phunny phellows" and Broadway. Dialect is the chief ingredient of this humor, but the narrator speaks in genteel prose, sparing the reader the difficulties of an entire volume in dialect. The narrator's impeccable English, contrasted to the dialect of the characters, constantly emphasizes their bizarreness, how low they remain and how far the narrator has come. Bernstein's *The Grove,* a series of short pieces tied together by a summer-town setting and a first-person youthful narrator, is in this tradition. The names of the summer residents give the lie to their pretentious demeanor: Abe Slobodkin, I. G. Katz, Ben Ruttman.

Wouk's *The City Boy* uses the device of mock-formal prose without, however, a cast of dialect characters. A quotation serves to illustrate the style:

"O.K.," retorted Herbie, *"then who made the world?"* There was a general laugh at Lennie's expense this time. Herbie had managed to twist the age-old circular argument so that he was now chasing his opponent. The athlete said angrily, "Well, if there's a God, let Him make a can of ice cream appear right here in front o' you 'n' me."

All the boys stared at the patch of grass between the debaters, half expecting a cylinder of Breyer's Special Chocolate to materialize. The Creator, however, seemed to be in no mood for showing off.[14]

The effect is that of *Tom Sawyer* and *Penrod:* the droll-
ness of boyhood with its alarums and pretensions is man-
ifested by the formal treatment of the above trivialities.
In the section of *The Adolescent in the American Novel*
called "Upper-class City Environment," J. Tasker
Witham calls Herbie Bookbinder a "fat, urbanized, semi-
tized Penrod." In the appendix, he classifies the book as
"H" and "Se" in style: "Humorous" and 'Sentimental."[15] Also seeing the resemblance, the publishers aimed
the 1951 edition of *The City Boy* at the children's market. Illustrations in an anachronistic style reminiscent of
those of Penrod were added, as was an introduction by
J. P. Marquand claiming for Herbie Bookbinder (funny
names are indispensable to the comic writer) the universal appeal of Tom Sawyer.

Dialect

The patronizing device of contrasting the well-bred
prose of the narrator with the broken English of the
characters was used in the long series of volumes of Po-
tash and Perlmutter stories by Montague Glass. In Leo
Q. Ross's (Leo Rosten) two volumes of Hyman Kaplan
stories, the contrast was provided by the English in-
structor in a night school for immigrants. Arthur Kober's three volumes of stories about the unkindly-named
Gross family contrast the formal narration with an ex-
cessively exaggerated dialect. Mr. Gross arrives to an
empty house after a half-Saturday at the shop:

"Say, what kine place is this?" Mr. Gross was now talking to himself petulantly. "A fine femily is here! The wibe, who knows
where she is? The dutter, I'll betcha she's gung to a moompickcheh
show! Is empty the whole house!" he cried. "It pays awready
to come home fomm shop! Better I should stay donntonn and
play a little pinochle, fife cents a hundritt, so I should lose the
whole bunch waitches!"[16]

Part of the humor lies in the spelling, but another part lies in the distortion of the accent. There is enough actuality in the speech and the personality of Mr. Gross to furnish genuinely funny caricature, but, finally, the distortion is excessive.

Over the century, the trend in the transcription of dialect has been toward a less phonetic rendering, one which hints at distinctive idioms and rhythms rather than laboriously transcribing them. The advantage in this change is a greater ease in reading with little loss in flavor. In the work of serious Jewish novelists, the re-creation of Yiddish speech has been stripped of what Daniel Bell calls 'stilted ideographs of inverted spelling or neologism."[17] The contemporary style is exemplified by Burt Blechman in *The War of Camp Omongo:* " 'You come from a lovely part, Mr. Tannenbaum. Personally I've never visited Mamaroneck, but in the papers you should notice the high rentals they're charging out there!' "[18] This is cruelly strong, but concise and free of the strain of phonetic transcription. The purpose is the satiric revelation of character rather than the more frivolous dependence on dialect for comedy of Kober, Glass, and Rosten.

Beyond trends in transcription lies the question of the writer's sharpness of ear; this is usually not divorced from his facility as a satirist. The comic novelists in the nostalgic group, relying heavily on dialect, fall short of the serious writer in their ability to use dialect to artistic effect. The following passage from Elick Moll's *Memoir of Spring* achieves merely the effect of a gag: " 'Minnie, I'm going to tell you something . . . Plain out. For your own good. You are not going to make a silk suit out of a cow's ear.' "[19] *The City Boy,* dealing with American-born Jews, relies on the pompous behavior of adults to children and on that standby of the inferior novelist, the minor character who displays his distinguishing characteristic at each appearance. The halting, noncommittal speech of Bookbinder's partner is so odd as to defy belief: "'Jake, why excited? I say this way, peaceable. Powers honest man. One way, another way. Maybe better off. Talk, decide. Friendly. Nobody rob us. Lot of cash. Reliable people. I say this way, cool off!' "[20] Wilson, in *Hurray for Me,* is skilled at Yiddish dialect but over-exaggerates his Italian barber: "'Shut up you crazy mouth, you strega, you . . . Shut da mouth, or I give you such a whoom-bam I knock every tooth out of your crazy head.' "[21] None of these achieves the verbal charm, funnily accurate, of Daniel Fuch's *Homage to Blenholt.* A street vendor sells imitation pearls: "'For your sweetheart,' he said hopefully. 'Fifty cents. Worth a dollar, I should live so.' . . . 'Thirty cents. Twenty cents,' the old man begged. 'You got a mother, ain't it? Ten cents! Give a man a show!' "[22]

The evocation through speech of the quality of Jewish life has been analyzed by Robert Warshow in an essay on Clifford Odets' *Awake and Sing.*[23] Warshow finds New York Jewish life to be the image of life for all American Jews. "It is what a Jew remembers, it is what he has in his mind when he experiences his more private emotions about being a Jew—affection, pity, delight, shame." Odets is a "poet of the Jewish middle class" because he communicates, through the self-revealing speech of the characters, the complexity of their lives. The mother Bessie is bitter, "In a minute I'll get up from the table. I can't take a bite in my mouth no more." The grandfather reveals his make-up, "All you know, I heard, and more yet . . . This is a house? Marx said it—abolish such families." Successful Uncle Morty reminds himself of how far he has come, "Where's my fur gloves?" In skillful hands, such an outrageous speech, crammed with malapropisms, solecisms, rich phonemes, and odd twists is genuinely funny; in the hands of a literary artist, it is funny and revealing.

Food in the Nostalgic Novel

By definition, nostalgia demands that past times be recalled as happier than they actually were. Popular nostalgia in America is easily aroused over the ante-bellum South, the "gay Nineties," "the old West," and the "roaring Twenties." As subjects for popular treatment, the first two have gone quite threadbare, while the "old West," which excites dark regions in the American psyche, maintains itself as a timeless era and a discrete world. The Twenties carried within itself the materials of myth; little time elapsed before it was adopted as a symbol of a good time gone. The decade of the Thirties is another matter. Granville Hicks, calling for a reappraisal of the period in the *Saturday Review,* cites the Depression and the political reactions which it provoked as the chief phenomena of that time.[24] One can hardly long for the misery of the one and the dismal failures of the other. But in a burst of genuine sentiment, Diana Trilling laments the loss of the "racial-depressed" Jewish world.[25] As the decade recedes into the past, it will be fully analyzed. It is likely that the Jewish experience of the Thirties will figure largely in the reassessment.

The Jewish writer is the literary executor of the Thirties and the neighborhood provides the pattern for that experience. The depiction of the Thirties in sentimental terms requires a refurbishing of the same slum life that the Depression novelist found so hideous. Wilson's *Hurray for Me,* the most overtly affirmative of the nostalgic novels, illustrates this process, using an important particular of Jewish fiction, food. The penny-candy counter is an institution which genuinely recalls the past. When

it is seen in *Hurray for Me* in the charge of white-haired
Mr. Goodman, the most skeptical reader will concede
its appeal. Table food is similarly persuasive—the familiar cold cuts, the vanished mustard "toot," the celery
tonic. In this day, in a strange land suffering from over-
abundance, where everyone is on a reducing diet, the
enumeration of gaudy delicatessen is irresistible. Even the
delights sold by the streetvendors—flavored ice and the
more robust "sweet corn" and *hayse arbes* (hot chick
peas)—are pleasing to remember.

At its crudest level, the evocation of the table resembles the efforts of the nightclub comedian before a
Miami audience; his patronizing interjection of Yiddish
phrases are met with a gratified snicker. Yuri Suhl's
chapter titles for *One Foot in America* make the point:
"What Happened to My Chicken Liver?", "Two Hot
Knishes and a Warm Feeling," "Easy as Kugel." Wit is
unnecessary. The mere mention of the homely, inelegant
dish suffices.

The stereotyped bill of fare of the Jewish table reappears in Jewish fiction with a suggestive persistence.
The favorite scene is the Friday night *Shabbes* dinner.
The *shtetl* tradition of the Sabbath as a holy day of rest
involving a complex of ritualized customs has so degenerated that the novelist now has available as material
only the elaborate meal, consisting of dishes which appeared on the table of the wealthier Jewish families in
the Pale. The efforts of the writer to recall the vanished
grandeur of the Sabbath are an empty litany, unintentionally symbolic of the hollow life of the deracinated
Jewish family which has retained the meal but not the
customs connected with it. A favorite phrase of the Jewish mother is *kleibing naches;* the meaning in America is
"receiving gratification," usually through the attainments
of the children. This Yiddish term is derived from the
Hebrew *lanuach,* to rest (on the Sabbath). This shift in

meaning traces a good deal of Jewish social history.

The invariable list of Sabbath food in fiction includes the following, each dish named in a reverential tone. (The passage is from Kazin's *A Walker in the City*.)

On the long white table cloth were the "company" dishes, filled for some with *gefillte* fish on lettuce leaves, ringed by red horse-radish, sour and half-sour pickles, tomato salad with a light vinegar dressing; for others, with chopped liver in a bed of lettuce leaves and white radishes; the long white *khalleh,* the Sabbath loaf; chicken soup with noodles *and* dumplings; chicken, meat loaf, prunes, and sweet potatoes that had been baked all day into an open pie; compote of prunes and quince, apricots and orange rind; applesauce; a great brown nut-cake filled with almonds; the traditional *lekakh;* all surrounded by glasses of port wine, seltzer bottles with their nozzles staring down at us waiting to be pressed; a samovar of Russian tea, *svetouchnee* from the little red box, always served in tall glasses, with lemon slices floating on top.[26]

The list recalls an old joke mocking the effect that Kazin seeks. A convert to Christianity, strolling in his old neighborhood, sniffing the flavorsome aroma of *erev shabbes* (the eve of the Sabbath) muses aloud: "From this religion a man converts?"

A second important, recurrent scene in Jewish novels is the *Pesah seder* (Passover ceremonial meal). Here the array of food reappears, but the particular dishes associated with the holiday bear more elaborate religious meanings. The holiday commemorates the passage out of Egypt of the Jews under the leadership of Moses. The *Haggadah* service, an ordering of song, prayer, and narrative reciting of the history of this event, conducted at the table responsively, is intimately connected with the foodstuffs; and, consequently, a religious service appears in the narrative. A passage from Halper's *The Golden Watch* combines the naming of foods with symbolic interpretation:

My restless glance strayed to the shankbone of a lamb on a plate
—symbol of the paschal sacrifice in biblical times; I saw the
dishes of parsley and radishes, the hard-boiled egg, the bitter herbs
floating in water—all religious and historical symbols which did
not interest me, though I knew the bitter herbs were very important tonight because they were a reminder of the bitter years
of bondage the Israelites had suffered under the yoke of the cruel
Egyptians . . . at my father's elbow was a plate covered with a
snowy linen napkin, which we all knew hid three big unbroken
squares of matzos, in keeping with the ritual. . . . He halted to dip
his wine into the big, cut-glass base upon which the decanter rested,
and we followed suit, dribbling a few drops of the red, red wine
in unison as he intoned the command to dip. I stared at the large
filled goblet of wine standing in the center of the table which was
for the prophet Elijah. As an unseen guest in our home on this
auspicious night, we welcomed him as the precursor of the Mes-
siah.[27]

The same baffling effect as Kazin's is created. There is a
quality about these lists which bring to mind Kazin's remark that some Jewish writers can succeed with these
materials without really knowing why. The addition of
religious explanations to Halper's set piece adds little;
the golden aura of the scene suggests that its effect is
that of the genre still life by Steen, the remembrance
of a time of comfort and peace.

Like the Sabbath, the Passover ceremony is the token
of a nullified choice to the serious novelist—"You can't
go home again," a basic postulate of the education novel.
Rosenfeld infuses his Passover scene with extra-religious
meanings: the grandfather's hand trembles as he pours
the ten drops marking the plagues visited upon the
Egyptians and the family avert their heads from the
stain, a reminder of approaching death. The occasion
also provides Rosenfeld with a dramatic scene. The *seder*
becomes a duel between the father and the cousin. As
Daniel Bell points out, despite the warmth of the scene,
for the protagonist it is only a "mirage within the im-
personal Gentile world."[28]

An attempt, couched in popular style, to account for the importance of food among Jews was made by Harry Golden in "Ess, Ess, Mein Kindt."[29] He lays it to the concern with survival, to the association of food with strength and growth. The Sabbath with its special food was the compensation for the degrading life in the European *golus* (diaspora). It was the table around which the family gathered to make decisions and conduct family services.

Golden refers in the essay to *kreplach,* dumplings of dough wrapped around chopped meat and served in chicken soup. Another attempt to analyze the significance of food to the Jews, "Kreplach" by Isaac Rosenfeld in *Commentary,*[30] treated the dish irreverently, seeing a pun in the name, but with serious intent, exploring the magical significance of Jewish food. Carrying on in *Commentary* with his mythological analysis of food in "Adam and Eve on Delancey Street,"[31] Rosenfeld considered the Jewish food restrictions which require the separation of *milkhik* and *fleyshik* (dairy and meat) foods. He theorizes that there is an unconscious analogue between food taboos and sex: feminine milk must be separated from masculine meat by a purification period. A Reichian, he considers all prohibitions to be sexually repressive, but also guesses, like Golden, that Jews eat to excess to satisfy the hunger of insecure *golus* life. (Excessive drinking, another form of allaying insecurity, has never been charged to the Jews. The sociological explanation is that their ritualization of drinking, the ceremonial use of wine, has prevented this.) Rosenfeld's provocative speculations were abruptly cut off by protests from the president of the American Jewish Committee (the sponsors of *Commentary*), whose letter in the December 1949 number includes such phrases of "offending the religious sensibilities," "violated every canon of good taste," "an abuse of the editorial freedom accorded you." Reassurances from the editor against a similar occurrence marked the unfortunate end to Rosenfeld's analyses.

In *Life Is with People*,[32] not the magical view but the psychological one is supported: when the mother offers food, "she is offering her love, and she offers it constantly." An entire chapter is devoted to the kosher home. Food plays a major part in religious, social, and family life. For the proscription upon combining meat and milk, a humanitarian explanation is provided: "Thou shall not seethe the kid in the milk of its mother."

The Lore of Childhood

To conclude the analysis of the literary creation of nostalgia, to dialect humor and food we must add the lore of childhood. Wilson's *Hurray for Me,* the story of a five-year-old whose world is stirred by the knowledge that mothers are mortal, presents a full account of the city child's rhythmic chants and street cries: "Minnie and a Minnie and a hot-cha-cha!," "I'm Bertha the sewing machine girl," "There was a man, he went mad," "My mother, your mother lives across the way," "Mr. Schmeckel-Peckel," "King of the mountain."[33]

Hurray for Me enjoyed the benefit which accrues to affimative books: the attention of the reviewers who call for books that show America in a favorable light. The history of its reception in the Chicago *Tribune* "Books Today" section is edifying. It received a cover review on February 23, 1964, climbed to fifth position on the Chicago best-seller list, then quickly dropped. Robert Cromie, Book Editor, praised the book repeatedly through the spring months. The book reappeared on the Chicago best-seller lists and stayed on through summer and fall. According to the publisher, Crown, in actual sales figures this meant a jump in the Chicago area from about one hundred twenty-five copies weekly to five hundred weekly.

A letter to Cromie from a Lake Forest bookseller, however, discloses the suburban reader's reaction to this general theme: "But when I recommend this book to our customers and tell them it is about a little boy and his family, living in the Bronx in 1930, they smile wanly and ask what else I have to offer."[34] Never very prepossessing, the Jewish education novel has had to make its way anew with each attempt.

THE SERIO-COMIC NOVELS

In contrast to the comic nostalgic novels are the serio-comic novels. More intense in tone, they alternate comedy scenes harsher and more grotesque than those of the comic novels with pathetic or violent scenes absent from the latter. Arthur Granit, author of the serio-comic *The Time of the Peaches,* believes that fiction requires intensity, a tension which can be naturally achieved by the use of Jewish materials—the dichotomization of life in America, with its "pull in two directions," Jewish and American, makes "'American' writing seem pallid by comparison and compelled to adopt physical violence in order to produce intensities."[35]

The Time of the Peaches depicts Brownsville during the late Thirties as an enclave surrounded by enemies and facing an inexorable destruction. The sense of this pressure is expressed by an accelerated tempo, wild incidents, and larger-than-life characters. The novel is dominated by the image of the Podolsky cellar, filled with the accumulated ashes of years, with cats, and with screaming hysterics. Benjamin DeMott, comparing the book to *A Walker in the City,* finds Granit's voice to be nervous and sentimental, finds that he fails to order his details and reconstruct Brownsville as a "process of self-emergence," a myth.[36] The serio-comic novelist seeks the effect of excess, but at the risk of exhausting and irritating the reader.

Another novel which starts, like *The Time of the Peaches*, by circumscribing the boundaries of its locale (this time Williamsburg in the middle Thirties) is *The Neighborhood* by David Mark. The ingredients of serio-comic nostalgia are here: the dense population crowding the summer streets; the petty criminals, prostitutes, small-time gamblers and the like; the quick succession of various ill-matched couples; and the odd nicknames, "Rip-apart" and "Hesh." The education of fifteen-year-old Arnie Aronson is effected by means of the election campaign of ward politician Sam Shapiro, "The Grand Old Man," the last of the breed of "Illiterate Immigrant Leaders." A realistic relief-line scene brings Arnie home with a disappointing store of government goods: unlabeled cans, a coal sack, a stale bread, and, incongrously to the Jewish family to whom it is *treyf* (unclean), a can of lard. Although the action sometimes borders on paperback violence (Arnie faces his friend, the Negro Jesse, in a senseless confrontation out of "West Side Story"), the novel is a well-wrought example of the serio-comic school.

The prefatory epigraph to *The Breakwater* by George Mandel turgidly expresses the intent of the serio-comic nostalgic novelist: ". . . and now he recognized these things that seemed too long gone to be immediate, past and present were an equation through which he labored and the future was a dream begun long ago." Like Fuchs's *Low Company*, *The Breakwater* is set in Coney Island in the Thirties and deals with gang rivalry for the local rackets. Pathos is achieved in the figure of Daniel, lover of the protagonist's mother. He is ostracized by the Communist Party as discipline for a *petit-bourgeois* act: a furrier, he has sewn a coat for his love. The Communist

Party always hovers in the background of these novels but does not figure integrally in the plot of *The Breakwater,* which is concerned with matter more sensational and less prepossessing to treat.

On the Shore and The Golden Watch

Turning back to an older generation, to Albert Halper and Charles Angoff, one finds the re-creation of a vanished Jewish-American life realized through simpler techniques than those of the serio-comic novelist. Halper and Angoff's nostalgic novels elicit a response free of false sentiment, and a sympathy that makes sophistication seem irrelevant.

Most of Albert Halper's novels were published in the Thirties. In these years he wrote a series of "proletarian novels," *Union Square* (1933), *The Foundry* (1934), *The Chute* (1937), and *The Little People* (1940). *The Chute* could serve as a representative dreary Depression novel. It describes a large mail-order firm as seen by the seventeen-year-old son of a West Side Chicago Jew who operates a grubby retail shop, the milieu with which Halper is most comfortable. After returning to Jewish materials in *Sons of the Fathers* (1942) (a Jewish grocer resists the war spirit of 1917), he published *Only an Inch from Glory* (1943) and, in paperback edition only, *Atlantic Avenue* (1956), a "slice-of-life" novel deserving revival in a more dignified form. Halper's career, built on these honest, solemn Naturalistic novels seems to have run its course, although four of his novels recently have been republished as paperbacks, and another novel, *The Fourth Horseman of Miami Beach,* appeared in 1966.

Halper's Chicago Jewish material was used for two volumes of stories, the first, *On the Shore,* in 1934, the second, *The Golden Watch,* in 1952. Although the stories in both volumes originally were published over a thirty-year period in sixteen periodicals, they are sufficiently unified to justify their consideration as novels in this study. Halper calls them neither short-story collections nor quite novels but "family albums."[37] Autobiographical in spirit, the stories in both volumes recount the experiences of David, a grocer's son, growing up on Chicago's West Side in the years before World War I.[38] While all of Halper's work is directly in the Naturalistic tradition, his volumes of stories of Jewish life in Chicago seem likely to outlive his dated proletarian novels.

The elements of nostalgic fiction are present in both volumes, which can be treated together. The stories revolve around the family and the grocery, a family enterprise. In "The Date," the sister undergoes a typical *rite de passage;* in "My Aunt Daisy," the mother's unmarried sister comes to visit; in "My Father's Broad Shoulders," Father cooks while Mother escapes the summer heat. Halper demonstrates Naturalistic fiction at its best, with its compassion for people and sense of the city. He represents poverty without resorting to violence or the flat prose which reproduces the tone of poverty at the price of monotony. The absence of details, laboriously drawn from popular culture and designed to identify the period, is no handicap to the narrative; the stories fix the timeless reactions of the characters within a surely conceived setting. The warm depiction of the family and the sympathy for even the minor characters are the stuff of fiction, making the contrived literary effects of the serio-comic novels seem arbitrary and precious. Only when Halper thinks of himself self-consciously as a young realistic writer does his occasionally breezy prose become obtrusive, as in "Young Writer Remembering Chicago."

The David Polonsky Series

Unquestionably, the greatest venture into nostalgia and the enterprise which rivals Thomas Wolfe's four-volume *Kunstlerroman* in scope is Charles Angoff's David Polonsky series, an autobiographical re-creation of boyhood and youth in Boston and manhood in literary New York. Wolfe had in Lloyd McHarg his Sinclair Lewis; Angoff has in Henry Brandt his H. L. Mencken, the counterpart in criticism of Lewis in fiction. The series originally was conceived as a trilogy but since has grown to seven substantial volumes bringing Polonsky into the mid-Thirties. *Journey to the Dawn,* the boyhood of David Polonsky in the Taft era; *In the Morning Light,* his adolescence during World War I; and *The Sun at Noon,* his Harvard years, comprise a trilogy. The subsequent novels concern David's New York experience, a second unit outside the scope of this study.

Angoff's novels differ in quality from the light tone of the comic group and the intense one of the serio-comic group. They are the kind of books that are described approvingly by reviews as old-fashioned Victorian narratives with plenty of story and solid characterization. The leisurely pace—possible in an unlimited number of five-hundred-page volumes—permits the inclusion of the life histories of David's many relatives, making the reader wish for the table of characters which formerly prefaced such novels.

Angoff's accomplishment, the re-creation of immigrant life with all its social currents, recalls the education novels written thirty years earlier by men who were, after all, Angoff's contemporaries. The theme, like theirs, is the dual identity of the European-bred immigrant, part Orthodox Jew and part "Zionist-Revolutionary." There is also the sympathetic portrayal of the older generation, from their viewpoint, really, and the thorough knowledge of *shtetl* customs and religious rituals. One difference is that Angoff's protagonist reads Thomas Huxley but finds him less enlightening than did the Darwinian novelists of the early group. But more important is the similarity in the handling of the protagonist: in Angoff's series, the interest really lies in the characters who surround David. As Angoff says in "Why I Wrote a Jewish Novel," they take over the narrative, particularly in the first volume. Angoff's affectionate attitude toward his immigrant Jews has seldom been seen since the novels of the first generation.

Religion in the Polonsky Series

In the second novel, David's dawning religious doubt, as he begins the process of assimilation which is already befuddling his elders, receives more treatment. The first incident of *In the Morning Light* is David's *bar mitzvah,* the first major event in the religious life of a Jew, the moment when he is assigned adult responsibilities. David finds the ceremony perfunctory and disappointing. The *bar mitzvah,* despite its ritual importance to Jewish youth, is seldom a set piece in Jewish novels as are the *Shabbes* dinner and the Passover *seder.* A modest post-confirmation party lessens David's disappointment, but his doubts reappear in a symbolic form. The catchy melody of "Onward Christian Soldiers" runs through his mind; even humming "Hatikvah," the Zionist national anthem, fails to drive it out; but an American popular song, "Rings on My Fingers, Bells on My Toes," does.

David's religious education continues after his *bar mitzvah.* He studies the *Gemara* and *Talmud* (rabbinic commentaries on the *Torah,* the first five books of the Old Testament) but finds them remote from contemporary American life, as are the irksome thrice-daily prayers,

with their obligatory tying on of *tefillim* (phylacteries).
Angoff takes pains to define the religious artifacts and
the Yiddish and Hebrew words, another resemblance to
the first-generation novelists who were ever conscious
that they were introducing the American reader to an
exotic culture. "Each man had his *tefilin* and *talis* as well
as a *sider, chumesh,* and *tehilim* (prayer book, copy of
the Pentateuch, and Book of Psalms)."[39]

One day, David is late for players because he stops at
a window display of toys. Particularly enchanting to him
are the baseballs, another sign of the rupture of his Orthodox life by Americanization. Baseball has been a particularly intriguing sport to Jewish-American writers.
Bernard Malamud and Mark Harris have written baseball novels. The emphasis on baseball in David's assimilation reinforces the view that the game has a special attraction as a symbol of the purest Americanism to the
son of immigrants.

Immigrant Life in the Polonsky Series

Angoff's novels are most notable, however, for their
encyclopedic account of immigrant life, related through
the highly elaborate sub-plots involving David's extended
family. Angoff's profound understanding of the first
generation early in the century can be determined by comparing some of his insights to the comprehensive an-
thropological study of life in the Pale of Settlement in
Life Is with People. The story in *In the Morning Light*
of Uncle Pinchus, who devotes his life to the synagogue,
leaving to his wife the care of their children and grocery
store, had its counterpart in the *shtetl* marriage, where
it was common for the wife to put in long hours in the
family business while the husband fulfilled his obligation
to the *Torah.* In *Journey to the Dawn,* Uncle Moshe resists such American innovations as tomatoes and lettuce,

food which he regards fit for horses, not people. Raw vegetables, except for radishes, cucumbers, and onions, played little part in the *shtetl* diet.[40]

A twist is given to the standard portrait of the *heder melamed* in *In the Morning Light*. The *melamed* is usually seen from the viewpoint of the young student. His incompetence, a compound of old-fashioned severity and sheer ignorance of his subject, is blamed for his charges' lack of interest in Judaism. The *melamed* in *In the Morning Light* is seen from the inside as David's *zayde* (grandfather). True to the type, unable to support himself as a synagogue *shammes* (beadle), he announces that he is available to teach the "rudiments of Judaism— the Pentateuch, the 613 mitzvahs, the prayers, and so on."[41] Selfless and kindly, unlike the usual *melamdim,* *zayde* cannot bring himself to demand full payment of fees, nor can he provide the summer picnic entertainments of his competitors.

Angoff explores the contradictory systems which had begun to dissolve the unity of *shtetl* life even before the exodus to America. Enlightenment and such Messianic movements as Sabbatianism were countered by the revival in the eighteenth century of the ecstatic approach to religion called *Hasidism*. Father Moshe in *The Sun at Noon* is the product of a *Hasidic* household, but his wife's family is more modernized. To maintain the peace, Zionism, socialism, and *Hasidism* are not discussed in the home, although Moshe does find himself moved by the Balfour Declaration. Believing in the medical powers of a *guter Yid,* a sort of *Hasidic* shaman, Moshe obtains from one the prescription for a mentally ill friend: spend the night praying in *shul,* where the *shechineh* (the holy spirit) resides. The maternal side of the family is enlightened, believing in *die revolutze* and Zionism, although the two are by no means parallel. As a small child, David had sat on the lap of Theodor Herzl,

Shmarya Levin, and Ahad Ha'am, overhearing details of the return to the homeland. At other times, however, he overheard talk of Kropotkin, Tolstoy, Bakunin, and Marx from his outspokenly socialistic brother and sister. In the United States, the conflict between religion and the modern heresies is embodied in Uncle Aryeh, who starts his career as a research chemist under the tutelage of professors whom he labels atheists and agnostics. It is Aryeh's desire to work with people instead of test tubes, and not religiosity, which turns him to a new career, Hebrew teacher. Through the medium of the sub-plots, Angoff achieves a memorable historical re-creation of Jewish life.

Writers on their Jewish Novels

Some of the nostalgic education novelists have attempted to account for their novels. Referring to *Journey to the Dawn* in "Why I Wrote a Jewish Novel," Angoff stresses the emotional impact of the theme, a Jewish boyhood, in terms similar to those of David Mark, stating that the theme and the characters developed through their own power.[42] In the same article, Yuri Suhl, who wrote two boyhood novels, refers to his "subjective attitude and emotional involvement" and his refusal to be alienated from his historical heritage.[43] Suhl ascribes the vitality of his work to his Jewish heritage, contrasting himself to writers who approached Jewish material as outsiders or "gropers." As a Yiddish poet, Suhl is more deeply immersed in Jewish material than most of the writers in this study; but the best scenes in his novels are the European flashbacks recalling a lost friendship, rather than the American scenes, which are light, innocuous humor. It is the "gropers," rather than the novelists grounded in Judaistic lore, who have written the best education novels. Fuchs and Henry Roth had literary

intelligences developed on Western models; Angoff and
Isaac Rosenfeld returned to their Jewish material after
a career in the general American culture.

Suhl maintains a dual heritage. Along with his Yiddish
masters—Mendele, Aleichem, Bergelson, Asch, Kobrin,
Rosenfeld, and Edelstadt—he discovered Jack London,
George Eliot, Edgar Allen Poe, and Walt Whitman.
Albert Halper, who had no Jewish education, was awak-
ened by Anderson, Dreiser, Frank Norris, and Stephen
Crane, and was later influenced by European writers:
Gogol, Turgenev, Chekhov, and Joyce. It was not the
Yiddish writers, but Isaac Babel, a Jew who wrote in
Russian, who touched him.[44]

A fourth novelist in whose work we must survey Jewish influences is Arthur Granit. Yiddish was his first
language (as was the case with several Jewish-American writers even since the first generation, Rosenfeld and
Bellow among them). Granit spent a year in a New York
Yiddish school run by Socialists. The son of a militant
atheist and of a "believer on the simple folk level," he
avoided Yiddish writers, especially after a friend pointed
out the similarity in style between his short stories and
those of Sholom Aleichem.[45]

In the United States, Jewish fiction has been a realistic
fiction drawing more on life for motifs and characterization than on the great body of Hebrew religious writings,
whether biblical, rabbinical, Kabbalistic, or folkloristic.
Yiddish literature has often been discovered by the
writers after their indoctrination in Western literature.
Always, Yiddish literature occupies a lower position than
Western literature in their scale of literary values.

Therefore Be Bold

Herbert Gold's *Therefore Be Bold* and two related
short stories collected in *Love and Like,* "The Heart of

the Artichoke" and "Aristotle and the Hired Thugs," are in the vein of the serio-comic nostalgic education novel, but are distinguished by their sensitive rendering of the psychology of the adolescent. The time of *Therefore Be Bold* is again the late 1930's, which falls within the remembered boyhood past of Gold, Granit, Mark, and Mandel.

The setting is new—Lakewood, a suburb of Cleveland —but the father's occupation is familiar, the retail grocer. Gold makes of the father a considerable figure, more in keeping with the father in non-Jewish adolescent novels who dominates the submissive mother. Appearing as Sam Stein in *Therefore Be Bold* and as Berman in the two stories, the father is described as a workman by the "non-executive ectomorph" narrator son. Jealous of the sensuous alternation of hard physical labor and expansive ease which he imagines such a life to hold, the son re-creates the romance between the writer and the laborer.

The style is very like that of *The Adventures of Augie March*, which was not published until 1953, but excerpts of which had appeared in various periodicals since 1949. One of these was in the *Hudson Review* which published "The Heart of the Artichoke" in 1951. The opening paragraph of "The Heart of the Artichoke" illustrates the elaborate sentences, the off-beat rhythms and falls, the hard details, and the flamboyance that mark the style:

My father, his horny hands black with sulphur, lit a cigar with a brief, modest, but spectacular one-handed gesture, his thumbnail crr-racking across the blue-headed kitchen match; when he described his first job in America, selling water to the men building the skyscrapers, teetering across the girders for fifteen cents a pail, green flecks fumed and sailed in his yellowish Tartar eyes; he peeled an artichoke with both hands simultaneously, the leaves flying toward his mouth, crossing at the napkin politely tucked at the master juggler's collar, until with a groan that was the

trumpet of all satisfaction he attained the heart; he—but he was
a man of capabilities, such feats apart.[46]

This style is shared by a number of writers beside the
progenitor Bellow, Edward Adler in *Notes from a Dark
Street* (1962) and Daniel Gordon in *A Likely Story*
(1962) among them. It has been labeled a Jewish style
and, therefore, requires some analysis.

Addressing himself to the questions raised by this
fictional style of the 1950's, Philip Roth, in "Writing
American Fiction,"[47] asks, "Why is everybody so bouncy
all of a sudden?" His answer: driven to extremes by
the bizarre modern age, a group of urban, mostly Jewish
writers have become "specialists in a kind of prose-poetry
that often depends for its effectiveness as much on how
it is ordered . . . as it does on what it is expressing."
The style is influenced by the Jewishness of the writers,
according to Roth. Freed of the English literary tradition and recalling the spoken English of their boyhood,
a language which reflected the rhythms and folk expressions of Yiddish, they attempt to reproduce in written
prose "the excitements, the nuances and emphases of
urban speech, or immigrant speech . . . [The] result can
sometimes be a language of new and rich emotional subtleties, with a kind of backhanded grace and irony all its
own. . . ." Roth finds the style in Bellow to have a tough-
minded exactitude which, in Gold's *Therefore Be Bold,*
is mere exhibitionism.

There is more than a touch of the derivative in *Therefore Be Bold,* with its conscientious inclusion of Americana, circa 1930, and its humor, based on the braggadoc-
cio and sneering of adolescent mannerisms. But the final
effect of the novel is to dignify adolescence by regarding
it with unpatronizing sympathy. Thesis is subordinated
to the examination of the protagonist as an adolescent;
as a result, a timelessness is achieved which marks the

THE INVENTION OF THE JEW

nostalgic novel at its best. Granville Hicks calls this novel
Gold's major effort to "find the truth by finding the meaning of childhood." He finds to discover Gold the "struggle
to define the self and relate to others" is richer in possibilities than in frustration.[48] This discovery has been
made repeatedly in education novels, but Gold brings to
it a certain freshness.

Jewish-American fictional prose style had progressed
from the kitchen realism of the first generation through
a long period when Naturalism predominated. The in-
fusion of a surrealistic spirit into realism in the late
1940's by the alienated school did not end straight-
forward realism, which continued into the 1950's. A
prose finally freed from Naturalism's lugubrious tone and
drawing freely on both surrealism and realism is best
demonstrated by Bernard Malamud and a tougher-
minded group of satirists whose work will be treated in
the next chapter.

NOTES TO CHAPTER 6

1. Lionel Trilling, "Another Jewish Problem Novel," *The Menorah
Journal,* XVI, No. 4 (April 1929), 378.

2. Stephen Longstreet, "Why I Wrote a Jewish Novel," in *Mid-
Century,* ed. Harold U. Ribalow (New York: The Beechhurst Press,
Inc., 1955), p. 327.

3. C. Bezalel Sherman, *The Jew Within American Society,* (Detroit:
Wayne State University Press, 1965), p. 94.

4. Blanche Gelfant, *The American City Novel,* (Norman, Okla.: University of Oklahoma Press, 1954), pp. 228 ff.

5. In conversation with the present author.

6. Herbert Gold, *Love and Like* (Cleveland: World Publishing Co.,
1961), p. 302.

7. Quoted in Harry T. Moore, "The Fiction of Herbert Gold," *Contemporary American Novelists* (Carbondale, Ill.: Southern Illinois University Press, 1964), p. 171.

8. Theodore Solotaroff, "Philip Roth and the Jewish Moralists,"
Chicago Review, XIII, No. 1 (Winter 1959), pp. 87-99.

9. Jane Howard, "The Belated Success of Henry Roth," *Life,* LVIII,
No. 1 (Jan. 8, 1965), 76.

10. Herbert Gold, *Therefore Be Bold* (New York: Dial Press, Inc.,

1960); Albert Halper, *On the Shore* (New York: The Viking Press, 1934); Albert Halper, *The Golden Watch* (New York: Henry Holt & Co., 1953); Charles Angoff, *Journey to the Dawn* (New York; Thomas Yoseloff, 1951); Charles Angoff, *In the Morning Light* (New York: The Beechhurst Press, 1952).

11. David Mark, *The Neighborhood* (New York: Popular Library edition, 1960); Arthur Granit, *The Time of the Peaches* (New York: Abelard-Schuman, 1959); George Mandel's *The Breakwater* (New York: Holt, Rinehart & Winston, 1960).

12. Herman Wouk, *The City Boy* (Garden City, N. Y.: Doubleday & Co., Inc., 1948 and 1952); Yuri Suhl, *One Foot in America* (New York: Macmillan Co., 1951); Yuri Suhl, *Cowboy on a Wooden Horse* (New York: The Macmillan Co., 1953); S. J. Wilson, *Hurray for Me* (New York: Crown Publishers, Inc., 1964).

13. Elick Moll, *Memoir of Spring* (New York: G. P. Putnam's Sons, 1961); Burton Bernstein, *The Grove* (New York: McGraw-Hill Book Co., Inc., 1961).

14. Wouk, *The City Boy*, p. 30.

15. J. Tasker Witham, *The Adolescent in the American Novel,* (New York: Frederick Ungar Publishing Co., 1964), p. 317.

16. Arthur Kober, *Treasury of Jewish Stories,* ed. Harold U. Ribalow (New York: Thomas Yoseloff, 1958), p. 219.

17. Daniel Bell, in *Mid-Century,* ed. Ribalow, p. 144.

18. Burt Blechman, *The War of Camp Omongo* (New York: Random House, 1963), p. 12.

19. Moll, *Memoir of Spring,* p. 100.

20. *The City Boy,* p. 50.

21. Wilson, *Hurray for Me,* p. 143.

22. Daniel Fuchs, *Three Novels* (New York: Basic Books, 1961), p. 24.

23. Robert Warshow, *The Immediate Experience* (New York: Anchor Books, 1964), pp. 22-23.

24. Granville Hicks, "The Thirties: A Reappraisal," *Saturday Review* (May 4, 1963), p. 27.

25. Diana Trilling, *Claremont Essays* (New York: Harcourt, Brace & World, 1964), p. 160.

26. Alfred Kazin, *A Walker in the City* (New York: Harcourt, Brace & Co., 1951), pp. 53-54.

27. Halper, *The Golden Watch,* pp. 103-105.

28. Bell, *loc. cit.*

29. In Harry Golden, *Only in America* (Cleveland: World Publishing Co. edition, 1958), p. 91.

30. Isaac Rosenfeld, "Kreplach," *Commentary,* VI, No. 5 (Nov. 1948), p. 488.

31. Rosenfeld "Adam and Eve on Delancey Street," *Commentary,* VIII, No. 4 (Oct. 1949), pp. 385-387.

32. Mark Zborowski and Elisabeth Herzog, eds., *Life Is with People: The Culture of the Shtetl* (New York: Schocken Books, 1962), pp. 361-380.

33. *Hurray for Me*, p. 106 *Passim.*

34. *Chicago Tribune*, Aug. 9, 1964, Sec. 9, p. 2; *Chicago Tribune*, June 29, 1964, Sec. 2, p. 2.

35. Letter to the present author.

36. Benjamin DeMott, "Vanished Island," *Midstream*, VI, No. 4 (Fall 1960), 98-102.

37. Letter to the present author.

38. John E. Hart, "Albert Halper's World of the Thirties," *Twentieth Century Literature*, IX, No. 4 (Jan. 1964), 194.

39. Angoff, *In The Morning Light*, p. 161.

40. Zborowski and Herzog, *Life Is with People*, pp. 240, 371.

41. *In The Morning Light*, p. 190.

42. Charles Angoff, "Why I Wrote a Jewish Novel," in *Mid-Century*, ed. Ribalow, p. 324.

43. Suhl, *ibid.*, p. 319.

44. Letter to the present author.

45. Letter to the present author.

46. Gold, *Love and Life*, p. 3.

47. Roth, "Writing American Fiction," *Commentary*, Vol. 3, No. 31, March, 1961, pp. 223-233.

48. Granville Hicks, "Generations of the Fifties: Malamud, Gold, and Updike," *The Creative Present* ed. N. Balakian and C. Simmons (Garden City, N. Y.: Doubleday & Co., 1963), pp. 230–231.

7

Third Generation:
The Black Comedians

BLACK HUMOR

The popular and critical success of Bellow, Malamud, and Philip Roth in the 1950's was followed by the appearance of a whole new generation of young writers, men closer in age to Roth than to Bellow and Malamud. As the children of parents born in the United States, they came of age after World War II rather than during the Depression. Their novels, which will be examined in this chapter, are similar enough in style and premise to comprise what can be called a school. Members of the group (by no means all of the young writers who use Jewish materials) are Burt Blechman, Bruce Jay Friedman, L. S. Simckes, Jeremy Larner, Jack Ludwig, Stanley Elkin, and Irvin Faust.

Appellations attached to the work of the group are "vaudeville Americana," "The Critical Eye," and, most accurately, "Black Comedy" and "Black Humor." The black comedians have been compared to Kafka, Nathanael West, Beckett, Chagall, and Chaplin, to slapstick comedy and the cartoon-strip.[1] (George Herrimen's Krazy Kat would be the closest in style.) Other novelists writing within this loose tradition, using even more avant-garde and anti-realist techniques and viewing society with a more detached and pessimistic attitude, were Joseph Heller, Terry Southern, John Barth, James Purdy, and Thomas Pyncheon.

These books are alike in more than their unreality, compression, and sharpness. As commentary on American life, they are devastating. As representations of Jewish-American life, they are far harsher than the uncomplimentary novels of the past such as Ben Hecht's *A Jew in Love* (1931). In contrast to the older novels, as a sign not only of the current acceptability of Jewish fiction, but also of the greater freedom for novelists, general critical reception of the black comedy novels has been favorable. In the Jewish press the novels have been received with much less enthusiasm, but also with less vituperation than was directed to the earlier negative portrayals of Jews.

Just as depiction of the Jew in fiction has undergone change, so has humor in the Jewish-American novel. The earliest and most common kind was dialect humor directed toward the popular audience. Despite the unfashionableness of humor exploiting ethnic groups, it persists in the slight novels of Louis Heyward and Ethel Rosenberg. More significant to the novel as an art form is the serio-comedy of Malamud, Bellow, and Roth. As the chief means of these important writers, serio-comedy flourishes. Humor here is integral, the outcome of juxtapositions of the incongruous with the basically serious situations of the novels. Humor here is an expression of the absurd *weltanschauung* of the novelist, an indication that he finds the world a place of disparities and disconnections. A branch of this comedy, fathered by Nathanael West and Daniel Fuchs and bringing comedy and tragedy into sharper opposition, is black humor. Substantially different from serio-comedy, it is narrower in scope; having departed from the realism of serio-comedy, it is limited to a febrile satire.

In the anthology *Black Humor,* Bruce Jay Friedman defines this school, stressing the fading line between reality and fantasy in the modern world. He mentions an important influence: "a nervousness, a tempo, a near-hysterical new beat in the air, a punishing isolation and loneliness of a strange, frenzied new kind."[2] This tempo is indeed caught by the rhythms of black humor.

Anticipations of black humor have appeared already in this study. Roth's *Goodbye, Columbus* and Richler's *The Apprenticeship of Duddy Kravitz* use black comedy in some of their scenes. Richler's next novel, *Stick Your Neck Out* (1963), although completely in the vein of black comedy, departed from the Jew as subject; and Roth's *Letting Go* (1962), a double love story of two young Jews, moved toward a realism perhaps designed to classify Roth as a major novelist.

Black comedy education novels are not lacking, however—the school finds the tale of a young man thrust into a series of rudely instructive experiences to be a most convenient framework. The novels to be examined in this chapter are Mark Harris' *Something about a Soldier* (1957), which prefigures the school in its fantasy but is otherwise too gentle in its humor and spirit to be a true work of black comedy; and David Karp's *Enter Sleeping* (1960), a novel fulfilling some of the requirements of black comedy but lacking its savage anger.[3] Other examples directly displaying the style are Burt

Blechman's *How Much?* (1960) and *The War of Camp Omongo* (1963), L. S. Simckes' *The Seven Days of Mourning* (1963), and Bruce Jay Friedman's *A Mother's Kisses* (1964).[4]

THE LUFTMENSCH IN
SOMETHING ABOUT A SOLDIER
AND
ENTER SLEEPING

Something about a Soldier is of interest chiefly for its protagonist, Jacob, a true example of the *luftmensch,* the ineffectual dreamer of Yiddish literature. The *luftmensch* sometimes appears in Jewish-American literature as the father. His equally frequent appearance as the protagonist is marked by an exaggeration of the usual sensitivity and unworldliness of that figure, Max Balkan in Fuchs's *Homage to Blenholt,* for example. Howe and Greenberg call the "sainted fool" a basic character type of Yiddish literature, an offshoot of *dos kleine menschele,* the long-suffering, persistent, poor Jew, a mixture of pride and humility.[5] In the latest phase of the Jewish-American novel, in which the anti-hero is a favorite character, the *luftmensch* is more useful than ever.

Harris' Jacob is the opposite of his Biblical namesake. He is not shrewd but ingenuous, not grasping but giving, not studied but spontaneous. His story is that of the civilian in the military. His eager willingness, underlaid by an insoluble strata of idealism, provokes riot and disorder where Schweikean compliance would have ensured adjustment. Leaving the shelter of the Jewish home and the provinciality of the city as he knows it, Jacob proffers himself to the world with excruciating innocence: "If you want to know my name it's Jacob Epstein, I'm a private, United States Army. I'm Jewish." He encounters the American South in the forms of Sergeant Toat and Joleen, the PX girl. As a vision of bureaucratic life, the army provides situations comparable to those in the Yiddish novel in which the *shtetl* householder confronts the Czarist official.

The *luftmensch* appears in *Enter Sleeping* as Julius Schapiro. Anglicized Jewish names (Moishe to Morris to Maurice to Milton to Michael) offer an entire social history, but also the uncanny potency of a conjure word. Since few protagonists' names bear the poeticized mystery of Norman Moonbloom in Edward Lewis Wallant's *The Tenants of Moonbloom* (1964), or the Biblical echoes of Joseph, Jacob, and Moses, their evocativeness must be laid to extra-literary causes, e.g., that they serve as a yellow star of David proclaiming the identity of the bearer. Anglo-Jewish names offer both the wry music of modern poetry and the persuasive particularity of the realist.

In *Enter Sleeping,* Julius, would-be song writer and putative play-reader for a fraudulent theatrical producer, undergoes a number of fanciful experiences which illuminate the modern scene only intermittently, despite such topical bits of business as an FBI agent's infiltration of a group of eccentrics. Julius' colorless presence as antihero is insufficiently delineated to contrast with the vivid aberrants of the novel. A greater flaw of the book, however, is its failure to be funny. The humor is especially important because Karp's only intent is to entertain, to use the materials of black comedy inoffensively—an impossibility.

THE SEVEN DAYS OF MOURNING

L. S. Simckes' *The Seven Days of Mourning* is similar to the work of the central practitioners of Jewish black comedy, Friedman and Blechman. The resemblances are marked enough to remove any doubts about its labeling

THE INVENTION OF THE JEW

—the racy tempo, the scatology, the mingling of hysterical comedy with a perfervid pathos, the overlay of horror. There is, however, a substantial difference between Simckes and the others. Simckes' comedy is turned not to a savage indictment of American society, but to the development of a moral fable. The story details the efforts of a quack doctor, Vossen Gleich, to pull Barish Shimansky, a bitter cripple living with his abnormal family, back toward life. "Vossen Gleich" means "knowing what is right" in Yiddish; the phrase reveals the author's fabulistic intent.

The immediate progenitors of this novel are Bellow for the sentence rhythms and Malamud and Isaac Bashevis Singer for the type, the nightmarish little tale which mingles the homely with the magical and phantasmagoric. Singer currently is producing such stories in Yiddish with settings in the vanished Pale of Settlement. A close equivalent in painting is found in the work of Marc Chagall with its mixture of nineteenth-century subjects and twentieth-century surrealism—the fiddler on the roof. Going further back, one finds Yiddish folk fables and the stories of Peretz with their madmen and miracles, such as "The Mad Talmudist" and "Bontsha the Silent." The folk traditions of European Jewry are rich in superstition and belief in magic. Simckes, as the descendant of rabbis, educated at *yeshivas* in Israel as well as at Harvard, has the credentials of a writer in this vein.

The fabulistic intent of the novel is carried out in a manner appropriate to black comedy. John Gross, reviewing *The Seven Days of Mourning* in tandem with Blechman's *The War of Camp Omongo*, found the characters of Blechman to be reduced by scorn to marionette proportions, while Simckes' are "inflated like great carnival monsters."[6] The image does indeed suggest the amorphous loomings and apprehensions of the novel. The pathology of the Shimansky household is shown in a series of insect images. Barish wheels around "like some noisy insect," and "they're all over, spiders, beetles: leggers from the window." Barish, confined to his wheelchair and his apartment, baleful, speaking "like an evil insect," is, of course, another version of Gregor Samsa in Kafka's "Metamorphoses." Almost everyone in the book is some kind of physical cripple.

Another dimension is provided by the extensive use of Yiddish, more sustained than the usual *"sei gesund"* of the Jewish novel, and of folklore, the "tumtums," cripples, and "Ogs." (The novel's title refers to the *shiva* the period of mourning prescribed by Orthodox tradition.) Vossen Gleich makes the function of these references and the theme of the novel apparent in his address to the Shimanskys:

Is that how you live together and hold peace? Don't bear tales, so many of them. . . . You don't talk Yiddish, and you're an old timer. What, am I, in a Jewish home, a stranger, or something dead, God Forbid, like your Bracha? I'm a doctor, no more, but I know things, I study, I learn, even in the bathroom. There's always enough light. Me, every day I speak something in Yiddish. We all must be scholars. Look here, every time to be a Jew must be taken. You don't know that? That's why I'm here. . . . Oh, Shimansky people, who are you? What brings you together? Better go over and study, and mourn. Like myself, the doctor, Vossen Gleich, all the time I mourn. Can you see my black bag? I have medicines for everybody.[7]

The idea here is not that Yiddish is essential to Judaism—a notion always rejected by the Jewish-American novelist—but that Jews are obligated by their identity to live a moral life informed by Jewish learning—a commandment seldom given by the Jewish novelist.

Gleich is finally evicted by the Shimanskys despite Barish's dream that Gleich, transformed into an insect, sacrifices himself to save Barish. The family continues as before, with only the most ambiguous hope that they can emerge from the curse of hatred. Gleich's message remains, however, a reminder of the transcendence possible to man amid the squalor of life.

A Mother's Kisses

At its most typical, black comedy finds in man less potential sublimity, and more ignoble actuality. Friedman's *A Mother's Kisses* has a sour quality because it emphasizes the ugliness of life, relying on the innocence of its protagonist, seventeen-year-old Joseph, to supply the intimations of goodness. Joseph is insufficient to the task, overwhelmed as he is by the power as a fictional character of his mother. The anti-hero protagonist of Friedman's first novel, *Stern* (1962), is an older version of Joseph; but the existential absurdities which plague Stern are the specters of his mind and, therefore, are credible. The horrors that follow Joseph as he travels from resort to college, pursued by his mother, are all too real and, therefore, incredible.

With *Stern*, Friedman found a stylistic device which he repeats in *A Mother's Kisses*. Both Stern and Joseph are continually revealed by their uncontrolled secret thoughts, the distorted image of their daily travails. Joseph is as innocent as a child. Although he knows he is underpaid as a summer camp waiter, he pridefully hangs his head when complimented for his skill. But Joseph suffers a series of surrealistic visions which mingle his altruistic impulses with dark streaks of precocious sexuality. One of these fantasies occurs at a party at which he and his mother are the only Jews. He imagines a game requiring the two to face the guests in combat, his mother spinning off in defeat, exposing her undergarments. Another fantasy: Joseph gathers up oppressed wives protectively, lining them up along the "wall of a distant auditorium with no scheduled activities." The image recalls the vistas of di Chirico and Dali.

Like Stern, Joseph displays symptoms of morbidity. He sleeps the day through, stays indoors endlessly to avoid people, and develops a swollen arm. After being rejected for matriculation at Columbia University, he promptly steals a few dollars from each of the camp waiters.

Joseph's half-mad impulses are filtered through the screen of adolescence. His attempts to conceal his sexual interests convey the sordidness of this stage of maturation. At the theater, he guiltily thrills at the glimpses of panties as the chorus twirls. To simulate indifference, he casually turns his head to miss an occasional one, wondering if the choreographer had planned these divertissements.

Joseph's fantasies, his tearful dependence on his mother, and his ill-conceived chivalrous gestures (he yanks a too-forward friend of his mother into the soup at Lindy's) are a predictable syndrome in the world of black humor. The world of Friedman, Simckes, and Blechman is peopled by fantastic, frantic victims of the commercial society. The dream of success is now seen in the unnatural, glaring, fluorescent light of the 1960's— the same harsh light which illuminates the dream world of Yves Tanguy.

All the events of *A Mother's Kisses* are seen in this light. Joseph's contemporaries at Kansas Land Agricultural College (which appears to have a rooming house full of Jewish students) are a wildly repellent lot, already lost to the twisted values of adult society. The invariable monstrousness of the characters and Joseph's fantasies are matched to similar weird flights of the narrator; the imagery of the novel abounds with sado-masochistic touches that sometimes exceed the probable intent of the author. The failure to provide relief from the grotesquerie gives the book a wearing quality. Black humor requires short scenes and chapters, and the books tend to be brief, just as were Nathanael West's. The reliance on unsustainable effects and nightmare terrors resembles the Theater of the Absurd with its short scenes and plotlessness, and, above all, its vision of the world as a nightmare landscape. But a little horror goes far.

THE CAMP SETTING

The summer camp and resort setting has been a staple of Jewish fiction at least as far back as Montague Glass's *Lucky Numbers* (1927). Since then, Arthur Kober, Herman Wouk, Paul Goodman, Sidney Offitt, Richler, and Friedman have done camp or resort scenes. The Jewish summer camp is seen most often as the arena where evil contends with good for the soul of the child. Burt Blechman's *The War of Camp Omongo*[8] recounts the struggle for the soul of Randy Levine, camper.

The venal camp owner-director is an inevitable figure in this fiction. He is the master of revels whose greed wars with his twisted attempts to provide "character-building" activities. The values of Camp Omongo's Steiner are substantially those of the parents of his charges. (Campers appear to both Blechman and Friedman to be miniatures of their middle-aged fathers.) Steiner boasts of the American fighting spirit of former campers who have succeeded in life: a bomb-shelter manufacturer, an advertising executive, a comedian. Competitive struggle is the educational method of Camp Omongo: the game of war (a treasure hunt between red and blue teams), sports played to win, and World War II movies in the recreation hall. Rejecting the progressive philosophy of his arts-and-crafts counselor (the customary figure for the ineffective proponent of idealism), Steiner schedules a contest for the best Intermedi-

ate Pottery. "Philosophy's all right for the classroom . . .
But this is real life."

RELIGION IN THE BLACK HUMOR NOVEL

The competitive spirit of "The Great White Father"
with its mystique of pennants and prizes debars much
emphasis on religion. At Camp Omongo, a show-rabbi
is permitted to hurry through a few prayers, but it is
Steiner who has the last word to the boys: in the last
analysis, God determines who will win and who will fail.
The chapter entitled "The Chaplain" describes Rabbi
Yeslin's declining career as he falls from lost pulpit to
cemetery prayer-chanter to marriage broker to sausage-
factory *mashgiach* (supervisor of koshering) to cantor
at a Catskill hotel to the lowest rung, rabbi in a camp
for Reform Jews.

Formal religion is also treated irreverently in *A Mother's Kisses*. Joseph and his mother, Meg, attend a college
religious service held in the basketball court of the Bap-
tist Church. Meg is moved to the following: "Stay a
second, I want to keep this picture in my mind. As long
as I live, I'll never forget it. That right there, in a church
that God forbid we should have to resort to this again,
is your true Jewishness. They don't need a Torah, they
don't need those old hypocrites with their donations.
What you're looking at is your real religion."[9] Heedless
of this inspiriting setting, the rabbi promptly utters an
unsubtle request for a donation, a plea which Meg has
long anticipated, *baksheesh* being the chief tenet of her
code governing human intercourse.

THE JEWISH MOTHER IN BLACK HUMOR

The reviewers of *A Mother's Kisses* were very much
taken with Meg; and she is, indeed, a striking creation,

possibly destined to be the classic portrait of the Jewish mother. Stanley Kauffmann's review of *A Mother's Kisses* emphasizes the Oedipal nature of the mother-son relationship.[10] There is something oppressive in the hysterical embrace of the black comedy mother. By the third generation, the Yiddish idioms of the mother are the heritage of her childhood in Bensonhurst or Queens. She possesses ferocious energy and a massive load of fear and bitterness which she directs violently toward her inevitable companion, the passive, suppressed husband.

Ma Shimansky of *The Seven Days of Mourning* chose her mate. Fleeing home, she came upon him at the foot of Brooklyn Bridge, at his newspaper stand, taking pleasure in being short-changed by each customer. A Brooklyn-ite, he is unable to find his way to Ebbets Field. Pa Shimansky is the willing dependent of the wife who has turned his life into a great terror, his revenge is fits of shivering and choking and endless days spent roaming the apartment in his underwear. This is recounted in a prose with rhythms, turns of phrase, and allusions derived from Bellow's *Augie March* style: "Our last chance began with a meal of condolence, prepared by the doctor and his mistress in our own honor: eggs, lentils, grapes, things which had no mouth, like mourners."[11]

The father of *A Mother's Kisses* has been made an incompetent by Meg. The instant he loses his Depression job, he rushes home to awaken his son, tearfully crying that he can no longer provide dimes for "big little books." He, like Pa Shimansky, has had his psychosomatic revenge: he spends two years on a plank with back trouble. (He is finally cured by being thrust out of the apartment by Meg.) As ever with the Jewish-American novelist, it is the family which elicits the most intense imaginative treatment. The requirements of black comedy reinforce the acerbate picture of family life; but no alteration of the conventional outline is necessary.

What is the relationship between the Jewish writer and his family, his mother and father, the ever-present sister? Why do these continue to provide such a potent subject at this late date?

The relationship of the writer to his mother at its most antic is seen in Bernard Kops's autobiography, *The World Is a Wedding* (1963).[12] Kops, who suffered through mental illness and a series of ideologies, finally to become a playwright, assesses the meaning of the Jewish mother: "She is practically always a matriarch, holding the family together, bending it to her will, making a bit of sense out of the senselessness of the universe. When she dies the family is splintered, destroyed. The children become separate planets shooting their own directions into space."[13] In one of his more disordered moments at his mother's death ("Why don't you pull yourself together?"), Kops is unable to display emotions properly like his father, who wails upon the floor beating his breast. Instead, the perfect image of the writer, he sneaks into the bathroom to record the episode. Playing out the scene, Kops provides a sensation at the funeral. In a borrowed suit, unshaven, drugged, the madman brought out for the occasion, he recites the *Kaddish*, the prayer for the dead which exalts God rather than dwelling on the bereavement. Caught up in hysteria, unable to understand the words he recites, Kops sways to and fro uncontrollably. The ungovernable need of the son to *épater les bourgeois*, to disgrace the grieving family, is the result, one suspects, of the compulsive need of the parents to have the son succeed in terms that they define.

Die Yiddishe momme is a collection of stereotypical characteristics, whether she is imagined with benign sentimentality, as in the old popular song of that title, or malignly by the dark comic novelist. The mother's emotional force focused with single-minded devotion upon the family is the outcome of a process which somehow has survived the *shtetl*. The domineering mother, the monster of energy, the animated Punch of the black comic novelist, is the antithesis of Al Jolson's *Yiddishe momme*.

Malin and Stark make much of the Jewish father in *Breakthrough*. They find the repeated portrayal of the father as a source of "fear, love and spiritual authority" to signify an archetype, especially for the Jews.[14] In the first-generation education novel, the father was more important; in the dark comic version, it is the domineering mother who is the prominent figure in the writer's imagination.

BLACK HUMOR'S DREAM OF SUCCESS

The reading of these novels as an attack upon the dream of success should not be overlooked. As a glimpse of America after mid-century, they offer a more heightened and appalling vista than any conceived previously. John Gross calls the work of Blechman an "offensive against the American Way . . . patently aimed at a much wider target" than the boys' camp (or, by implication, the Jews); he cites the camp director's speech: "Fellow-Tribesmen, America and Omongo are one and the same!"[15] America in the Sixties desires chastisement. Its taste for it is reflected in the continuous appearance of books treating a number of "problems" or "issues." But novelistic sermons on such an abstract problem as the futility of material goals are hardly likely to do more than distract. The dark comedian is patently a court jester, the tinkle of his bells but the faint sound of his imprisoned rancor.

The Jewish setting can be excused the black humorist by socio-economic fact. The American Jew has completed his movement from the working class to the great middle class, where he shares in the vision of bounty. More than the realist's need for particularity and the availability of a ready target can be seen in the choice of the Jews as subject. In the Sixties, the Jew no longer threatens. The bland tolerance of the public at best makes the mockery of the Jew slightly shocking, but not frightening.

The favorite protagonist is still the also-ran, trapped in his pathetic efforts to guess at the formula which carried the rich uncle upward. Even in the black comedy novel, which should be the most free of introspection, the writer is unable to divorce himself from the materials of his life, from a tortuous self-examination which is more than a little self-mocking. The neuroticism of the alienated Jew, now a generation past, which was to illuminate our general condition, now has developed into a plaint against the ugly manners of the failure who scrambles too hard. In this choice of subject, there is a hint of the *selbst hass* (self-hate) of marginal man. Nonetheless, the satirist's inclusion of himself in the merciless attack is perhaps the one note of grace in these novels.

The relation of sons to parents is ever the key in the study of Jewish-American fiction. The education novel customarily examines the question of the American promise from the viewpoint of the son. In one work, however, it is the father who mistrusts the tolerance of America. Mark Harris, in the Preface to "Friedman and Son," records the father's recurrent question: "Are there any Jews here?"[16] The bright new buildings of the University of California campus symbolize the successful career Harris has built in his own American way. Harris contrasts his success with the terms of his father's life, with the rent collecting, and the suburban home never fully accepted by the father. The lugubrious, meditative rejection of America by the father and the son's acceptance of it, the oppositions of father and son—"I am all action and he all meditation, I am all society and he all solitude, I all jazz and he all Sunday symphony."— are resolved after the father's death when Harris discovers, by reading old letters, that he has become his father.[17] The father's writing style is exactly his. The implications of this become clear when Harris realizes that one can't assimilate. "Identity is a principle . . . Jewish identity gives sustenance for Jewish intellectuals not so much to religious forms and rituals as to points of character, principle, and social conviction."[18] The parents are the embodiment of this inescapable identity, the points of contact. Whether they are seen with hate or favor, whether or not the artist recognizes this major source of his art, as Harris has done, the parents are bound to reappear in his work; and the son is bound to continue writing education novels.

NOTES TO CHAPTER 7

1. Stanley Kauffman, "A Mother Who Would Have Scared Off Oedipus," *Life* (Aug. 21, 1964), p. 8; Richard Kostelanetz, "The Critical Eye," *Chicago Jewish Forum,* XXII, No. 4 (Summer 1964), 315; "The Black Humorists," *Time,* LXXXV, No. 7 (Feb. 12, 1965), 94.

2. Bruce Jay Friedman, *Black Humor* (New York: Bantam Books), 1965, p. viii.

3. Mark Harris, *Something About A Soldier* (New York: The Macmillan Co., 1957); David Karp, *Enter Sleeping* (New York: Harcourt, Brace and Co., 1960).

4. Burt Blechman, *How Much?* (New York: Ivan Obolensky, 1960); L. S. Simckes, *The Seven Days of Mourning* (New York: Random House, 1963); Bruce Jay Friedman, *A Mother's Kisses* (New York: Simon and Schuster, 1964).

5. Irving Howe and Eliezer Greenberg, eds., *A Treasury of Yiddish Stories* (New York: Meridian Books, Inc.: 1958), p. 39 ff.

6. John Gross, "Oy!", *New York Review of Books,* I, No. 4 (Oct. 17, 1963), 14.

7. Simckes, *The Seven Days of Mourning,* p. 90.

8. Burt Blechman, *The War of Camp Omongo* (New York: Random House, 1963).

9. Friedman, *A Mother's Kisses,* p. 215.

10. Kauffman, *loc. cit.*

11. *The Seven Days of Mourning,* p. 95.

12. Bernard Kops, *The World Is a Wedding* (New York: Coward Mc-Cann, 1963).

13. *Ibid.,* p. 195.

14. Irving Malin and Irwin Stark, eds., *Breakthrough* (New York: McGraw-Hill Book Co., 1964), p. 10.

15. Gross, *loc. cit.*

16. Mark Harris, *Friedman and Son* (New York: The Macmillan Co., 1963), p. 3.

17. *Ibid.,* pp. 42-43.

18. *Ibid.,* pp. 39-40.

Conclusion

Tracing the evolution of the education novel as a sub-
genre within Jewish-American fiction has promoted the
close examination of the themes of that literature (and
permitted the avoidance of the many thesis novels which
add to its bulk without raising its quality). Without
stretching the definition of the education novel excessive-
ly, I have included novels of most of the important Jewish-American authors. There are important omissions—
novelists who did not write education novels: Ben Hecht,
Waldo Frank, Nathanael West, Norman Mailer, Bernard Malamud, and Edward Lewis Wallant—and many
minor ones. The strategy which dictated the topic was
to narrow the compass of the study to a single type, to
explore it chronologically, and to uncover the characteristic themes and the successive theories of composition of
the Jewish-American novel.

A body of literature numbering authors in the hundreds may well be expected to show a considerable range
in quality; among the twoscore novels appearing in this
survey, such a diversity is apparent. Among the novels,
one has hoped (along with their readers, who have not

been characterized in these pages as being especially patient or encouraging and, perhaps, are owed some apology) to find some novelists of first quality, if not genius or enduring significance in the world of literature. A handful of finely wrought and even beautiful novels has been found, a number of "interesting failures," and fewer dreary books than critics have suggested.

Related to the question of quality, the critic's concern, is that of stylistic change, the literary historian's problem. An ideological component has been studied in those novels informed by more or less leftist approaches to society; from a more purely literary point of view, the line of development has been traced in the successive appearances of the biographical, the economic, the psychological, the comic, and, finally, the absurd form. These stages are related to the similar stages in the American novel which they have followed—albeit not closely at times, but still followed. The protagonist has traversed his own evolutionary path from socialist hero to rogue-hero to slum boy to alienated hero to anti-hero.

The changes in the protagonist, however, have been external, the sign of his relation to the world as a social being. In essence, no matter what his nominal identity, he remains the sensitive innocent, the artist-hero of Romantic tradition. He is ever the child of Yiddish fiction: "precocious, ingenious, deprived, yet infinitely loved," as Howe and Greenberg describe him. A basic character of Jewish fiction, he is, at the same time, a literary convenience in American fiction.

As Jewish books, the novels have described Jewish life in America with a degree of thoroughness, taking up many of the social concerns of a people, scornfully or mockingly demanding correction of injustice. The better novels have transcended ethnic themes and characteristics to achieve an aesthetic universality.

Description of the Jewish ethos, although it has figured

prominently in this study, is not what makes a religious novel even if it can be said to make a Jewish one. Novels which take up Jewish theology explicitly are rare. Chaim Potok's *The Chosen* (1967) is a notable exception. The novelists clearly have not been theologists in the narrow sense of the word. It is clear from their frequent denunciation, based on first-hand acquaintance, of the *heder,* an elementary school, that they lack a profound knowledge of Judaistic lore. The Judaism of the novels lies in the point of view of the novelist, which I have asserted, if not proved, is identifiably Jewish. It is found in the tensions which contribute to the novels their sense of yearning. It is found in the moral sense and the heightened vision of the novelists, expressed in wryly oblique terms and giving the novels whatever uniqueness may be claimed for them.

Bibliography

BOOKS AND PAMPHLETS

Aaron, Daniel. *Writers on the Left.* New York: Harcourt, Brace & World, Inc., 1961.

Angoff, Charles. *In the Morning Light.* New York: The Beechhurst Press, 1952.

————. *Journey to the Dawn.* New York: Thomas Yoseloff, 1951.

Balakian, N. and C. Simmons. (eds.). *The Creative Present.* Garden City, N. Y.: Doubleday & Co., Inc., 1963.

Bellow, Saul. *The Adventures of Augie March.* New York: The Viking Press, 1953.

———— (ed.). *Great Jewish Short Stories.* New York: Dell Publishing Co., 1963.

————. *Herzog.* New York: The Viking Press, 1964.

Bernstein, Burton. *The Grove.* New York: McGraw-Hill Book Co., 1961.

Blechman, Burt. *How Much?.* New York: Ivan Obolensky, 1960.

————. *The War of Camp Omongo.* New York: Random House, 1963.

Cahan, Abraham, *The Rise of David Levinsky.* New York: Harper and Brothers, 1917 and 1960.

Cohen, Hyman, and Lester Cohen. *Aaron Traum.* New York: Horace Liveright, 1930.

Cournos, John. *The Mask.* New York: George H. Doran Co., 1919.

Davis, Allison. *Social-class Influences upon Learning.* Cambridge: Harvard University Press, 1948.

Eisinger, Charles E. *Fiction of the Forties.* Chicago: University of Chicago Press, 1963.

Epstein, Seymour. *The Successor.* New York: Charles Scribner's Sons, 1961.

Farrell, James T. *Judgment Day.* New York: The Vanguard Press, Inc., 1935.

Fast, Howard. *The Children.* New York: Duell, Sloan & Pearce, 1937.

Ferber, Nat J. *The Sidewalks of New York.* Chicago: Pascal Covici, 1927.

Fiedler, Leslie. *The Jew in the American Novel.* New York: Herzl Institute Pamphlet No. 10, 1959.

———. *Waiting for the End.* New York: Stein & Day, 1964.

Freeman, Joseph. *An American Testament: A Narrative of Rebels and Romantics.* New York: Farrar & Rinehart, Inc., 1936.

Friedman, Bruce Jay. *Black Humor.* New York: Bantam Books, 1965.

———. *A Mother's Kisses.* New York: Simon and Schuster, 1964.

Fuchs, Daniel. *Three Novels.* New York: Basic Books, 1961.

Gelfant, Blanche. *The American City Novel.* Norman, Okla.: University of Oklahoma Press, 1954.

Glazer, Nathan. *American Judaism.* Chicago: The University of Chicago Press, 1957.

Gold, Herbert. *Love and Like.* Cleveland: World Publishing Co., 1961.

———. *Therefore Be Bold.* New York: The Dial Press, Inc., 1960.

Gold, Michael. *Jews without Money.* New York: Liveright Publishing Corp., 1930.

Golden, Harry. *Only in America.* Cleveland: World Publishing Co., 1958.

Gollomb, Joseph. *Unquiet.* New York: Dodd, Mead & Co., 1935.

Granit, Arthur. *The Time of the Peaches.* New York: Abelard-Schuman, 1959.

Halper, Albert. *The Chute.* New York: The Viking Press, 1937.

———. *The Golden Watch.* New York: Henry Holt & Co., 1953.

———. *On the Shore.* New York: The Viking Press, 1934.

Handlin, Oscar. *Adventure in Freedom.* New York: McGraw-Hill Book Co., 1954.

Harris, Mark. *Friedman and Son.* New York: The Macmillan Co., 1963.

———. *Mark, The Glove Boy.* New York: The Macmillan Co., 1964.

———. *Something about a Soldier.* New York: The Macmillan Co., 1957.

Hassan, Ihab. *Radical Innocence: Studies in the Contemporary American Novel.* Princeton, N. J.: Princeton University Press, 1961.

Hatcher, Harlan. *Creating the Modern Novel.* New York: Farrar and Rinehart, 1935.

Howe, Irving, and Eliezer Greenberg (eds.). *A Treasury of Yiddish Stories.* New York: Meridian Books, Inc., 1958.

Karp, David. *Enter Sleeping.* New York: Harcourt, Brace & Co., 1960.

Kazin, Alfred. *Contemporaries*. Boston: Little, Brown & Co., 1962.

————. *Starting Out in the Thirties*. Boston: Little, Brown and Company, 1965.

————. *A Walker in the City*. New York: Harcourt, Brace and Co., 1951.

Kops, Bernard. *The World Is a Wedding*. New York: Coward McCann, 1963.

Kostelanetz, Richard (ed.). *On Contemporary Literature*. New York: Avon Books, 1964.

Krim, Seymour. *Views of a Nearsighted Cannoneer*. New York: Excelsior Press, 1961.

Kunitz, S. *Twentieth Century Authors*. New York: The H. W. Wilson Co., 1942.

Kussey, Nathan. *The Abyss*. New York: The Macmillan Co., 1916.

Lewisohn, Ludwig. *The American Jew*. New York: Farrar, Straus & Co., 1950.

————. *The Island Within*. New York: Harper and Brothers, 1928.

————. *What Is This Jewish Heritage?*. rev. ed. New York: Schocken Books, 1964.

Levin, Martin (ed.). *Five Boyhoods*. Garden City, N.Y.: Doubleday & Co., Inc., 1962.

Levin, Meyer. *In Search*. New York: The Horizon Press, 1950.

————. *The Old Bunch*. New York: Simon and Schuster, 1937.

Lifson, David S. *The Yiddish Theatre in America*. New York: Thomas Yoseloff, 1965.

Liptzin, Sol. *The Jew in American Literature*. New York: Block Publishing Co., Inc., 1966.

Lynn, Kenneth S. *The Dream of Success: A Study of the Modern American Imagination*. Boston: Little, Brown & Co., 1955.

Malin, Irving. *Jews and Americans*. Carbondale, Ill.: Southern Illinois University Press, 1965.

———. Irwin Stark (ed.). *Breakthrough*, New York: McGraw-Hill Book Co., 1964.

Mandel, George. *The Breakwater*. New York: Holt, Rinehart & Winston, 1960.

Manners, William. *Father and the Angels*. New York: E. P. Dutton, 1947.

Mark, David. *The Neighborhood*. New York: Popular Library, 1960.

Mellquist, J., and L. Wiese (eds.). *Paul Rosenfeld: Voyager in the Arts*. New York: Creative Age Press, 1948.

Mersand, Joseph. *Traditions in American Literature: A Study in Jewish Characters*. New York: The Modern Chapbooks, 1939.

Modder, Montagu F. *The Jew in the Literature of England*. New York: Jewish Publication Society, 1939.

Moll, Elick. *Memoir of Spring*. New York: G. P. Putnam's Sons, 1961.

Moore, Harry T. *Contemporary American Novelists*. Carbondale, Ill.: Southern Illinois University Press, 1964.

Norris, Frank. *The Octopus*. New York: Doubleday, Page & Co., 1901.

Ornitz, Samuel. *Bride of the Sabbath*. New York: Rinehart & Co., Inc., 1951.

———. *Haunch, Paunch and Jowl*. New York: Boni & Liveright, Inc., 1923.

Podhoretz, Norman. *Doings and Undoings*. New York: The Noonday Press, 1964.

Potok, Chaim. *The Chosen*. New York: Simon and Schuster, 1967.

Raskin, Philip M. (ed.). *Anthology of Modern Jewish Poetry*. New York: Behrman's Jewish Book Shop, 1927.

Ribalow, Harold U. (ed.). *Autobiographies of American Jews*. Philadelphia: The Jewish Publication Society of America, 1965.

———. *Mid-Century*. New York: The Beechhurst Press, Inc., 1955.

———. *Treasury of American Jewish Stories*. New York: Thomas Yoseloff, 1958.

Richler, Mordecai. *The Apprenticeship of Duddy Kravitz*. Boston: Little, Brown & Co., 1959.

Rideout, Walter. *The Radical Novel in the United States*. Cambridge: Harvard University Press, 1956.

Rischin, Moses. *The Promised City*. Cambridge: Harvard University Press, 1962.

Rosenfeld, Isaac. *An Age of Enormity*. Cleveland: World Publishing Co., 1962.

———. *Passage from Home*. New York: The Dial Press, 1946.

Rosenfeld, Paul. *The Boy in the Sun*. New York: The Macmillan Co., 1928.

Ross, Sam. *The Sidewalks Are Free*. New York: Farrar, Straus & Co., 1951.

———. *Someday, Boy*. New York: Farrar, Straus & Co., 1948.

Roth, Henry. *Call It Sleep*. New York: Pageant Books, 1960.

Roth, Philip. *Goodbye, Columbus*. Boston: Houghton Mifflin Co., 1959.

Sacher, Howard M. *The Course of Modern Jewish History*. New York: Dell Publishing Co., 1963.

Schneider, Isidore. *From the Kingdom of Necessity*. New York: G. P. Putnam's Sons, 1935.

Schulberg, Budd. *What Makes Sammy Run?*. New York: Random House, 1941.

Schwartz, Delmore. *The World Is a Wedding*. Norfolk, Conn.: New Directions, 1948.

Sherman, C. Bezalel. *The Jew within American Society.* Detroit: Wayne State University Press, 1965.

Simckes, L. S. *The Seven Days of Mourning.* New York: Random House, 1963.

Spiller, Robert E., *et al.* (eds.). *Literary History of the United States.* New York: The Macmillan Co., 1962.

———. *A Time of Harvest.* New York: Hill and Wang, 1962.

Stampfer, Judah. *Sol Meyers.* New York: The Macmillan Co., 1962.

Suhl, Yuri. *Cowboy on a Wooden Horse.* New York: The Macmillan Co., 1953.

———. *One Foot in America.* New York: The Macmillan Co., 1951.

Swados, Harvey. *A Radical's America.* Boston: Little, Brown & Co., 1962.

Tarr, Herbert, *Heaven Help Us.* New York: Random House, 1968.

Tarr, Herbert. *The Conversion of Chaplain Cohen.* New York: Bernard Geis, 1963.

Tobenkin, Elias. *Witte Arrives.* New York: Frederick A. Stokes Co., 1916.

Trilling, Diana. *Claremont Essays.* New York: Harcourt, Brace & World, Inc., 1964.

Turnbull, Andrew. *Scott Fitzgerald.* New York: Charles Scribner's Sons, 1962.

Waldmeir, Joseph J. (ed.). *Recent American Fiction: Some Critical Views.* Boston: Houghton Mifflin Co., 1963.

Warshow, Robert. *The Immediate Experience.* New York: Anchor Books, 1964.

Weidman, Jerome. *I Can Get It for You Wholesale.* New York: Random House, 1937.

Wilson, Edmund. *The American Earthquake.* New York: Anchor Books, 1964.

Wilson, S. J. *Hurray for Me*. New York: Crown Publishers, Inc., 1964.

Wirth, Louis. *The Ghetto*. Chicago: University of Chicago Press, 1956.

Witham, J. Tasker. *The Adolescent in the American Novel*. New York: Frederick Ungar Publishing Co., 1964.

Wouk, Herman. *The City Boy*. Garden City, N. Y.: Doubleday & Co., Inc., 1948 and 1952.

Zborowski, Mark, and Elisabeth Herzog (eds.) *Life Is with People: The Culture of the Shtetl*. New York: Schocken Books, 1962.

NEWSPAPERS AND PERIODICALS

Aaron, Daniel. "Communism and the Jewish Writer," *Salmagundi*, I, No. 1 (Fall 1965), 22-36.

Adler, Renata. "The New Reviewers," *The New Yorker*, XL, No. 20 (July 4, 1964), 60-80.

Bellow, Saul. "From the Life of Augie March," *Partisan Review*, XVI, No. 11 (Nov. 1949), 1077.

———. "Hemingway and the Image of Man," *Partisan Review*, XX, No. 3 (May-June 1953), 342.

———. "Isaac Rosenfeld," *Partisan Review*, XXIII, No. 4 (Fall 1956), 565.

"The Black Humorists," *Time*, LXXXV, No. 4 (Feb. 12, 1965), 94.

Boroff, David. "An Authentic Rogue-Hero," *Congress Bi-Weekly*, XXI, No. 9 (May 25, 1960), 17.

———. "The Author," *The Saturday Review*, XLVII, No. 38 (Sept. 19, 1964), 77.

———. "Philip Roth and His Audience," *The Menorah Journal*, XLIX, Nos. 1 and 2 (Autumn-Winter 1962), 156-157.

Chase, Richard. "The Adventures of Saul Bellow," *Commentary*, XXVII, No. 4 (April 1959), 324.

Chicago Tribune, June 29, 1964, Sec. 2, p. 2.

―――. Aug. 9, 1964, Sec. 9, p. 2.

Cohen, Richard. " 'Best Novel'—Worst Award," *Congress Bi-Weekly,* XXVII, No. 19 (Dec. 19, 1960), 12-14.

Cournos, John. "Truth and Fiction," *The Menorah Journal,* XXIV, No. 2 (April-June 1936), 151-153.

Daiches, David. "Breakthrough?" *Commentary,* XXXVIII, No. 2 (Aug. 1964), 63.

DeMott, Benjamin. "Vanished Island," *Midstream,* VI, No. 4 (Fall 1960), 98-102.

Fiedler, Leslie. "The City and the Writer," *Partisan Review,* XIX, No. 2 (March-April 1952), 240-241.

―――. "Henry Roth's Neglected Masterpiece," *Commentary,* XXX, No. 2 (Aug. 1960), 102-107.

Freedman, Morris. "The Jewish Artist as Young American," *Chicago Jewish Forum.* X, No. 3 (Spring 1952), 213.

Glicksberg, Charles. "The Jewish Element in American Drama," *Chicago Jewish Forum,* X, No. 2 (Winter 1951-52), 115.

―――. "The Theme of Alienation in the American Jewish Novel," *The Reconstructionist,* XXIII, No. 13 (Nov. 1, 1957), 8-13.

Gross, John. "Oy!" *New York Review of Books,* I, No. 4 (Oct. 17, 1963), 14.

―――. "Zangwill in Retrospect," *Commentary,* XXXVIII, No. 6 (Dec. 1964), 54.

Hart, John E. "Albert Halper's World of the Thirties," *Twentieth Century Literature,* IX, No. 4 (Jan. 1, 1964), 194.

Hayman, Jane. "Futile and Uncertain," *Commentary,* XXXI, No. 6 (June 1961), 550.

Hicks, Granville. "The Thirties: A Reappraisal," *The Saturday Review.* (May 4, 1963), p. 27.

Howard, Jane. "The Belated Success of Henry Roth," *Life*, LVIII, No. 1 (Jan. 8, 1965), 76.

Howe, Irving. "Daniel Fuchs: Escape from Williamsburg; The Fate of Talent in America," *Commentary*, VI, No. 1 (July 1948), 29-34.

――――. "Life Never Let Up," *The New York Times Book Review*. (Oct. 25, 1964), p. 1.

――――. "Our Country and Our Culture," *Partisan Review*, XIX, No. 5 (Sept.-Oct. 1952), p. 575n.

――――. "The Stranger and the Victim," *Commentary*, VIII, No. 2 (Aug. 1949), 147-156.

Isaac, Dan. "In Defense of Philip Roth," *Chicago Review*, XVII, Nos. 2 and 3 (1964), 84-106.

"Jewishness and the Creative Present," *Congress Bi-Weekly*, XXX, No. 12 (Sept. 16, 1963).

"Jews in America," *Fortune*, XIII, No. 2 (Feb. 1936), 79-144.

Kauffmann, Stanley. "A Mother Who Would Have Scared Off Oedipus," *Life*, (Aug. 21, 1964), p. 8.

――――. "Our New Cultural Heroes—American-Jewish Writers," *Chicago Tribune Books Today*, (May 30, 1965), p. 7.

Kazin, Alfred. "The Bitter 30's," *The Atlantic*, CCIX, No. 5 (May 1962), 99.

――――. "The Most Neglected Books of the Past Twenty Five Years," *The American Scholar*, XXV, No. 5 (Autumn 1956), 486.

――――. "My Friend, Saul Bellow," *The Atlantic*, CCXV, No. 1 (Jan. 1964), 53.

Kostelanetz, Richard. "The Critical Eye," *The Chicago Jewish Forum*, XXII, No. 4 (Summer 1964), 315.

Kronenberger, Louis. "Gambler in Publishing: Horace Liveright," *The Atlantic*, CCXV, No. 1 (Jan. 1965), 97.

Larner, Jeremy. "The Conversion of the Jews," *Partisan Review*, XXVII, No. 4 (Fall 1960), 760-768.

Levin, Meyer. "When I Was a Book Peddler," *Congress Bi-Weekly*, XXVIII, No. 19 (Dec. 25, 1950), 6-8.

Magid, Marion. "Mocking Heroics," *Commentary*, XXXVII, No. 5 (Nov. 1964), 81.

Popkin, Henry. "Jewish Writers in England," *Commentary*, XXXI, No. 2 (Feb. 1961), 136.

Ribalow, Harold U. "Fifty Basic Works of American-Jewish Fiction," *Chicago Jewish Forum*, X, No. 3 (Spring 1952), 193-198.

———. "A Note on Meyer Levin," *Chicago Jewish Forum*, IX, No. 1 (Fall 1950), 9-11.

Rosenfeld, Isaac. "Adam and Eve on Delancey Street," *Commentary*, VIII, No. 4 (Oct. 1949), 385-387.

———. "Kreplach," *Commentary*. VI, No. 5 (Nov. 1948), 488.

———. Review of Graham Greene's *Nineteen Stories*, *Partisan Review*, XVI, No. 7 (July 1949), 754.

Roth, Henry. "At Times in Flight," *Commentary*, XXIX, No. 1 (July 1959), 51-54.

———. "The Dun Dakotas," *Commentary*, XXX, No. 2 (Aug. 1960), 107-109.

Roth, Philip. "Writing about Jews," *Commentary*, XXXVI, No. 6 (Dec. 1963), 446-452.

"Second Dialogue in Israel," *Congress Bi-Weekly*, XXX, No. 12 (Sept. 16, 1963), 12-14.

Sloan, Jacob. "The Jewish Novel of Education," *The Reconstructionist*, XXV, No. 7 (May 15, 1959), 15-20.

Solotaroff, Theodore. "Philip Roth and the Jewish Moralists," *Chicago Review*, XIII, No. 1 (Winter 1959), 87-131.

Syrkin, Marie. "Revival of a Classic," *Midstream*, VIII, No. 1 (Winter 1961), 89-92.

Trilling, Lionel. "Another Jewish Problem Novel," *The Menorah Journal*, XVI, No. 4 (May 1929), 378.

"Under Forty: American Literature and the Younger

Generation of American Jews," *Contemporary Jewish Record*, VII, No. 1 (Feb. 1944), 17-20.

Waller, I. "The 'Jewish Book' Myth," *Chicago Jewish Forum*, IV, No. 1 (Fall 1945), 32.

Weber, Brom. "Some American Jewish Novelists," *Chicago Jewish Forum*, IV, No. 3 (Spring 1946), 179.

Wrong, Dennis. "Jews, Gentiles, and the New Establishment," *Commentary*, XXXIX, No. 6 (June 1965), 23-25.

Index

249